The Behavior of State Legislative
Parties in the Jacksonian Era

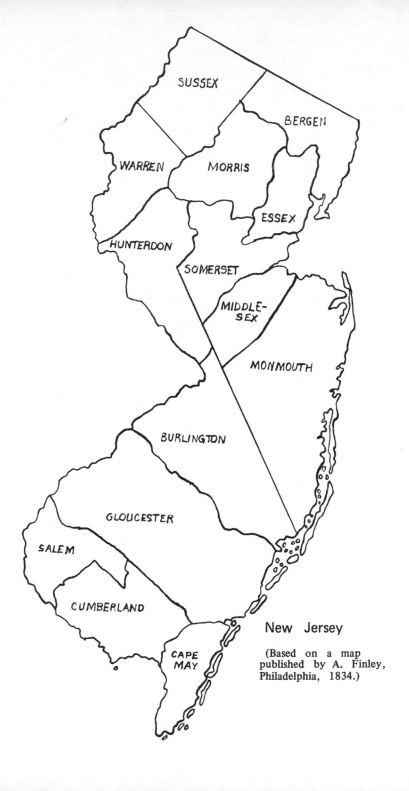

SUSSEX

BERGEN

WARREN

MORRIS

ESSEX

HUNTERDON

SOMERSET

MIDDLE-
SEX

MONMOUTH

BURLINGTON

GLOUCESTER

SALEM

CUMBERLAND

CAPE
MAY

New Jersey

(Based on a map
published by A. Finley,
Philadelphia, 1834.)

The Behavior of
State Legislative Parties
in the Jacksonian Era
New Jersey, 1829–1844

Peter D. Levine

Rutherford • Madison • Teaneck
Fairleigh Dickinson University Press
London: Associated University Presses

Portions of this work originally appeared as a dissertation,
Party-in-the Legislature: New Jersey, 1829–1844, ©1971 by Peter David Levine.

Associated University Presses, Inc.
Cranbury, New Jersey 08512

Associated University Presses
Magdalen House
136-148 Tooley Street
London SE1 2TT, England

Library of Congress Cataloging in Publication Data

Levine, Peter D   1944–
 The behavior of state legislative parties in the
Jacksonian era, New Jersey, 1829–1844.

 Portions of this work originally appeared as the
author's thesis, Rutgers University, 1971, published
under the title: Party-in-the legislature, New Jersey,
1829–1844.
 Bibliography: p.
 Includes index.
 1. Political parties—New Jersey—History.
 2. New Jersey — Politics and government — 1775–1865.
 I. Title.
JK2295.N62L38   328.749'07'69   75-18248
ISBN 0-8386-1800-6

In Memory of
My father, Sam Levine
My mother, Pearl Levine
My brother, Jon Levine
and for Gale

Contents

7

List of Tables and Figures

Tables

9

Figures

Acknowledgments

From its origins in a graduate seminar at Rutgers University, this study owes much to the guidance of Professor Richard P. McCormick. I benefited greatly from his careful criticism, his occasional proddings, and his moral support. Special thanks are due to Rudolph Bell, who first introduced me to the computerized techniques that made this work possible, and to Douglas T. Miller, who as a friend and colleague offered many useful suggestions. Neither Warren Cohen nor Norman Pollack read a word of this book, yet their friendship was vital to its completion.

The staffs of the computer centers at Rutgers and Michigan State Universities facilitated the processing of my data and solved the seemingly innumerable technical problems that arose. The task of creating computer programs relevant to my investigation was expertly done by

Mr. Neil Polo. Mr. Robert Culp provided valuable help in the visual presentation of my findings.

Customary thanks to library staffs are a standard part of these proceedings. Certainly those of the Columbia University Library, the Princeton University Library, the New Jersey State Library, and the New Jersey Historical Society deserve acknowledgment. The staff of the Special Collections department of the Rutgers University Library, however, merits particular mention. Their assistance, both as friends and as professionals, made my work considerably easier than it might have been.

Portions of this work have appeared previously in *New Jersey History* as "The Rise of Mass Parties and the Problem of Organization: New Jersey, 1829–1844" (Summer 1973), pp. 91–107; and in the *Journal of American History* as "The Behavior of State Legislative Parties in the Jacksonian Era: New Jersey, 1829–1844" 62 (December 1975): 591–607.

Finally, in their own ways, Gale, Ruth, and Cleo have all made this book possible.

Introduction

The purpose of this study is to investigate a neglected aspect of party development during the period of the second American party system, namely, the role of party in the state legislature. This era witnessed the emergence of mass parties that were aware of the requirements of a democratized political environment and that created elaborate electoral organizations capable of securing political power.[1] How parties utilized power once in control of state governments and what that usage indicates about the nature and the structure of ante-bellum parties, however, remain open questions.

Examination of party behavior in the New Jersey legislature permits investigation of these questions and other relevant concerns for a highly competitive two-party situation.[2] Between 1829 and 1844 elections for seats in the New Jersey legislature were contested by two parties on a

closely competitive basis. Legislators bore clear party attachments. This investigation seeks to determine by appropriate techniques the manner in which the behavior of
party activists in the legislature correlated with their identities as partisans. An understanding of their conception of
party function and of the influence of party on legislative
behavior will afford important insights into the role of
legislative parties and their relationship both to party organization and government operation in a competitive
two-party system.[3]

Recent investigations of the role of party in shaping state
legislative voting alignments reflect a new awareness
among Jacksonian scholars of the need to test interpretations of party behavior based solely on the national experience.[4] Although much of this work is important, it raises
several problems of methodology and theory. Specifically,
the tendency to emphasize the voting records of legislators
on selected substantive issues as the single criteria for
evaluating the performance of elected representatives with
partisan identities has excluded from analysis a variety of
other factors that together define legislative behavior. Assumed as well is the notion that evidence of partisan division on these questions reflects sincere ideological differences not only between Democratic and Whig legislators,
for instance, but also between all members of the electorate who identified with one party or the other. Assumptions such as these predispose conclusions to fit expected
formats, while restricting the search for relevant information.

As a first step in avoiding such problems, it seems desir-
able to explain briefly the guiding assumptions of this
study of New Jersey politics, the questions to be asked, and
the approaches to be employed. The first assumption concerns the meaning of party voting in the legislature. Stated
simply, evidence of party voting is viewed as a manifestation of the role of legislative parties rather than the single
factor that defines it. Consequently any conclusions about

party function must be based on an examination of the entire range of activities that engaged the legislators' attention.

Evaluation of different voting patterns among party legislators also deserves mention. As noted, it is often assumed that such evidence is solid proof that the major contesting parties maintained distinctly different ideologies. In similar fashion it has become popular to classify party activists either as ideologues or as political brokers with no middle ground in between.[5] The dangers inherent in these assumptions are obvious. Recognition of different voting tendencies among party legislators without further investigation of other kinds of evidence leaves scholars in doubt as to whether these differences represented distinct ideologies, distinct constituencies, a sophisticated sense of political opportunism, or some combination of forces. Party activists can not readily be distinguished solely as ideologues who seek election in order to enact specific public policy or as political brokers who devote themselves entirely to preserving the party organization in order to maintain themselves in power. Consistency in policy positions and attention to the mechanics of party organization are not necessarily mutually exclusive concerns. Strongly principled men who view party in Burkean terms, for instance, may recognize the need to build and maintain effective electoral organizations in order to achieve power. So, too, might party elites in a competitive situation see the need to manufacture and to manage issue conflict in order to secure politically advantageous positions. Nor do these choices exhaust the possibilities.[6]

This study proceeds on the premise that certainly within the aggregate, and no doubt for the individual, the behavior of party activists in the New Jersey legislature was a product of a variety of forces.[7] As much as possible it seeks to identify these forces and to explain their significance in terms of understanding the role of legislative parties. It does not, however, assume that matters that generated intense elite engagement had similar effects on the mass public.[8] The concern is primarily with political activists and one can not assume that their positions defined by voting in the legislature or by other means reflected the views of their electoral constituencies.

Awareness of this distinction appropriately provides a definition of party and of party structure. This study views American political parties as the chief agencies responsible for organizing political power. Their most prominent characteristic is their ability to dominate the contesting of elections. As to party structure, the legislative party or the party in office is considered as but one branch of the political party. It represents an organized wing of party that functions on the basis of its own perception of its goals and responsibilities and with its own system of rewards. These goals and responsibilities may or may not correspond to those of the second major element of party structure, the party organization proper. Composed of party officials and party workers, this component has direct responsibility for organizing effective machinery capable of electing party candidates to office. Finally, there is the mass membership—individuals who identify with a party by their support at the polls or who for a variety of reasons choose to adopt a specific party label.[9]

Close attention to the operation of legislative parties does not preclude examination of other elements of party structure. The degree of coordination between the demands and the activities of all three parts will indicate much about party behavior in New Jersey.

Of particular relevance is the relationship between the party organization proper and the party in office. Did party organization in the legislature allow for cooperation and communication with the party organization proper? What were the specific links between the two branches? Did party representatives in the legislature consciously work to serve the party organization proper as an interest group? Did the closeness of party competition positively affect partisan cohesion in the legislature? If so, was this influence uniform or did it vary according to the specific types of legislation or activity before the legislature?

Answers to these questions will help define the role of legislative parties as well as what the major parties were after in the New Jersey political arena. On another level they provide the basis for tentative speculations about broader concerns. The continuing debate over the ability of parties involved primarily in contesting elections to act as responsible channels for the enactment of public policy will be discussed in the context of the New Jersey experience. Whether or not partisan conflict in New Jersey in any way reflected division over the basic structure and values of an expanding American liberal-capitalist state will also be examined.

Procedure and method follow logically from the questions this study seeks to answer. Chapter 1 establishes the high degree of party competition in New Jersey, its relationship to party organization in and out of the legislature, and the immense powers of that body. Chapter 2 focuses on the interaction between the legislative environment and the parties that functioned within it. The manner in which legislative parties mobilized the support of party members for such purposes as choosing legislative officials and naming committees receives special attention. So, too, does a description of the nature of legislative business and its implications for legislative party action. Comparative biographical analyses of New Jersey's legislators in chapter 3 provide a challenge to traditional interpretations of party elites in the Jacksonian era, while setting the stage for an intensive examination of legislative roll-call voting behavior.

Because the chief way in which legislators express themselves is through their votes on roll calls, I have made an exhaustive study of this phase of legislative behavior. The specific methodology employed is clearly presented in the context of the analysis that occupies chapters 4, 5, 6, 7, and

8. Although concerned primarily with the influence of party on the decision-making process, I have attempted to identify as well the influence of variables other than party on the formation of voting alignments. Rather than a narrow investigation of selected roll calls on particular issues, I have examined virtually every roll call, including unanimous votes, recorded in both houses of the legislature over a sixteen-year period.

The first of these five chapters surveys Assembly voting behavior on the entire range of issues subject to roll-call vote, as well as to roll calls on appointments controlled by the legislature. This investigation establishes important connections between legislative parties and their larger party organizations that provide the basis for an interpretation of party role in the legislature. The following three chapters deal separately with legislation in the general field of banking and fiscal policy, the incorporation of businesses and related economic measures, and social enactments. Chapter 8 involves a body of legislation so distinctively political in character as to deserve a special category.

Through this investigation of party as a factor bearing upon legislative behavior, there emerges an understanding of what legislative parties meant in New Jersey between 1829 and 1844. Legislative parties assumed an organized form through the caucus. They mobilized through the caucus to organize the legislature. With respect to the influence of party on legislative outputs, the assessment varies in relation to the specific measures under consideration and the conditions maintaining at a particular time. In general, those matters defined as highly political, that affected party and particularly party activists as an interest concerned with winning elections and enjoying the perquisites of power, evoked strongly partisan behavior. On questions vital to the successful operation of the party organization proper, legislative parties delivered admirably.

Introduction 21

Only a detailed answer will suffice to explain voting behavior on substantive questions. A variety of factors including constituency pressure, devotion to specific public policies, and party considerations explain the decision-making process. Party voting in the legislature on all categories of legislation increased over time as party alignments stabilized and as intense party competition continued. Only on selected occasions, however, did partisan cohesion on substantive matters attain the levels reached on questions that clearly concerned party as an interest.

Legislative parties in New Jersey functioned as integral parts of larger institutions with their own vested interests capable of exerting a real influence in behalf of those interests. Their ability to satisfy the demands of state party organizations did not impede the evolvement of party influence on the whole range of questions before the legislature. Nor did it obviate partisan differences over public policy. In no way, however, did such differences reflect basic division about the nature of government or society. The development of parties in New Jersey as political organizations capable of effectively maintaining power for self-sustaining purposes along with their ability to mediate the demands of other interest groups seeking favors from the legislature underlines rather than contradicts their acceptance of the American liberal consensus.

Notes

1. The literature on party development during the period of the second American party system is extensive. General bibliographies on the subject can be found in Alfred A. Cave, *Jacksonian Democracy and the Historians* (Gainesville, Florida: University of Florida Press, 1964); Edward Pessen, *Jacksonian America: Society, Personality, and Politics* (Homewood, Illinois: The Dorsey Press, 1969), pp. 352–93; and Charles G. Sellers, Jr., "Andrew Jackson versus the Historians," *Mississippi Valley Historical Review* 44 (March 1958): 615–34. Of particular note is Richard P. McCormick, *The Second American Party System: Party Formation in the Jacksonian Era* (Chapel Hill, North Carolina: University of North Carolina Press,

22   THE BEHAVIOR OF STATE LEGISLATIVE PARTIES

1966). *Also see* William N. Chambers, "Party Development and the American Mainstream," in *The American Party Systems: Stages of Political Development,* ed. William N. Chambers and Walter D. Burnham (New York: Oxford University Press, 1967), pp. 3–32; and Richard P. McCormick, "Political Development and the Second Party System," in *The American Party Systems: Stages of Political Development,* ed. William N. Chambers and Walter D. Burnham (New York: Oxford University Press, 1967), pp. 90–116.

2. Richard P. McCormick, "Party Formation in New Jersey in the Jackson Era," *Proceedings of the New Jersey Historical Society* 83 (July 1965): 161–73, offers a brief but accurate account of party formation in New Jersey. Also useful are: Herbert Ershkowitz, "New Jersey Politics During the Era of Andrew Jackson, 1820–1837" (Ph.D. dissertation, Dept. of History, New York University, 1965); and Walter Fallaw, Jr., "The Rise of the Whig Party in New Jersey" (Ph.D. dissertation, Dept. of History, Princeton University, 1967).

3. Theodore J. Lowi, "Party, Policy, and Constitution in America," in *The American Party Systems: Stages of Political Development,* ed. William N. Chambers and Walter D. Burnham (New York: Oxford University Press, 1967), pp. 238–76; Frank J. Sorauf, "Political Parties and Political Analysis," in *The American Party Systems: Stages of Political Development,* ed. William N. Chambers and Walter D. Burnham (New York: Oxford University Press, 1967), pp. 33–55; and idem, *Political Parties in the American System* (Boston: Little, Brown and Co., 1964) were particularly useful in posing certain questions concerning the operation of legislative parties in a competitive two-party situation of the American variety. *Also see* David Derge, "Urban-Rural Conflict: The Case in Illinois," in *Legislative Behavior: A Reader in Theory and Research,* ed. Heinz Eulau and John Wahlke (Glencoe, Illinois: The Free Press, 1959), pp. 218–27; Maurice Duverger, *Political Parties: Their Organization and Activity in the Modern State* (New York: John Wiley, 1954); Thomas R. Dye, "State Legislative Politics," in *Politics in the American States: A Comparative Analysis,* ed. Herbert Jacob and Kenneth N. Vines (Boston: Little, Brown and Co., 1965), pp. 151–206; Malcolm E. Jewell, "Party Voting Behavior in American State Legislatures," *American Political Science Review* 49 (September 1955): 773–91; William J. Keefe, "Parties, Partisanship, and Public Policy in the Pennsylvania Legislature," *American Political Science Review* 48 (June 1954): 450–64; V. O. Key, Jr., *Politics, Parties, and Pressure Groups* (New York: Alfred A. Knopf, 1956), pp. 310–402; Austin Ranney, "Parties in State Politics," in *Politics in the American States: A Comparative Analysis,* ed. Herbert Jacob and Kenneth N. Vines (Boston: Little, Brown and Co., 1965), pp. 61–100; E. E. Shattschneider, *Party Government* (New York: Rinehart and Co., 1942) and Julius Turner, *Party and Constituency: Pressures on Congress* (Baltimore: Johns Hopkins Press, 1951).

4. Thomas B. Alexander, *Sectional Stress and Party Strength: A Computer Analysis of Roll-Call Voting Patterns in the United States House of Representatives, 1836–1860* (Nashville, Tennessee: Vanderbilt University Press, 1967) Joel H. Silbey, *The Shrine of Party: Congressional Voting Behavior, 1841–1852* (Pittsburgh: University of Pittsburgh Press, 1967) and Alan Bogue, "Bloc and Party Voting in the United

States Senate, 1861–1863," *Civil War History* 13 (September 1967): 221–41, represent recent attempts at quantitative analysis of congressional voting behavior during the ante-bellum period. Rodney O. Davis, "Illinois Legislators and Jacksonian Democracy, 1834–1841" (Ph.D. dissertation, Dept. of History, University of Iowa, 1966); Herbert Ershkowitz and William G. Shade, "Consensus or Conflict? Political Behavior in the State Legislatures During the Jacksonian Era," *Journal of American History* 58 (December 1971): 591–621; and James R. Sharp, *The Jacksonians Versus the Banks: Politics in the States After the Panic of 1837* (New York: Columbia University Press, 1970), place a heavy emphasis on understanding party behavior in the state legislatures during the Jacksonian period.

    5. Sharp, pp. 14–15.

    6. Herbert McCloskey, Paul Hoffman, Rosemary O'Hara, "Issue Conflict and Consensus among Party Leaders and Followers," *American Political Science Review* 54 (June 1960): 406–427.

    7. Sorauf, *Political Parties in the American System*, pp. 82–84.

    8. Ronald P. Formisano, *The Birth of Mass Political Parties, Michigan 1827–1861* (Princeton, New Jersey: Princeton University Press, 1971), p. 12. *Also see* Philip E. Converse, "The Nature of Belief Systems in Mass Publics," in *Ideology and Discontent*, ed. David E. Apter (Glencoe, Illinois: The Free Press, 1964), 206–261; and Murray Edelman, *The Symbolic Uses of Politics* (Urbana, Illinois: The University of Illinois Press, 1964).

    9. Sorauf, "Political Parties and Political Analysis," pp. 33–55.

The Behavior of State Legislative
Parties in the Jacksonian Era

All roll calls referred to specifically in the text will appear in appropriate footnotes at the end of each chapter in the following manner:

18—Council or Assembly, C.R.C. (cleavage roll call) or U.R.C. (unanimous roll call) number, page. The page number will refer to the page in the appropriate house journal in which the roll call appeared.

26

1
Competitive Politics and Party Organization

Between 1829 and 1844 the Jacksonian Democratic party and the National Republican, then Whig, party comprised a balanced, competitive two-party system in New Jersey. Unchallenged by any third party movements and confronted by electoral machinery well adapted to mass political participation, these parties maintained elaborate organizations in order to effectively contest Presidential, Congressional, and state elections. The ever-present possibilities for electoral success and the close competition this condition engendered were central determinants of party formation in New Jersey. Party organization in a legislature constitutionally sanctioned as the most powerful branch of state government was also influenced by these considerations.

I

The establishment of the second party system in New Jersey resulted from new opportunities for political power generated by the collapse of the state's Democratic-Republican party. Except for Federalist victories in one Congressional election and one state legislative election, the Democratic-Republicans dominated New Jersey politics between 1800 and 1824. The development of an effective party organization with its network of township committees, annual county conventions, and state conventions held biennially to nominate candidates for Congress and quadriennially to select Presidential electors had much to do with the party's success. So too did the party's legislative caucus that enabled the Republicans to dispense patronage and to provide party majorities on particular issues. The consistent inability of the Federalists to challenge the party on the national or state level, however, eroded the elaborate apparatus that the Democratic-Republicans had constructed. While certain of the party's county organizations remained active and cohesive to meet the Federalist threat in particular counties, the statewide organization gradually deteriorated as the danger of Federalist competition for national office diminished.[1]

Internal party disintegration emerged clearly during the Presidential election campaign of 1824. Representatives to the state Democratic-Republican convention failed to unite behind any one of the five Presidential candidates seeking their support. Delegates of William Crawford and Andrew Jackson joined forces and successfully nominated a slate of Presidential electors that included five supporters of Jackson and three supporters of Crawford. Appalled at this turn of events, John Quincy Adams's spokesmen withdrew from the convention and formed their own ticket. Jackson's supporters subsequently held another meeting where they replaced the Crawford electors with their own. Faced with a choice between Adams and Jackson, the Garden State backed "Old Hickory" at the polls.

Out of a divided and lethargic party, the Jackson men, sensing new opportunities for political power, created their own organization, nominated a set of electors, and won the state for their candidate.[2] The collapse of the state convention in 1824 as a device for marshaling party support and maintaining party unity behind candidates for national office was as clear a sign as Jackson's victory that a process of party realignment was taking place.

Further indication of the formation of new political alignments was not forthcoming until 1826 when the Democratic-Republican biennial state convention met to choose candidates for the House of Representatives. Again the question of whether those who called themselves Democratic-Republicans should support Jackson or Adams disrupted the meeting. Failing to agree on a single list of candidates, each faction met separately and nominated its own ticket. Although the party labels of Federalist and Democratic-Republican still retained some meaning in certain areas of the state, political contests in New Jersey were henceforth to be waged under the banners of the Jackson Party and the Adams or Administration Party.

Congressional and state elections between 1826 and 1828 provided the opportunity for both parties to strengthen their forces and to organize effective party machineries. Opportunistic Federalists who had played an active role in the initial thrust of the Jacksonians now flocked to both sides, attracted by promises of political office and partisan favors.[3] As the Presidential campaign of 1828 approached, the Jackson Party and the Adams Party were both prepared to wage well-organized campaigns throughout the state. The participation of seventy-two percent of all eligible adult, white males is evidence of the effectiveness with which both sides carried out their tasks.[4]

In terms of this study, the fact that John Quincy Adams won the state by some 2,000 votes is less important to remember than that by 1829 there existed in New Jersey a highly structured, close competition between two new party groupings—the Jacksonian Democrats and the National Republicans. Antedating the creation of a national two-party system, these parties, after a period of coalitional reshuffling and stabilization, emerged in 1834 as state components of the Democratic and Whig parties. Andrew Jackson's assault on the Bank of the United States, providing as it did an issue on which the state parties could establish their identities, was a key element in this final stabilization of party alignments.[5]

II

New prospects for political power arising out of the shambles of the Democratic-Republican party and the Presidential elections of 1824 and 1828 gave rise to new party formations in New Jersey. Between 1829 and 1844 the incentive of electoral success and the evenness of competition compelled both sides to maintain elaborate organizations to accomplish their electoral function.

Voting returns for Congressional and Presidential elections indicate the balanced, competitive nature of the second party system in New Jersey. Tables 1 and 2 summarize the frequency with which percentages of the total popular vote in these contests achieved victory for either the Democrats or their opposition on the county level.[6] Although certain counties overwhelmingly supported one party, on a balance these statistics suggest a high level of competition throughout the state. Over 43 percent of all county Congressional returns between 1828 and 1840 and over 39 percent of all county Presidential returns between

TABLE 1

NEW JERSEY CONGRESSIONÀL ELECTIONS,
1828-1840

County	No. of Elections	No. of times counties carried by either Democrats or National Republican/Whigs with winning percentage of total vote between:				
		100-70	69-60	59-55	54-50	49-0
Atlantic	3		2	1		
Bergen	6			1	5	
Burlington	6		3	2	1	
Cape May	6	3	3			
Cumberland	6		1		5	
Essex	6		4	2		
Gloucester	6			4	2	
Hudson	1			1		
Hunterdon	6		2	3	1	
Mercer	2			2		
Middlesex	6			1	5	
Monmouth	6				6	
Morris	6				6	
Passaic	2			2		
Salem	6			2	4	
Somerset	6			1	5	
Sussex	6	5	1			
Warren	6		5	1		
TOTAL:	92	8	21	23	40	

1828 and 1844 registered winning percentages between 54% and 50%. For both categories of elections, over 68 percent of all victories were gained with winning percentages between 59% and 50%.

Analysis of state legislative elections also indicate the existence of a competitive two-party system. Utilization of a measure of party competition known as the *index of competitiveness* suggests that these elections were hotly contested. Calculation of the mean number of seats held by one party in the Council and the Assembly between 1829

TABLE 2

NEW JERSEY PRESIDENTIAL ELECTIONS,
1828-1844

County	No. of Elections	No. of times counties carried by either Democrats or National Republican/Whigs with winning percentage of total vote between:				
		100-70	69-60	59-55	54-50	49-0
Atlantic	2		2			
Bergen	5			2	3	
Burlington	5		2	3		
Cape May	5	3	2			
Cumberland	5			1	4	
Essex	5		2	3		
Gloucester	5		1	2	2	
Hudson	2		1	1		
Hunterdon	5			3	2	
Mercer	2			2		
Middlesex	5			1	4	
Monmouth	5				5	
Morris	5				5	
Passaic	2		2			
Salem	5			3	2	
Somerset	5			1	4	
Sussex	5	5				
Warren	5		5			
TOTAL:	78	8	17	22	31	

and 1844, along with the percentage of terms that party controlled both houses and the governor's chair, provides the necessary data for generating this measure. The mean of these three figures is the index of competitiveness. Its range is from 1.0000 to .0000, with .5000 representing absolutely even two-party competition.[7] The figure for New Jersey is .5034.

Table 3, a tabulation of party majorities in the Council and the Assembly, illustrates the keen competitive balance that existed between the state's major parties. Between

TABLE 3

Party Majorities in the Two Houses of the
New Jersey Legislature, 1829-1844

	Council		Assembly	
Year	Democratic Members	National Republican/ Whig Members	Democratic Members	National Republican/ Whig Members
1829	5	9	19	24
1830	10	4	33	10
1831	10	4	37	13
1832	8	6	26	24
1833	6	8	22	28
1834	12	2	41	9
1835	8	6	27	23
1836	9	5	34	16
1837	7	7	30	20
1838	6	10	18	35
1839	7	10	20	33
1840	7	10	20	33
1841	5	13	12	41
1842	9	9	23	35
1843	8	10	25	33
1844	12	6	35	23
TOTAL:	129	119	422	420

1829 and 1844 each side was able to secure majorities in these houses an equal number of times. The National Republicans achieved majorities in 1829 and 1833, while Whigs predominated in the six legislative sessions between 1838 and 1843.[8] Democrats secured victories in the three sessions between 1830 and 1832, the four sessions between 1834 and 1837, and in 1844. Like their opponents, the Democrats' mean majority in the Assembly during their eight years in control was sixteen. When dominant, both sides maintained at least a two-seat margin in the Council. The only exceptions were the 1837 and 1842 sessions when Council seats were evenly divided along party lines.[9]

III

Recent scholarship suggests that prior to 1840 Whigs were less efficient in creating voter-oriented mass-party organizations than the Democrats.[10] In his study of Michigan politics, Ronald Formisano even argues that the disparate social and religious beliefs of Michigan's Democrats and Whigs resulted in Whig antipartyism and a consequent lack of organizational ability.[11] However provocative such notions are, it appears that crucial factors in determining the nature of party organization are the closeness of party competition and the prospects for victory. National anti-Jackson coalitions were unsuccessful until 1840, while in Michigan the Democrats dominated state-election contests into the 1850s. In contrast, New Jersey's activists on both sides responded to the realities of electoral success by instituting and maintaining vigorous party organizations.

The party organizations developed to contest for the Presidency in 1828 were sustained throughout the Jackson period to supervise the selection of candidates, to devise and coordinate campaign strategies, and to mobilize voter support. From the records of the state conventions down

to the procedures adopted by township vigilance committees, there is an abundance of evidence to indicate that
both sides took their work seriously. The smallest units of
party organization were the ward and township meetings.
Here candidates for local office and delegates to the party's county and state conventions were selected. These
meetings also appointed the poll and vigilance committees
responsible for bringing out the vote on election day.
County conventions, like ward and township meetings,
were held yearly. Delegates to these conventions nominated the party's ticket for the annual state legislative elections and for elective county posts. State conventions were
held every four years to select a slate of presidential electors and every two years to nominate congressional tickets.[12]

These various party gatherings usually convened in
July, August, and September in order to prepare for the
October elections. Party activity, however, was not limited
to these few months. There is evidence, for example, of
county and state party meetings held as early as April.[13]
Moreover, close party associations with particular
newspapers allowed both sides to present their cases to the
state's voters.[14]

The decentralized nature of party-in-the constituency or
the party organization proper resulted from the formal
procedures that governed elections in New Jersey.[15] Regardless of whether the election was for local, county,
state, or national office, the township served as the election
unit. Rather than journeying to the county seat to cast
their ballots, eligible voters could usually exercise their
franchise without venturing far from their homes. Secret
ballots, either printed or written, were required. Suffrage
was restricted to free, white, male citizens, twenty-one
years of age or older, who paid taxes. Aliens, women,
slaves, and blacks were officially disenfranchised. For the
most part the tax requirement was not enforced. With few
modifications, these procedures were maintained up to

1844, thus resulting in an electorate that by 1840 included over four-fifths of all the adult, white males in the state.

The need to extend their appeals to the smallest unit of state government in order to reach a mass electorate compelled parties to organize extensively. The frequency of elections and the virtual absence of district representation in both congressional and state legislative contests were also factors in this process. Congressional elections took place on the same days as state elections, except in Presidential election years when they were held on the first Tuesday in November. Up to 1842 the general ticket method of election prevailed. A federal law of that year requiring all states to use only the district method relieved New Jersey's candidates from the burden of statewide campaigns.

Annual elections were held to elect individuals to the two houses of the state legislature. The size of the Council and the Assembly and the apportionment of their county representatives changed over the years. Each county was represented by one councillor and, after 1830, by one assemblyman for each of its 6,000 inhabitants.[16] By 1844 the Council contained eighteen councillors, while the Assembly membership equaled fifty-eight.[17] Candidates for office were always chosen by the entire voting population of their counties.

IV

Concern for organization was not limited to the maintenance of the party organization proper. Having expended great effort in order to obtain state legislative majorities, partisans on both sides recognized the need for some kind of organization in the legislature in order to convert their mere presence into important determinants of legislative behavior. The broad constitutional powers possessed by the legislature encouraged party efforts in this direction.

The New Jersey constitution of 1776 conferred the major responsibility for governing the state on the legislature.[18] Both the Council and the Assembly chose their own leaders, the vice-president and the speaker respectively, as well as other minor legislative officers. Each house decided upon its own adjournments and judged the qualifications and the elections of its members.

The legislature's power to supervise its own conduct matched its authority over the enactment of legislation and the appointment of officials. Both the Council and the Assembly were empowered "to prepare bills to be passed into laws." Majority approval in both houses were the sole requirements necessary for a bill's passage. The governor, annually elected by the legislature, had no constitutionally defined role in the lawmaking process. With the absence of the executive veto, the only checks on the legislature's lawmaking power were the constitution's explicit instructions that the citizen's rights to religious freedom, trial by jury, and annual legislative elections remain sacred. Except for these specific limitations, the legislature was left alone to decide for itself what subjects to consider.

The legislature's control over appointments was also constitutionally sanctioned. Together, the Council and the Assembly were instructed to hold joint meetings during each legislative session. At these meetings legislators selected, by a majority vote, numerous state officials, including the governor, state treasurer, attorney-general, and supreme court justices, as well as a variety of county civil, judicial, and military officers. The legislature also set its own criteria for evaluating the suitability of potential officeholders.

The joint authority given to the Council and the Assembly concerning the enactment of legislation and the appointment of officials was supplemented by certain exclusive powers given to each house. Only the Assembly could initiate the preparation or the alteration of money bills. The Council, in concert with the governor, served as the

38   THE BEHAVIOR OF STATE LEGISLATIVE PARTIES

court of appeals in the last resort. Finally, the Assembly was authorized to initiate impeachment proceedings against any official appointed by the legislature but only the Council could try such cases.

Between 1829 and 1844, parties in New Jersey clearly functioned in a setting in which the legislature maintained uncontested and exclusive control over the passage of legislation, the appointment of officials, and the organization of its affairs. The opportunity for true party government thus existed. Although hardly proof that this situation was realized, the legislative party caucus provided the means for the effective manipulation of party majorities to that end. This device was employed by New Jersey's partisans to organize themselves as legislative parties. Although its application in New Jersey between 1829 and 1844 was neither unique to the period nor to the state, it was the caucus that gave the party representatives in the legislature the potential to overcome internal differences and problems and to operate as cohesive forces within it.[19]

When called, caucus meetings were usually held at night in rooms in the statehouse.[20] Here the legislators of each party met separately to debate questions of partisan interest and to come to decisions on these matters by the majority vote of those in attendance. All votes cast at these sessions were by secret ballot.[21] Although there might be vigorous debate and disagreement, the unanimous support of all was expected once a decision had been reached.

Participation in caucus meetings was not limited solely to legislators. Party leaders who were not legislators and certain governors, acting as partisans, attended caucus sessions. In some instances these individuals were responsible for drawing up the agenda of the party conclaves.[22] Referring to Garret Wall, James Green, and James Parker, all important leaders of the Democratic party in New Jersey, one newspaper reporter in 1832 noted that the power of these "outsiders" in the Democratic legislative party caucus was so great, that they "controlled and will still control to the uttermost the members of that party [Democratic] in the Legislature."[23]

On one level the caucus provided the means by which a party could achieve some measure of continuity in legislative matters that were of partisan interest. At the same time the caucus served as a liaison between the party in office and the party organization proper. By allowing close cooperation between stable outside party leadership and the parties' legislative representatives, the potential for coordinating and integrating the goals and incentives of both sectors of the party existed.[24]

In his study of New Jersey's Democratic-Republicans, Carl Prince notes the stultifying impact of one-party rule after 1817 on party organization in and out of the legislature. The political situation in New Jersey between 1829 and 1844, however, marked as it was by a balanced, competitive two-party system in which both sides had equal success in securing legislative majorities, was a constant spur to party organization. So, too, were the broad constitutional powers possessed by the legislature. The adoption of a new state constitution in 1844 altered somewhat this constitutional environment, thus posing a new set of problems for analyzing party-in-the legislature. By terminating this study in 1844, then, attention remains fixed on a period characterized by competitive party politics and by a framework of government with its emphasis on legislative dominance that remained constant.[25]

Notes

1. Carl E. Prince, *New Jersey's Jeffersonian Republicans: The Genesis of an Early Party Machine, 1789–1817* (Chapel Hill, North Carolina: University of North Carolina Press 1967) provides an excellent account of the formation and the power of New Jersey's Democratic-Republicans. I have relied on Prince's account for an understanding of New Jersey politics between 1800 and 1824. Also useful in this respect are McCormick, "Party Formation," pp. 161–73; and Peter D.

Levine, "The New Jersey Federalist Party Convention of 1814," *The Journal of the Rutgers University Library* 33 (December 1969): 1–8.

2. McCormick, "Party Formation," p. 165.

3. Walter R. Fee, *The Transition From Aristocracy to Democracy in New Jersey, 1789–1829* (Somerville, New Jersey: Somerset Press 1933), pp. 244–68.

4. McCormick, "Party Formation," p. 167.

5. Ibid., pp. 168–72. As McCormick indicates, along with the Bank of the United States, Jacksonians and National Republicans divided over support of the Joint Companies, a powerful transportation company in New Jersey that will be discussed at length in chapter 6. Fallaw, "The Rise of the Whig Party in New Jersey," attempts, rather unconvincingly, to argue that the transition from National Republican to Whig was something more than the relative stabilization of party alignments already clearly noticeable as early as 1828.

6. Election data was obtained from the Historical Archive at the Inter-University Consortium for Political Research, Ann Arbor, Michigan. Congressional elections included in Table 1 include those held in 1828, 1830, 1832, 1834, 1838, and 1840. No data at all were available for the 1836 election. Election data for congressional elections after 1840 were too spotty to warrant inclusion.

7. Ranney, p. 64, describes the index of competiveness. Included in this description is an additional calculation, that is, the inclusion of the average percent of the popular vote won by the party's gubernatorial candidate. Because New Jersey's governors were chosen by the legislators rather than by popular vote prior to 1844, this figure was omitted.

8. Legislative sessions began in late October and usually continued to March of the following year. For convenience, sessions will be referred to by the year in which they ended. Thus the session that began in October 1843 and ended in March 1844 will be referred to as the 1844 session.

9. One-party dominance in particular counties appeared more frequently in state legislative contests than in national or congressional elections. With minor exceptions, Sussex, Warren, Hunterdon, and Atlantic always elected Democrats, and Essex, Mercer, and Cape May only National Republicans or Whigs to the legislature. Four other counties presented slightly less of a one-party situation. The remaining counties found each party winning a minimum of twenty-five percent of the annual legislative elections held between 1829 and 1844. Rarely, however, did the minority party in any county fail to either nominate candidates or actively campaign in their behalf. *See* chapter 3, Tables 10 and 11 for information on party participation by county for legislative elections.

10. For example, *see* Robert Remini, *The Election of Andrew Jackson* (New York: J. B. Lippincott, 1963), pp. 121–166; and Lynn L. Marshall, "The Strange Stillbirth of the Whig Party," *American Historical Review* 72 (January 1967): 445–468.

11. Formisano, pp. 56–81.

12. Contemporary newspapers, particularly the *Newark Daily Advertiser*, provide abundant evidence of party organization. *Also see* Ershkowitz, "New Jersey Politics," pp. 70–220.

13. For example, *see State Convention of the National Republican Young Men of New Jersey,* June 1832, Peter Voorhees Papers, R.U.L.

14. A full discussion of party relationships with newspapers appears in chapter 8.

15. Sorauf, "Political Parties and Political Analysis," pp. 37–39, distinguishes three sectors of the party. The party organization proper "is the political party of the party officials, the activists, and the members; it is the purposeful, organized, initiating vanguard of the party." I use this term interchangeably with party-in-the constituency to connote the organized wing of the party that involves itself in conducting elections. The party in office is Sorauf's designation for the legislative party organization, what I refer to as the legislative party or party-in-the legislature. Sorauf identifies a third sector, the party-in-the electorate, as composed of "those partisans who attach themselves to the party either by regular support at the polls or through self-identification."

16. Richard P. McCormick, *The History of Voting in New Jersey, A Study of the Development of Election Machinery, 1664–1911* (New Brunswick, New Jersey: Rutgers University Press, 1953), p. 120. All information concerning suffrage requirements and election procedures was taken from this book, pp. 64–159.

17. *J.N.J.L.C.,* 1829–1844; *P.N.J.G.A.,* 1829–1844. At the beginning of the proceedings of the Council and the Assembly for every session a list of delegates, by county, is provided.

18. Charles R. Erdman, Jr., *The New Jersey Constitution of 1776* (Princeton, New Jersey: Princeton University Press, 1929). *Also see Proceedings of the New Jersey State Constitutional Convention of 1844,* comp. and ed. New Jersey (Federal) Writer's Project, with Introduction by John Bebout (n.p., 1942), pp. 16–19. Information concerning the specific powers of the legislature was taken from a copy of the constitution located in this volume, pp. 1–6. Cited hereafter as Bebout, Introduction, or *Proceedings 1844.*

19. Prince, pp. 107–130, discusses the use of the legislative party caucus by New Jersey's Democratic-Republican party between 1801 and 1817. Ralph V. Harlow, *The History of Legislative Methods in the Period Before 1825* (New Haven, Connecticut: Yale University Press, 1917), dates the origin of the caucus to colonial times and notes that it was used in the United States Congress as early as 1790.

20. *Proceedings 1844,* p. 354.

21. Ibid.

22. Stacy Potts to Garret D. Wall, 30 October 1829, Charles Philhower Collection, R.U.L.

23. *Newark Daily Advertiser,* 21 September 1832. Garret D. Wall, Peter D. Vroom, James Green, and James Parker were named as Democratic party leaders. For an example of Whig organizational ability, *see* Herbert Ershkowitz, "Samuel L. Southard: A Case Study of Whig Leadership in the Age of Jackson," *New Jersey History* 88 (Spring 1970): 5–24.

24. Sorauf, "Political Parties and Political Analysis," pp. 37–38, recognizes this relationship as a crucial determinant of party behavior.

25. *Proceedings 1844*, pp. 614–33, contain a copy of the 1844 constitution. The most important changes involved the office of the governor. The chief executive was then granted veto power over the enactment of legislation and was to be elected annually by the eligible voters of New Jersey. In addition, a number of judicial posts, formerly appointed in Joint Meeting, were to be chosen by the people. The term of office for members of the Council was also extended from one to three years.

2
The Legislative Setting

By 1829 New Jersey legislators functioned in a setting that facilitated the execution of the legislature's broad constitutional powers. The legislative session consisted of two sittings, committees processed the legislature's varied agenda, and definite rules and precedents governed the lawmaking process and the day-to-day operation of the Council and the Assembly. Modifications involving the number of committees and the legislature's relations with the governor altered this system only slightly over the next sixteen years. This legislative environment had direct consequences for the organization, operation, and influence of legislative parties.

I

New Jersey's statehouse, constructed in 1790, was located in the city of Trenton on a plot of land between State

Street and the Delaware River. Separate chambers were provided for the Council and the Assembly. Here the state's legislators convened annually during the last week of October. The work of the legislature was divided into two sittings. The first sitting usually lasted two weeks. The second, or adjourned sitting, generally began at the end of the first week in January and lasted to late February or early March. Except for an emergency third sitting in 1837, these two meetings comprised the only time during the year that legislators performed their duties.[1]

A clear division of labors existed between the first and the second sitting. The work of the first sitting was essentially preparatory, "a mere coming together for the purpose of organizing—a setting the wheels of government in motion. . . ."[2] At this time the members of both houses separately selected their own officers. In Joint Meeting they chose the governor and filled other vacant state and county posts. Legislators then considered unfinished business from the previous session, renewed the annual accounts of the treasurer and of the state prison, composed an agenda for the current session, and introduced legislation. Committee assignments in both houses were also decided upon.[3]

Even the few laws enacted during the first sitting dealt primarily with readying the legislature for the decisive adjourned sitting. Only 154 of the 1,795 acts approved between 1829 and 1844 were processed during first sittings.[4] Of these, fourteen were public or general acts; legislation that affected the entire state or which enunciated a policy position by the state on a particular subject. The remaining 140 enactments involved private or special legislation and certain procedural measures that concerned the expenditure of state monies necessary for the operation of government. Special acts concerned specific, named concerns: individuals, corporate bodies, townships, or counties.[5] Fifty-one such acts approved during the first sitting involved the granting of divorces and the execution of trusts.

Described by one newspaper editor as "legislative bores," they comprised nearly one-third of all the legislation that was enacted during the first sittings.[6] The passage of government-support acts and of acts to defray incidental expenses accounted for another twenty-eight measures.

As with legislation, few resolutions received legislative approval before recess. Between 1829 and 1844 the Council and the Assembly enacted 134 joint resolutions on a variety of national and state issues. The evils of drink, the necessity of state-supported internal-improvement projects, the conduct of Andrew Jackson, the Bank of the United States, relations with France, tariff laws, and the disposition of the nation's public lands were all subjects of resolutions. Only thirty-eight of these resolutions were approved during the first sittings. Of these, three dealt with national issues, while twenty concerned procedural matters, such as the appointment of a clerk to engross bills or of a printer to publish the state's laws.

The appointment of legislative officials, the distribution of committee assignments, and the enactment of some legislation that for the most part elicited little debate during the first sittings of the legislature, all allowed the lawmakers to get down to the major part of their agenda during the second sittings. The preparation of bills and the investigation of particular problems that often led to additional legislation occupied much of the time of these sittings. Over ninety-one percent of all laws enacted by the legislature between 1829 and 1844 were processed at this time. Passage votes usually came in a flurry during the last weeks of session after many hours spent in preparing and debating proposed legislation. The only exception to the division of labors between the first and the second sittings concerned the Joint Meetings. Of sixty-one of these sessions held between 1829 and 1844, thirty-three were held during the first sittings. More than 3,240 of the 7,146 appointments approved by the legislature were handled at these meetings.[7]

II

Although the major part of the legislative agenda awaited the adjourned sitting, legislative organization depended upon the appointment of legislative officials and the allocation of committee assignments accomplished in October and November. Partisan control over these offices and committees was not, by itself, a motivating force behind party efforts to elect their candidates to the statehouse. Nevertheless, the potential inherent in such control for cohesive legislative party behavior was not lost on either the Democrats or their opposition.

The chief officers of the legislature—the vice-president of the Council and the speaker of the Assembly—were responsible for prescribing the order of business in their respective chambers and for determining all questions of order regarding house rules.[8] If loyal party men, they could arrange the agenda of the legislature to suit party needs. The simple matter of giving precedence to certain legislation or of recognizing the right of one member to speak before another, maneuvers allowed by the powers of their offices, could be used in partisan fashion. Democratic, National Republican, and Whig legislators recognized the advantages inherent in controlling these positions.

The selection of candidates for these positions was a primary task of the legislative party caucuses held in Trenton immediately prior to the opening of the first sitting.[9] Speakers and vice-presidents were always members of the majority party in their respective chambers. In those years where the minority party offered its own candidates, the nominees of the majority party always won election by a strict party vote; all of the members of each party in the respective house supporting the favorites of their own party.[10]

Aside from their duties as presiding officers, the speaker and the vice-president appointed their colleagues to Assembly and Council committees.[11] Like most state legislatures in the first half of the nineteenth century, the New Jersey legislature organized and employed a system of standing and select committees in both houses. These committees were the essential elements in transacting the legislature's agenda. Standing and select committees received the petitions and memorials of the state's citizens. These agencies also initiated all general legislation. Regardless of committee recommendations, all bills were presented on the floor of the house to which the committee belonged.[12] At this time committee members offered their opinions as well as any information that had influenced their decision. The legislature was not bound to abide by committee suggestions. Nor did these reports always receive the unanimous support of all committee members. Their presentation, however, was the necessary prerequisite for legislative action.[13]

Newspaper correspondents and legislators themselves made it quite clear that the committees were responsible for the smooth functioning of legislative affairs. One reporter noted in 1837, for instance, that "the legislature had done little as they are waiting the reports of several committees. . . ."[14] William Stites, speaker of the Assembly in 1840, put it more precisely; addressing his fellow assemblymen, Stites informed them "that for the dispatch of business much depends on the Chair, yet it by no means rests there altogether. In the ordinary course of legislation, almost the entire business of the house, must, of necessity, pass through the hands of some one of its committees."[15]

The number of standing committees increased over the years, while the number of select committees varied from year to year.[16] From 1829 to 1837 the Assembly functioned with five standing committees: unfinished business, rules, support, incidental expenses, and taxes. For these same years the Council operated with committees on rules and unfinished business. In 1838 both houses added standing committees to deal with matters relating to agriculture, corporations, education, judicial proceedings, the militia, and military pensions.[17] The Assembly also created committees on elections and on ways and means. The unusually large volume of legislation during the 1837 session undoubtedly influenced the decision to organize additional committees. [18]

Standing joint committees composed of members of both houses also existed. Separate committees were responsible for settling the treasurer's accounts, reviewing the expenditures and the income of the state prison, and receiving proposals for the public printing. In 1831 a fourth joint committee was established to wait upon the governor. Its function was to relate to the legislature whatever the chief executive wished to communicate concerning the affairs of the state.

Select committees dealt with special bills and with any kind of extraordinary circumstances that required action on the part of the legislature.[19] When concerned with special legislation these committees usually included one legislator from the county in which the bill originated. On occasion select joint committees were utilized to frame particular pieces of general legislation that were likely to provoke much debate and disagreement.[20]

Party dominance in committee would create a situation in which the majority party could shape legislative activity as it desired. Although it is not certain that the legislative caucus of the majority party provided direct advice on committee assignments, the individuals who served as speaker and vice-president, elected as partisans, made them with an eye toward securing this party advantage.

During the eight years of National Republican and Whig legislative supremacy, members of these parties maintained at least a one-seat advantage over their Democratic counterparts on thirty-six of forty-five standing Council committees. Democratic councillors controlled two committees, while seven were composed of one individual from each party. National Republican and Whig assemblymen held majorities on fifty-three of fifty-nine standing committees. The selection of the membership of the joint committees showed similar results, for all of the twenty-six appointed in these years contained either National Republican or Whig majorities.[21]

The pattern of Democratic control during that party's stay in power was just as impressive. Of eighteen standing Council committees appointed during the eight years of Democratic dominance, fourteen contained Democratic majorities. Only one committee had more opposition legislators than Democrats, while three were composed of one member from each side. Democrats also held majorities on thirty-six of thirty-eight Assembly committees and on twenty-six of twenty-nine joint committees.

With few exceptions, minority control of standing committees, when it did occur, was limited to those bodies concerned with unfinished business, incidental expenses, support bills, and rules.[22] On those Assembly committees where the majority party held more than a one-seat advantage over the minority, no committee recorded such a margin more than twice. In the Council only the committee on unfinished business, which registered a 2–0 margin for the majority party in six sessions, the rules committee, which accomplished the same advantage in three sessions, and the committee on corporations, which had a Whig majority of two during the 1838 session, ever obtained more than a one-seat edge for either the majority or the minority party. The joint committees on the treasurer's reports, the state prison, and the public printing recorded at least a two-seat advantage for the majority party in five, six, and seven sessions, respectively.

Additional steps were taken by both sides to name experienced partisans to committee chairmanships. All but six chairmen of standing Council and Assembly committees selected in National Republican and Whig years were members of these parties. All but five of the chairmen of these committees in Democratic years were Democrats. In the Council over sixty-four percent of National Republican and Whig chairmen and over seventy-three percent of Democratic chairmen had prior legislative experience. In the Assembly over ninety percent of all committee chairmen previously occupied Assembly seats.[23]

The composition of standing committees also reflected this emphasis on experience. Out of a total of sixty-three standing Council committees, only three were comprised solely of freshmen legislators. Ten contained only men with prior service, while fifty included a combination of newcomers and experienced legislators. Of the Assembly's ninety-seven standing committees, three were composed entirely of first-year men, nine were occupied solely by experienced hands, and eighty-six included a mixture of both types. Thus, the speakers and the vice-presidents, regardless of party affiliation, by emphasizing party identity and legislative experience in choosing the membership of the standing committees created a situation where machinery crucial to the processing of legislation remained in the hands of loyal and experienced partisans.

Although similar data were not obtainable for the select committees of both houses, appointments to these bodies were obviously not immune to partisan considerations.[24] A Democratic newspaper editor charged that Whig legislators during the 1839 sessions "made a great and successful struggle to pack a committee by ballot, which being devoted to partisan purposes, would throw off public pursuit on a false scent."[25] A similar charge leveled against the Democrats by a Whig editor during the 1834 session presents a clear illustration of the manner in which select committees were chosen. After reporting that a committee of five Democratic assemblymen had been appointed to propose a resolution on the Bank of the United States, he noted that "the Speaker does certainly believe that it is very unparliamentary to appoint any other than Jackson men on a committee, if the subject had the most distant connection with politics."[26]

III

Partisan control over legislative offices and committees suggest the availability of legislative parties for channeling demands before the legislature. Examination of the rules governing the lawmaking process and the nature of proposals before the legislature indicate the kinds of situations in which this influence might be felt.

For every session the members of the Council and the Assembly adopted formal rules to govern their proceedings. Although each house drew up its own set, these procedural regulations were similar and changed little from year to year. The variations between those for the Council and those for the Assembly were usually factors of the difference in the size of the two bodies.[27] As stated in these rules, both houses began their day with the reading of their journals. Presentation of documents, letters, petitions, memorials, committee reports, and resolutions followed. Permission to introduce bills or to request leaves of absence could be sought. Bills and resolutions previously introduced were discussed. Amendments might be offered and passage votes taken. Preference was given to the unfinished business of the preceding meeting and general legislation was given priority over special legislation.

Bills and resolutions presented in the Council and the Assembly received three readings and an engrossment before passage votes were taken. Both houses required the consent of the majority of the members present to move a bill along to the next reading. A majority of the full membership of each house was necessary for final passage. After receiving approval in one house, each bill was sent to the other chamber for consideration. If amendments were added, the bill returned to the original house for reconsideration. On those occasions when an impasse was reached, committees of conference, composed of dissenting members from both houses, were called to try to work out a compromise.

These rules established procedures with which the legislature performed its most important responsibility; namely, the enactment of legislation. Between 1829 and 1844 these practices were applied most often to the processing of private or special legislation; the category of proposals that generated the least disagreement among the state's lawmakers, but which took up a good deal of their time.

Special legislation, comprising eighty-seven percent of all of the laws enacted by the legislature in these years, was not the subject of as much disagreement as the enactment of general legislation. The source of special legislation and the nature of the response that it elicited from the state's lawmakers supports this contention. Although there is no way of accurately determining the percentage of bills originating through petitions, it appears that literally all special legislation was in response to the specific demands of interested citizens. Requests for bank or business charters, divorces, and other special matters were presented to the legislature in the form of petitions.[28] In many instances these papers were worded as bills so as to expedite the lawmaking process.[29]

The types of motions in both houses eliciting recorded roll-call votes indicates that much legislation occasioned little opposition. Although legislators were required to vote upon motions to give every bill, whether general or special, three readings and to engross it, recorded roll-call votes were limited almost entirely to final passage votes and to proposals to amend bills. During the 1837 Assembly session, for instance, of 298 recorded roll-call votes, 198 were on motions to amend or to enact particular bills. Only fourteen concerned motions to engross bills and only five

to give them second readings.[30] The infrequent requests
for polling members on motions other than amendments
and final-passage votes on legislation predominately special in nature indicates little disagreement over such questions.[31]

The distribution of roll-call votes in the Council and the
Assembly between general and special legislation offers
conclusive proof that special legislation produced less disagreement than general legislation. Excluding roll calls
needed to approve the 185 divorces and 370 laws involving
the conveyance and the execution of estates, 1,999 roll
calls were recorded in Council and 2,592 roll calls were
recorded in the Assembly between 1829 and 1844. In the
Council, 1,129 roll calls found at least 85% of those members voting in agreement on each ballot. The remaining
870 roll calls found councillors taking different sides, at
least 15% of those members voting against the majority
position on each measure. On roll calls producing substantial agreement, 60% involved special legislation, 22% involved general legislation, and 18½ involved procedural
questions. Where measurable disagreement existed, 54%
of the bills were special in nature, 26% concerned general
proposals, and 20% dealt with procedural matters.[32]

A similar pattern occurred in the Assembly. Of the
2,592 Assembly roll calls, 944 found at least 85% of those
members voting on each ballot in agreement. The remaining 1,648 roll calls found at least 15% of those assemblymen voting on each roll call opposed to the majority position. On those questions where there was near unanimity,
64% were concerned with special legislation, 21% with
general legislation, and 15% with procedural questions.
Where measurable disagreement existed, 48% of the bills
involved special legislation, 31% dealt with general legislation, and 22% involved procedural concerns.

Excluding roll calls concerned with divorces and estates,
more than 55% of all Council roll calls and 37% of all
Assembly roll calls did not engender sharp conflict among

New Jersey's lawmakers. Significantly, general enactments, although a small percentage of the total number of laws approved, occasioned more division than special legislation. Uncovering patterns of partisan response on special and general legislation will help determine party attitudes on substantive matters, while leading to an understanding of both the functions and the goals of legislative parties.

IV

The presence of established procedures and an organizational structure for conducting legislative business complemented the legislature's relationship with the executive branch of state government. Constitutionally deprived of formal authority to influence legislative action, the governor as party leader nevertheless exerted clear pressure on party representatives in the legislature.

Expansion of the governor's powers during the period of the second party system coincided with the reconstitution of the state's political parties in the late 1820s and early 1830s.[33] Individuals who served as governors between 1829 and 1844 were prominent men in their parties.[34] All of them were chosen by the legislature and every man who occupied the post belonged to the party that had a majority in the legislature during the year in which he served. By becoming involved in the organization of the legislature's agenda and by exerting an informal influence over the deliberations of individual legislators, they expanded the scope of the governor's office. Their desire to further party interests most often explained their actions.

Peter D. Vroom of Somerset, a key Democratic party leader who served as governor for six sessions between 1829 and 1836, was the most important figure in the development of increased participation by the chief executive in legislative affairs. Shortly after his first election, Vroom sent to the legislature his personal comments and recommendations on those matters that he felt demanded its attention. In particular, he called for action on the common school system, the need for prison reform, and for a positive response by the legislators to the proposals concerning the chartering of the Delaware and Raritan Canal Company and the Camden and Amboy Railroad Company.[35]

This address was presented on 7 January 1830. Seven weeks later a joint resolution unanimously enacted by the Council and the Assembly made it the duty of the governor to address the legislature each October for the purpose of "recommending such measures in relation to resources, finances, laws, and policy of the state, as may tend to promote the happiness and prosperity of the people."[36] Other governors had delivered messages to the legislature on special occasions. Now, however, the presentation of these addresses became a required part of the legislature's proceedings.

These annual addresses often dealt with specific proposals for government action. At the least they provided the legislators with general comments on the prosperity of the state and the condition of its finances. In 1832, for example, Vroom recommended that the legislature seriously consider a new tax bill that would equalize the payments made by landholders with those whose wealth was not in the form of land. In addition the governor urged that the Orphan's Court system be reformed and that a new state prison be built.[37] Two years later he proposed that the "multiplication of banks be stayed" and that the law passed in 1830 prohibiting the passage and circulation of foreign bank notes under $5 be reenacted.[38] The next year Vroom reiterated his concern over banks and urged that "corporations, of any description . . . be sparingly created."[39] Elias P. Seeley, Whig governor during part of the 1833 session, after reporting on the condition of the treasury, proposed a legislative program that called for the abolition of public executions and of the militia system, revision of the School Fund, and legislation regarding the influx of "colored persons" into the state.[40]

It is clear that after 1830, New Jersey's governors en-hanced their own roles by presenting their views on state affairs to the legislature. Nor were these annual messages received merely out of courtesy. The establishment of the joint committee to wait upon the governor in 1831 is only one example of the seriousness with which New Jersey's legislators considered the programs of the state's chief executives. The building of a new penitentiary, planned reform of the Orphan's Court system, legislation limiting the circulation of small bank notes, and a general law con-cerning the formation of limited partnerships are just a few instances of legislative action generated from specific suggestions of New Jersey's governors between 1829 and 1844.[41] In most years the various proposals offered by the governor were referred to select committees where they were transformed into bills or resolutions for presentation to the legislature.[42] Although not always acted upon posi-tively, the messages of the governor represented a major program of priorities considered by the legislature.

These messages often were designed to provide the dominant legislative party with a program on which it could take positive action. In meeting this party need, the governor's involvement and hence his authority became increasingly more noticeable. For instance, during his term as governor in the 1833 session, Samuel Southard, the undisputed leader of New Jersey's National Republi-cans, urged the National Republican-controlled legislature to approve the construction of a new prison and to revise the state's legal code and court system so that his party could structure its campaigns, in part, on the basis of its legislative achievements. In his message Southard also demanded the legislature make its opinions known on Andrew Jackson's role in destroying the Bank of the United States, a move clearly designed to distinguish his party from the Democrats in the minds of the state's voters.[43]

The ability of the governor to influence the appointment of local officials, almost nonexistent under the constitution of 1776, also naturally expanded between 1829 and 1844. The appointment of notary publics, masters in chancery, and flour inspectors devolved on the governor.[44] In 1837 when no Joint Meeting was held during the second sitting, Governor Philemon Dickerson was able to appoint the clerks and the surrogates for two newly created counties. On occasion, the men who served in the post were asked to obtain certain county appointments for various individuals.[45] In one instance, a governor was offered a substantial bribe to obtain an appointment for a particular individual. Invariably, governors acted as partisans in these matters by seeking to gain the appointment of individuals who belonged to their own party.[46]

Intrusions into the legislators' domain were not limited to governors acting as party leaders. Throughout the 1830s and the 1840s the legislature permitted professional lobbyists in its midst whose sole purpose was to shape the content of legislation to suit the needs of their clients. A variety of special interests, party included, made use of this service.

The special needs of the state's citizens, be they the desire of one individual to receive a divorce, or the wish of a number of people to form a new community or to obtain a business charter, were often guided through the legislature by lobbyists. One newspaper correspondent noted that "people would be astonished to hear how fully and familiarly these gentlemen offer the votes of their representatives, to those who wish them. . . . I very much suspect that they lay claim to quite as much influence as they possess: and if they do not exaggerate, the other two houses are little more than merely the 'mouthpieces' to express their decisions."[47]

Although no direct references in the records of the legislature exist regarding lobbying and little of a specific nature is mentioned in the newspapers, scattered evidence indicates that this informal pressure-group activity was quite prevalent.

In 1835, the *Newark Daily Advertiser* ran a series of articles authored by a "Spy in Trenton" about lobbying. An excerpt from an interview with a fictitious expresident of the lobby, "Dick Bonus," provides a description of its operation.

> Formerly [Dick] observed he got his board and lodging out of the Banks; the water powers found him in terapins and champaigne [sic]—the manufacturing incorporations supplied incidental expenses, and the divorces furnished grog and cigars; but now, said he, Banks are all cried down, the water powers have run dry; nothing going on but those abominable Rail Roads, who are always too poor or too stingy to fork out a fee to us gentlemen of the third house.[48]

The struggle for power between the Camden and Amboy Railroad and Delaware and Raritan Canal Company—the Joint Companies as they were called—and the New Jersey Railroad, between 1833 and 1836, affords a more specific illustration of how lobbyists utilized their skills. At issue was control of all passenger and freight transportation between New York and Philadelphia; control that the Joint Companies already possessed and that the combined interests of four companies, led by the New Jersey Railroad, wanted to share. The members of the "third house" were also quite interested in the "conflict between the two great railroads." As one correspondent wrote, "the lobby seems anxious to have a finger in the pye [sic], and every stage and railroad car brings us several of the younger and promising members of that valuable appendage to the house."[49] As events indicate, these individuals did quite well.

Between 1833 and 1836 the Trenton and New Brunswick Turnpike Company, one of the four companies attempting to wrest control from the Joint Companies, employed twelve men to act as their lobby in Trenton. The total expenses and fees paid to these individuals came to $2,738.15, with a scale ranging from as little as $34 to as much as $900 per lobbyist. One lobbyist eventually sued the Trenton and New Brunswick Turnpike Company in order to recover funds spent in behalf of securing a charter for the Bergen Port Company. Two other lobbyists in the employ of the turnpike company testified in his behalf. One related how in return for working on the same charter he was promised the post of secretary in the company at a salary of $500 a year. In the course of his testimony, he described how unfriendly legislators were assigned to various members of the "third house" who in turn entertained their charges with "champagne suppers." The other individual who testified at this case concurred that these free dinners were the most effective way of influencing New Jersey's legislators.[50]

The influence exerted by lobbyists on behalf of special concerns, although difficult to document in every instance, indicates the presence of a variety of interests seeking favors from the legislature. In terms of the lawmaking process, effective operation of legislative parties depended upon their ability to sift through a diverse agenda and to mediate the demands of these interests, including those of party. Party control of the offices of speaker and vice-president and of the committees responsible for processing legislation certainly created the potential for party influence on legislative decisions. The effective operation of the legislative party caucus in controlling this legislative machinery indicates its ability to marshal votes on crucial questions. The governor's influence, dictated by partisan considerations, also encouraged decisive party action. Only careful investigation of the careers of New Jersey's legislators and of their voting records, however, can determine the effect of party on legislative voting behavior.

Notes

1. The journals of both houses indicate the time at which the legislature convened. *See also Proceedings 1844,* p. 2. In 1834 the first sitting lasted only nine days, while in 1832 it was prolonged to thirty-nine days. The mean length of the second sitting was fifty-three days. In 1832 it lasted for thirty-seven days, while in 1837 it was extended to seventy-two days.

2. *Proceedings 1844,* p. 135.

3. Ibid. *J.N.J.L.C.,* 1829–1844 and *P.N.J.G.A.,* 1829–1844 contain information on committee memberships.

4. *N.J.L.,* 1829–1844. The number of laws and resolutions approved each session were tabulated from these records. References to the number of roll calls taken in the Council and the Assembly were similarly tabulated from the journals of the two houses.

5. Charles Sitgreaves, *Manual of Legislative Practice and Order of Business in the Legislature of the State of New Jersey* (Trenton, New Jersey: B. Davenport, 1836), p. 203, provides definitions for special and general legislation.

6. *Newark Daily Advertiser,* 15 January 1841.

7. These figures, which appear at the end of the journal of the Council for each session, were tabulated from the records of the Joint Meeting. A detailed discussion of these appointments is provided in chapter 3.

8. Sitgreaves, p. 191. Sitgreaves also notes that these officials could vote on all roll calls, although the speaker's right to participate in debate required the majority consent of the Assembly.

9. *Newark Daily Advertiser,* 27 October 1843; *New Jersey State Gazette* (Trenton), 23 October 1843.

10. In some years the minority party did not offer candidates. Elias Seeley, for example, was unanimously elected vice-president in 1832 and 1833, while Alexander Wurts was unanimously chosen as speaker in 1830 and in 1831.

11. Sitgreaves, p. 191.

12. Ibid., p. 208.

13. Although the individual legislator, upon the consent of the majority of his colleagues of his house, could introduce a bill without prior action by a committee, this practice was quite rare. Sitgreaves, pp. 200–203.

14. *Newark Daily Advertiser,* 3 November 1837.

15. Ibid., 23 October 1839.

16. *J.N.J.L.C.,* 1829–1844; *P.N.J.G.A.,* 1829–1844.

17. There is some evidence that these functions were performed by committees prior to 1837, though not necessarily by standing committees. For example, *see Newark Daily Advertiser,* 14 January 1833, where references to judiciary committees are made.

18. During the 1837 session, the Assembly voted on twice as many roll calls as in any other session between 1829 and 1844. The regular two sittings of the

legislature produced the longest session for these years. A special third sitting was convened to complete legislative action on certain matters.

19. Sitgreaves, p. 220.

20. *P.N.J.G.A.*, 53d sess., 2d sitting, 1829, p. 95; *J.N.J.L.C.*, 60th sess., 1st sitting, 1836, p. 115.

21. Although Democrats and their opposition each maintained legislative majorities for eight years, Democrats appointed fewer committees. The increase in the number of committees after 1837 coinciding with Whig majorities between 1838 and 1843 explains this fact.

22. In 1843 the Democratic minority maintained a one-seat advantage on the Assembly education committee and a similar advantage on the agriculture and militia committees in Council.

23. Sitgreaves indicates that the first name mentioned in each committee listing was the chairman. Information was gathered on this basis.

24. No listings for select committees are given in the legislative journals.

25. *Emporium and True American*, 5 July 1839.

26. *Newark Daily Advertiser*, 11 February 1834.

27. *Rules for the Government of the Legislative Council of the State of New Jersey as well as to Their Proceedings When Sitting as a Court of Appeals and a Court of Pardon* (Trenton, New Jersey: 1829); *Rules for the Government of the Legislative Council of the State of New Jersey* (Trenton, New Jersey: 1835); idem (Trenton, New Jersey: 1839); idem (Trenton, New Jersey: 1842); *Rules and Orders to be Observed in the House of Assembly of the State of New Jersey Adopted 26 October 1831* (Trenton, New Jersey: 1831); *Rules for the Government of the General Assembly of the State of New Jersey, Adopted 24 October 1839* (Trenton, New Jersey: 1839), as well as additional rules found in Council and Assembly journals provide information on rules.

28. *Newark Daily Advertiser*, 15 January 1834, 22 January 1836, 24 January 1843; New Jersey Documents, Box 137, Southard Papers, P.U.L.; *J.N.J.L.C.* 60th sess., 1st sitting, 1836, p. 18.

29. For instance, see *J.N.J.L.C.*, 60th sess., 1st sitting, 1836, p. 18.

30. *P.N.J.G.A.*, 61st sess., 1837.

31. Roll calls in the Assembly were to be recorded on every question when moved and seconded by five members. In the Council the request of one member was sufficient to have the roll call recorded.

32. Roll-call totals, although stated in exact terms, should be considered as near approximations rather than as absolutely errorless computations. Totals were made for each year separately and then added together. A double check was made to avoid errors but, particularly with unanimous roll calls, the chance that some were missed is possible. Occasionally bills had cleavage and unanimous roll calls recorded on them. Roll calls of each type were included in their separate categories in such cases. Roll calls other than of the special or general categories were classified, for convenience, as procedural. They included roll calls on resolutions on national issues and house operation, the state prison, government operation, appointment of legislative officials, and the public printing.

33.   Prince notes that prior to 1829 certain governors who served during years when sharp division between Federalists and Democratic-Republicans existed exerted a good deal of power. The career of Joseph Bloomfield, governor in the early 1800s, illustrates the development of the extralegal powers of the office.

34.   The following is a list of those men who served as governor between 1829 and 1844 with their party affiliation.

Philemon Dickerson	Democrat	1837
Daniel Haines	Democrat	1844
William Pennington	Whig	1838–1843
Elias P. Seeley	National Republican	1833
Samuel Southard	National Republican	1833
Peter D. Vroom	Democrat	1830–1832, 1834–1836
Isaac Williamson	National Republican	1829

35. *P.N.J.G.A.*, 54th sess., 1st sitting, 1830, p. 77.

36. *N.J.L.*, 54th sess., 1830.

37. *J.N.J.L.C.*, 57th sess., 1st sitting, 1833, pp. 9–16.

38. *P.N.J.G.A.*, 59th sess., 1st sitting, 1835, pp. 13–18.

39. *J.N.J.L.C.*, 60th sess., 1st sitting, 1836, p. 17.

40. *J.N.J.L.C.*, 58th sess., 1st sitting, 1834, pp. 4–17.

41.   These examples come from the records of the 59th, 58th, 57th, and 61st sessions, respectively. Each was proposed in the governor's address and, as recorded in the *N.J.L.* for each session, were enacted.

42.   The records of both houses provide numerous examples of this procedure. For example, *see P.N.J.G.A.*, 55th sess., 1st sitting, 1831, pp. 27–29.

43.   Ershkowitz, "New Jersey Politics," p. 190. *See also J.N.J.L.C.*, 57th sess., 1st sitting, 1833, p. 44.

44.   The Southard Papers—P.U.L., for 1832–1833, when Southard was governor—provide numerous examples of the appointive powers of the governor. *Also see* Peter D. Vroom to Colonel James Miller, 23 November 1831, Vroom Papers, Columbia University Library.

45.   Isaac Brown to Samuel L. Southard, 7 January 1833; William Halsey to Samuel L. Southard, 7 January 1833; William Anderson to Samuel L. Southard, 16 January 1833, all in Southard Papers, P.U.L.

46.   Tunis J. Ten Eyck to Samuel L. Southard, 25 October 1832, Southard Papers, P.U.L.; and Ershkowitz, "New Jersey Politics," pp. 190–92. Scattered references of governors attempting to influence the decisions of individual legislators concerning particular legislation also exist. *See* Joseph Jackson to Mahlon Dickerson, 8 February 1836; Mahlon Dickerson Papers, all in N.J.H.S.

47. *Newark Daily Advertiser*, 14 February 1834.

48. Ibid., 28 January 1835.

49. Ibid., 27 January 1835.

50. Robert T. Thompson, "Transportation Combines and Pressure Politics in New Jersey: 1833–1836," *Proceedings of the New Jersey Historical Society* 57 (January 1939): 1–15, 71–86. All information used on lobbying relating to the New Jersey Railroad—Camden and Amboy conflict comes from this well-documented article.

3
New Jersey's Legislators

New Jersey legislators were readily distinguished by their partisan identities. Discriminating characteristics other than party that might have affected their performance are not as obvious. Information culled from federal census returns, genealogical compilations, newspapers, and legislative records yields meaningful comparisons of a variety of personal factors for these men.[1] Although measurement of the effect of these variables on legislative voting behavior awaits detailed roll-call analysis, the overall lack of difference in the social, economic, and career patterns of the state's lawmakers suggests the likelihood that their political affiliations were of considerable weight in determining their legislative roles.

64

I

Between 1829 and 1844, 561 individuals occupied seats in the Council and the Assembly. Data on the age, occupations, business interests, financial status, legislative service, and public careers of these men were collected and analyzed for the entire period and for each individual session. Unfortunately insufficient information prohibited discussion of religious and ethnic affiliations and of educational training.[2] Although not always complete, the evidence suggests that New Jersey's legislators, regardless of their different political persuasions, were quite alike in many ways. What is most striking about their collective profiles are not the contrasts but the similarities.

Examination of the age of New Jersey's legislators while in office shows clearly the lack of correlation between their differing party identities and particular personal characteristics. Data obtained from 87.5% of all councillors indicates that their mean age was forty-eight. This figure was matched by Democratic and Whig and National Republican members of that house when considered as separate groups.[3] In the Assembly the mean age of 75.5% of its members was forty-two. There was no difference between the mean age of the major party groupings. In both houses, for individual sessions, distribution patterns similar to those for the aggregates prevailed. Party labels, at least for the variable of age, did not obscure differences between party representatives in the legislature.

Although posing certain methodological problems, attempts to uncover relationships between legislators with different political affiliations and the occupations that they engaged in also point to similarities rather than to differences. The problems involved in occupational analysis are inherent in the nature of available sources. Census material and genealogical records rarely elaborate on the information they provide. The town grocer who serviced the basic needs of his local community and the importer of foreign goods were both engaged in commerce so far as the census was concerned. Similarly, the farmer who owned only a few acres and who produced little surplus fell under the same classification as the owner of extensive tracts who engaged in large-scale commercial farming. Thus, a wide range of difference between members of the same occupational group that might well have existed are not revealed by the data on New Jersey's legislators, summarized in Tables 4, 5, 6, and 7. Moreover these tables are based on the occupations of 83.5% of those individuals who served in the Council and of 74.6% of those who served in the Assembly. The proportion of legislators for whom no information could be found is sufficiently large to affect any attempts to be overly precise in evaluating the significance of occupational profiles. Despite these limitations, it is clear that neither party was strongly identifiable in terms of particular occupations. Although some differences emerge, the overall picture lacks sharp contrasts.

Table 4 classifies all legislators by party affiliation and by occupation. Here and elsewhere, as a matter of convenience, National Republican and Whig legislators are included under the Whig heading. This analysis indicates that comparable numbers of legislators with differing party identities engaged in the same occupations. Although anywhere from two to ten more Whigs, as compared to Democrats, were artisans, businessmen, doctors, or lawyers, and sixteen more Democrats, as compared to Whigs, were farmers, these differences are not substantial. Only for doctors and artisans, the two categories with the fewest number of legislators involved, did the difference in the percentage of Democrats and their opposition engaged in the same occupation exceed thirteen.[4] Examination of occupational groupings by year merely underlines this general congruent pattern.

Occupational analysis of the membership of each house also reveals few sharp distinctions (Tables 5 and 6). In both

TABLE 4

Occupations of Legislators by Party: Council
and Assembly Combined, 1829-1844 Inclusive*

Occupation (N)**	No. of Democrats	Percent of Democrats	No. of National Republicans/Whigs	Percent of National Republicans/ Whigs
Artisans (6)	2	33.3	4	66.7
Business*** (103)	49	47.6	54	52.4
Doctors (23)	7	30.4	16	69.6
Farmers (244)	130	53.3	114	46.7
Lawyers (80)	35	43.8	45	56.2
Unknown (139)	72	51.8	67	49.2
TOTAL: 595	295		300	

*Thirty-four individuals served in both the Council and the Assembly. Information on the occupations of these individuals, since it was summarized separately in Tables 5 and 6, was included twice in this table so that comparisons between the three tables might be made. Thus although only 561 different individuals held Council and Assembly seats, the total number of individuals summarized in this table comes to 595.

*N equals the number of legislators in each occupational category. In certain instances, more than one occupation was listed for an individual. Where possible, the occupation reported in either the 1840 or the 1850 United States Census was used to categorize the individual. If the information was drawn solely from genealogical material, then a judgment was made as to which occupation the individual engaged in primarily. This holds true for Tables 5, 6, and 7.

**The 1840 United States Census lists two categories relating to business, that is, manufacturing and trades and commerce. The 1850 United States Census occasionally listed specific businesses. All individuals designated so or listed elsewhere as involved in other types of business ventures (such as mining and transportation) are included under the business category. The same holds true for Tables 5, 6, and 7.

TABLE 5

Occupations of Councillors, 1829-1844 Inclusive

Occupation (N)	No. of Democrats	Percent of Democrats	No. of National Republicans/Whigs	Percent of National Republican Whigs
Artisans (0)	0	0.0	0	0.0
Business (30)	17	56.7	13	43.3
Doctors (10)	3	30.0	7	70.0
Farmers (43)	23	53.5	20	46.5
Lawyers (33)	14	42.4	19	57.6
Unknown (23)	11	47.8	12	52.2
TOTAL: 139	68		71	

TABLE 6

Occupations of Assemblymen, 1829-1844 Inclusive

Occupation (N)	No. of Democrats	Percent of Democrats	No. of National Republicans/Whigs	Percent of National Republican Whigs
Artisans (6)	2	33.3	4	66.7
Business (73)	32	43.8	41	56.2
Doctors (13)	4	30.8	9	69.2
Farmers (201)	107	53.2	94	46.8
Lawyers (47)	21	44.7	26	55.3
Unknown (116)	61	52.6	55	47.4
TOTAL: 456	227		229	

the Council and the Assembly a greater percentage of doctors, lawyers, and artisans tended to be either National Republicans or Whigs. In terms of actual numbers, however, the differences between the major party groupings were slight. With few exceptions, little imbalance in any of the occupational categories in either house was uncovered for individual legislative sessions.[5]

Reordering of the data in terms of the distribution of occupations within each party both for single sessions and for the entire sixteen-year period reinforces comparisons based on the number of legislators in both parties with the same occupations. Table 7, a summary of the occupational distribution of New Jersey's assemblymen by party, illustrates this point. Only for farmers does the percentage of Democratic legislators with that occupation exceed the percentage of Whig and National Republican legislators with the same occupation by more than ten.[6]

The most noticeable distinction that emerges from this occupational analysis concerns differences between councillors and assemblymen. Twenty-three percent more of the total number of assemblymen with known occupations as compared to the total number of councillors with known occupations engaged in farming. Similarly, fifteen percent more councillors, compared to assemblymen, were lawyers. Comparisons of Democratic councillors with Democratic assemblymen and Whig councillors with Whig assemblymen also reflect these contrasts.[7] The Council's performance of certain nonlegislative judicial functions when sitting as the Court of Errors and Appeals doubtless accounts for these differences.

Data describing the general composition of a party group in terms of a single variable do not necessarily explain the behavior of a particular party subgroup in the legislature. For instance, only if all Democratic legislators had been farmers and all Whig legislators had been lawyers could anyone say with any assurance that occupation was likely to be as significant as party in determining

TABLE 7

Occupations of Assemblymen by Party, 1829-1844 Inclusive

Occupation	No. of Democrats	Percent of total Democrats with known occupations in each category	No. of National Republicans/Whigs	Percent of total National Republicans/Whigs with known occupations in each category
Artisans	2	1.2	4	2.3
Business	32	19.3	41	23.6
Doctors	4	2.4	9	5.2
Farmers	107	64.4	94	54.0
Lawyers	21	12.7	26	14.9
Unknown	61		55	
TOTAL:	227		229	

roll-call voting behavior. The fact that neither party was strongly identifiable in terms of particular occupations, then, does not mean that a man's occupation was of no import in his performance as a legislator. It does indicate, however, that a legislator's partisan identity did not depend upon the way in which he earned a living.

The distribution of occupations between party legislators in New Jersey challenges the traditional historical models of party leaders in the Jacksonian era. Viewing American history within the "progressive" frame of reference, the most prominent Jacksonian historians up to 1945 conceived the emergence of the Whigs and the Democrats as part of the continuing struggle between the forces of "conservatism and liberalism, the few and the many, the rich and the poor."[8] Emphasizing economic and ideological conflict, this school of interpretation, with some variations, argued that the Democrats as the party of the common man were represented primarily by farmers and workers. In contrast, the Whigs, defined as aristocratic champions of privilege, were represented by well-to-do lawyers, professionals, and businessmen.

Along with numerous modern studies of party leadership in other states, the information on New Jersey's legislators indicates that such images do not fit the men who occupied Council and Assembly seats.[9] Although in both houses more Whigs were lawyers and doctors than their Democratic counterparts, the differences were not great. A total of 42 Democrats were either doctors or lawyers as compared to 61 Whigs. In both houses and for both parties farmers predominated. Altogether, 153 Democrats and 134 Whigs were farmers. Most significant, nearly as many Democrats engaged in business as did Whigs. In fact the Council showed 17 Democrats and only 13 Whigs so involved. Quite clearly the images of the agrarian Democrat and the commercial Whig are not reflected by the representatives of these parties in the New Jersey legislature.

The actual economic interests of New Jersey's legislators

were also remarkably alike. The similarities underline the lack of correlation between their differing party identities and their personal characteristics and interests. Scattered references concerning their financial worth indicate that both Democratic and Whig legislators lived comfortably. Part of the data was drawn from the 1850 United States census that lists the wealth in dollars of a portion of those included in its rolls. Because these figures only indicate the individual's worth as of 1850, they might be as much as twenty years out of date for legislators who served between 1829 and 1844. Additional information gathered from genealogical records may also be misleading, since these sources usually indicate the wealth of an individual at the time of his death. Nevertheless, they do provide a limited basis for comparison. From them data on 131 of the 561 men who held legislative office between 1829 and 1844 were obtained. Information on 63 National Republicans and Whigs showed their average estate to be worth some $12,890, while that of the Democrats amounted to $11,550.[10]

Examination of the lists of special incorporation charters granted by the legislature offers more accurate and persuasive evidence concerning the similar economic interests of New Jersey's legislators. Up to 1844 a special act of the legislature was required to undertake any incorporated business enterprise. Between 1829 and 1844 a total of 217 such charter acts for banks, manufacturing companies, transportation concerns, mining ventures, and insurance companies were so granted.[11] Each charter included the names of all individuals who were among the original incorporators or the directors of the enterprise involved. The large number of legislators from the major parties mentioned in these acts effectively challenges those interpretations that have proposed that the party allegiance of political activists during the Jacksonian era could be correlated with particular economic viewpoints and interests.

Table 8 indicates that at least one member of either the

TABLE 8

The Involvement of New Jersey's Legislators in Incorporated Enterprises, 1829-1844 Inclusive

Year	Banks Tot. No.*	Banks Leg. No.**	Manufacturing Tot. No.	Manufacturing Leg. No.	Mining Tot. No.	Mining Leg. No.	Transportation Tot. No.	Transportation Leg. No.	Insurance Tot. No.	Insurance Leg. No.
1829	—	—	4	1	—	—	1	—	—	—
1830	2	—	4	—	1	—	3	2	—	—
1831	1	1	3	1	—	—	7	4	1	—
1832	2	2	3	2	2	1	5	5	1	—
1833	—	—	8	—	—	—	3	1	1	—
1834	4	4	3	1	2	—	5	2	2	—
1835	—	—	6	1	1	—	2	2	1	—
1836	1	1	18	8	1	—	17	13	—	—
1837	5	5	24	10	2	—	12	12	2	2
1838	—	—	3	1	1	—	1	1	4	—
1839	1	1	7	6	1	—	4	3	1	1
1840	—	—	5	3	1	1	1	—	1	1
1841	—	—	1	1	—	—	3	2	3	1
1842	—	—	3	2	—	—	2	—	3	2
1843	—	—	1	1	—	—	—	—	—	—
1844	—	—	3	1	—	—	3	2	4	—
Total	16	14	96	39	12	1	69	49	24	7

*Tot. No. refers to the total number of charters in each category enacted into law. The source for these figures is John W. Cadman, Jr., *The Corporation in New Jersey, Business and Politics, 1791-1875* (Cambridge, Massachusetts: Harvard University Press, 1949), p. 206.

**Leg. No. refers to the total number of charters in each category that included the name of at least one legislator as an incorporator or as a director.

Council or the Assembly was named in 110 of the 217 charters granted between 1829 and 1844. Some 167 legislators, comprising over twenty-nine percent of the total membership of both houses, participated in these enterprises. These men were most frequently involved in banks and transportation projects. Many legislators were named in more than one charter and, in most instances, at least two legislators were named as incorporators of the same charter (Table 9). Legislators' names appeared 244 times in these charters. Of these, sixty-one appeared in charters that were granted by the legislature in which these individuals were serving. In most cases, the location of the business was in the same county in which the particular legislator, named in the charter, resided.

Party balance for participating legislators was maintained in terms of the number and the type of projects in which they were engaged. Of the 167 legislators listed in charter acts, 82 were either National Republicans or Whigs and 85 were Democrats. As indicated in Table 9, members of both parties, in equal numbers and on an equal number of occasions, engaged in these enterprises.

If Democrats and Whigs had different views about the development of corporate enterprise, they were not revealed by the personal conduct of the parties' legislative representatives in New Jersey. Not only were many individuals from both sides participants in the same kinds of economic ventures, but on a number of occasions members of the two parties also joined together as partners. The degree of involvement of these men in these projects, when viewed in conjunction with the information concerning their financial status and their occupations, casts serious doubts on the reliability of historians' stereotypes of Democratic and Whig leaders.

II

All of the men who served in the Council and Assembly had one occupation in common; they were all legislators.

TABLE 9

Party Affiliations of New Jersey Legislators Involved in
Incorporated Enterprises, 1829-1844 Inclusive

Category	Tot. No. * Leg.	No. involving Dems. **	No. involving National Rep./ Whigs	No. involving National Rep./Whigs and Dems. ***
Banks	14	3	3	8
Manufacturing	39	16	17	6
Mining	1	–	1	–
Transportation	49	17	12	20
Insurance	7	3	3	1
Total	110	39	36	35

*Tot. No. Leg. refers to the total number of charters granted by the legislature in each category between 1829 and 1844 that included at least one legislator as an incorporator or as a director.

**No. involving Democrats refers to the number of charters in each category that had one or more Democrats involved. The same column appears for National Republicans/Whigs.

***No. involving National Republicans/Whigs and Dems. refers to the total number of charters in each category that had one or more Democratic and one or more National Republican or Whig legislators listed.

Not all legislators, however, served the same number of years. Examination of possible correlations between legislative experience and party attachments among New Jersey's legislators indicates again the similar experiences of these men.

The legislative careers of the 561 men who occupied Council and Assembly seats between 1829 and 1844 were extremely brief. Only 39 remained in office for four or more years. Seventeen of these 39, nine Democrats and eight Whigs, served five or six years. No man served more than six years. Only 73 legislators held office for three years, while 216 served for two years and 233 served for one year.

Legislative membership lists indicate that this rapid rate of turnover was comparable for National Republicans, Whigs, and Democrats.[12] Further evidence of this point is revealed by analysis of the number of times individuals tried for office (Tables 10 and 11).[13] The frequency with which New Jersey legislators competed for Council and Assembly seats varied little from one party to another. Over 90% of Democratic and opposition candidates ran for office no more than three times. Approximately 50% tried only once and less than 10% on each side competed four or more times. This pattern prevailed both in counties that were highly competitive and in those where one party maintained dominant control over legislative elections.[14]

Individuals who did try for office more frequently achieved a fair amount of success. For instance, sixty-two of seventy-one men who ran four or more times were each elected to the legislature at least three times. Only three men out of this group of seventy-one failed to win election at least once. Of the sixty-eight men who registered one or more victories, twenty-two served in both houses of the legislature.[15]

The pattern of short tenure that developed in New Jersey was not unique. In the first forty-seven United States

TABLE 10

Democratic Electoral Tickets for the New Jersey
Legislature, 1829-1844 Inclusive

County	No. of years for which data were obtained	No. men running 1x	2x	3x	4x	more 4x
Atlantic	7 of 7	2	6	--	--	--
Bergen	15 of 16	10	10	3	2	1
Burlington	13 of 16	21	9	5	4	3
Cape May	Insufficient data available*					
Cumberland	Insufficient data available**					
Essex	12 of 16	30	9	3	--	--
Gloucester	14 of 16	28	8	3	1	2
Hudson	Insufficient data available*					
Hunterdon	16 of 16	11	21	5	2	2
Mercer	5 of 6	14	2	--	--	--
Middlesex	14 of 16	27	5	4	2	2
Monmouth	15 of 16	13	11	8	2	2
Morris	16 of 16	14	10	7	2	2
Passaic	7 of 7	6	4	2	--	--
Salem	13 of 16	22	10	3	1	--
Somerset	14 of 16	12	8	3	2	2
Sussex	16 of 16	5	15	1	2	3
Warren	16 of 16	5	11	4	3	1
TOTAL:		220	139	51	23	20

*With one exception, Cape May and Hudson elected National Republicans or Whigs to office every year.

**Information on only ten of sixteen years could be found. Presentation of it might be misleading, for too many individuals might be excluded.

TABLE 11

National Republican and Whig Electoral Tickets for the New Jersey Legislature, 1829-1844 Inclusive

County	No. of years for which data were obtained	No. men running 1x	2x	3x	4x	more 4x
Atlantic	Insufficient data available*					
Bergen	13 of 16	18	9	1	–	1
Burlington	14 of 16	15	10	8	1	2
Cape May	16 of 16	–	1	1	4	2
Cumberland	14 of 16	19	8	4	–	1
Essex	16 of 16	26	24	6	1	--
Gloucester	13 of 16	22	9	–	2	2
Hudson	4 of 4	3	1	1	–	--
Hunterdon	Insufficient data available*					
Mercer	6 of 6	7	7	–	–	--
Middlesex	15 of 16	18	11	4	3	1
Monmouth	Insufficient data available**					
Morris	13 of 16	12	12	1	3	1
Passaic	7 of 7	8	5	2	–	--
Salem	13 of 16	23	9	–	1	1
Somerset	13 of 16	8	6	6	3	–
Sussex	Insufficient data available*					
Warren	Insufficient data available*					
TOTAL:		179	112	34	18	11

*Atlantic, Hunterdon, Sussex, and Warren, with only one exception in one year, always returned Democrats to office.

**Information on only eleven of sixteen years could be found. Presentation of it might be misleading, for too many individuals might be excluded.

Congresses, the rate of turnover exceeded fifty percent in fifteen elections.[16] Similar patterns developed in New Jersey where a high percentage of the membership in any given year in both the Council and the Assembly were freshmen. In six of the sixteen sessions between 1829 and 1844 over forty percent of the membership of the Council were first-year men. In twelve sessions at least fifty percent of New Jersey's assemblymen were newcomers.

As it was in Congress, rapid turnover in the New Jersey legislature inhibited the development of continuous, mature leadership in key legislative offices.[17] Between 1829 and 1844 nine different individuals served as vice-president of the Council, while ten legislators presided as speaker of the Assembly. None of these men were chosen as house leaders for more than three years.

The enormous rate of turnover was not the result of consistent rejection of candidates by the voters. Service in the legislature appears to have been regulated by party county organizations. The Democratic organization in Hunterdon or the Whig organization in Essex could have offered the same candidates for legislative office year after year without jeopardizing their chances for victory. Both sides, however, chose to be represented by a constantly changing cast in the legislature. This decision prohibited the development of seniority and minimized the possibility that the factor of experience could be important in determining legislative behavior.

This lack of experience posed certain problems for New Jersey's legislative parties. The high percentage of freshmen in every session and the absence of continuity in the major offices of the Council and the Assembly had to be counteracted if party was to play a decisive role in the legislature. The existence of the legislative party caucus and the conscious efforts to stack committees with experienced partisans aided both sides in overcoming these obstacles to cohesive party action. The fact that many legislators were intimately involved in the work of party organization outside the legislature also contributed to the effective operation of legislative parties.

New Jersey legislators may not have been experienced lawmakers but a significant percentage of them were seasoned party workers. Data on state patronage appointments awarded these men suggest that many of them had been singled out for recognition by their parties before serving in the legislature. Between 1829 and 1844, 332 of the 561 individuals who served as state legislators received some type of state or county appointment to public office in Joint Meeting. Given primarily to individuals who actively participated in party election campaigns, the 1,013 appointments obtained by legislators accounted for over fourteen percent of the total number of Joint Meeting appointments distributed in these years.[18]

With few exceptions, Democratic legislators received their appointments during the years in which their party maintained legislative majorities, while National Republicans and Whig legislators were rewarded in those years when they were in power. Despite the fact that each party held majorities for eight years between 1829 and 1844, Democrats fared somewhat better than their opposition. Over 64% of all Democratic assemblymen and 85% of all Democratic councillors received some kind of appointment. For National Republicans and Whigs, 52% of their assemblymen and 50% of their councillors obtained jobs (Table 12). Of the 332 legislators who secured positions, 240 were appointed as either judges or justices of the peace.[19]

Desire to gain patronage appointments was not a major inducement to serve in the legislature. Over 230 of those individuals who received appointments obtained them before their election to the legislature, no doubt as rewards for loyal service to the party cause.

Further evidence of this concern for party comes from the records of party conventions held in New Jersey to select Congressional and Presidential tickets. Althouth a complete record of the proceedings of these meetings was not reconstructed, available information indicates that legislators from the major parties occupied important positions in the state party organizations.

Tables 13 and 14 summarize the involvement of party legislators in state conventions for which data could be found. Democratic totals are based on an analysis of a maximum of seven conventions. National Republican and Whig figures reflect participation in a maximum of nine meetings.

Legislators from the major parties were involved at

TABLE 12

Party Distribution of the Joint Meeting Appointments
for Members of the Assembly and the
Council, 1829-1844 Inclusive

House	No. of Dems.* serving	No. of Dems.** rec. appts.	No. of National Rep./ Whigs serving	No. of National Rep./ Whigs rec. appts.
Council	68	58	71	36
Assembly	227	147	229	121
TOTAL:***	295	205	300	157

*Refers to actual number of Democrats who held seats. A similar column is presented for National Republicans/Whigs.

**Refers to actual number of Democrats who received Joint Meeting appointments. A similar column is presented for National Republicans/Whigs.

***The totals indicate that 595 individuals served in the legislature and that 362 received appointments. Actually only 561 different individuals were involved. Thirty-four men served in both houses and were listed in the separate totals for each house. Only 332 men actually received appointments but 30 of these served in both houses, thus the total of 362 appointments reflected in this table.

TABLE 13

Participation of Democratic Legislators in Democratic State Conventions

	President[a]	Vice-Pres	Secretary	State Committee[b]	Resolutions Committee[c]	Address Committee[d]	Officer Selection Committee[e]	Committees of Correspondence[f]	Special Committees[g]	Delegates to National Convention[h]
Total number of positions examined	7	31	19	20	19	27	59	182	17	16
No. of legislators holding positions	4	12	7	8	8	15	24	56	8	4
No. of above legislators who were incumbents	1	1	2	3	2	4	5	16	1	2
Percent of individuals holding positions who were legislators	57.1	38.7	36.8	40.0	42.1	55.6	40.7	30.8	47.1	25.0

[a]President, vice-president, and secretary totals are based on the following seven conventions: 1828 to nominate Presidential electors; 1828 to nominate Congressional ticket; 1830 to nominate Congressional ticket; 1832 to nominate Presidential electors and Congressional ticket; 1834 to nominate Congressional ticket; 1836 to nominate Presidential electors and Congressional ticket; 1842 to nominate Congressional ticket. Sources for conventions in consecutive order are *Emporium and True American* (Trenton), 12 January 1828; 25 October 1828; 18 December 1830; 20 October 1834; 13 September 1834; 22 October 1836; 9 September 1842.

[b]Based on 1828 Presidential, 1830 Congressional, 1832 Presidential and Congressional, and 1836 Presidential and Congressional conventions.

[c]Based on 1828 Presidential and 1836 Presidential and Congressional conventions.

[d]Based on 1828 Presidential, 1832 Presidential and Congressional, 1836 Presidential and Congressional, and 1842 Congressional conventions.

[e]Based on 1832 Presidential and Congressional, 1834 Congressional, and 1842 Congressional conventions.

[f]Based on 1830 Congressional, 1832 Presidential and Congressional, and 1828 Presidential and Congressional conventions.

[g]Based on 1842 Congressional convention (committee to call a new convention if necessary).

[h]Based on 1828 Presidential, and 1836 Presidential and Congressional conventions.

TABLE 14

Participation of National Republican and Whig Legislators in National Republican and Whig State Conventions

	President[a]	Vice-Pres	Secretary	State Committee[b]	Resolutions Committee[c]	Address Committee[d]	Officer Selection Committee[e]	Committees of correspondence[f]	Delegates to National Convention[g]
Total number of positions examined	9	98	32	10	28	22	16	115	16
No. of legislators holding positions	7	35	11	2	12	9	8	31	7
No. of above legislators who were incumbents	4	0	1	0	3	1	3	5	0
Percent of individuals holding positions who were legislators	77.8	35.7	34.4	20.0	42.9	40.9	50.0	27.0	43.8

[a]President, vice-president, and secretary totals are based on the following nine conventions: 1828 National Republican Presidential, 1834 National Republican Presidential, 1834 National Republican, State 1834 Whig Congressional, 1836 Whig Presidential, 1838 Whig Congressional, 1839 Whig to select delegates to National convention, 1840 Presidential and Congressional, and 1842 Congressional conventions. Sources for conventions in consecutive order are *Proceedings and Address of the New Jersey Delegates in Favor of the Present Administration of the General Government Assembled in Convention at Trenton, 22 February 1828* (Trenton, 1828); *Newark Daily Advertiser*, 4 April 1834; 12 September 1834; 2 June 1836; 30 September 1836; 6 September 1838; 14 November 1839; 21 August 1840; 15 September 1842.

[b]Based on 1838 Congressional, and 1840 Presidential and Congressional conventions.

[c]Based on 1836 Congressional, and 1839 delegates to National Convention conventions.

[d]Based on 1839 delegates to National Convention, and 1840 Presidential and Congressional conventions.

[e]Based on 1839 delegates to National Convention.

[f]Based on 1828 Presidential, 1836 Presidential, and 1838 Congressional conventions.

[g]Based on 1828 Presidential, and 1839 delegates to National Convention conventions.

every level of their state party organizations. Seven of nine presidents of National Republican and Whig state conventions served in the legislature. Four of these men chaired meetings while in office. Of the two Whig conventions for which the composition of the party's state central committee was reported, two of the ten men named were legislators. Democratic legislators served as presidents of four of the seven conventions reported. Data on membership of four Democratic state committees show that eight of the twenty individuals named were legislators. Similar comparisons of active legislator participation in the other offices and committees are also apparent.

III

A major purpose of this chapter has been to analyze the backgrounds of New Jersey's legislators with a view to identifying characteristics that might be considered significant variables influencing legislative voting behavior. Because this study is concerned with examining legislative parties, of particular interest was whether the differing party identities of those who served in the Council and the Assembly could have accounted for patterned differences in the performance of their legislative duties.

Neither party was strongly identified with particular age groups, occupations, business interests, or levels of legislative experience. Party labels did not obscure other distinctions. Although the actual effect of variables such as age, occupation, prior service, and party on legislative behavior await detailed roll-call analysis, the similarities in the backgrounds of party legislators suggest that their political affiliations were likely to have influenced their activities in the Council and the Assembly.

Certain characteristics, common to New Jersey's legislators, while suggesting the significance of party as the operative factor in the legislature, also underline obstacles confronting such activity. The fact that party organization in the legislature and the partisan experience of legislators served to counteract these forces raises important questions about the function of New Jersey's legislative parties.

Theorists of party behavior often argue that legislative parties follow their own course. The legislative party maintains its own system of rewards in the form of favorable committee assignments, appointment to leadership posts, and success in enacting legislation. Its values and goals often differ from the party organization proper. Its members, while skilled campaigners and legislators, know little about the management of party organization. "Main loyalties are to the legislative party, the group life, and the traditions of the legislature."[20]

How well does this description fit New Jersey's legislative parties? Certain discrepancies are already obvious. Many of the men who held Council and Assembly seats, by virtue of their participation in state party conventions and their reception of patronage appointments, were recognized party activists. Their service in the legislature, quite brief by modern standards, was regulated by the party organizations in which they played important roles. The inclusion of outside party leaders in the legislative party caucuses and the organizational activities of legislators themselves meant that open communication between the legislative parties and the party organization proper existed. What effect did this connection have on the behavior of legislative parties in New Jersey? These parties were organized and they did control the leadership positions and the committees responsible for processing legislation. To what ends, however, were these efforts directed? Were their legislative roles defined solely by their responsiveness to the demands of party as an interest or did they serve other purposes as well? What bearing, if any, did the competitive nature of New Jersey politics have on these considerations? Focus on the most significant body of evidence concerning New Jersey's party legislators—their legislative roll-call voting records—provides answers to these questions.

Notes

1. The 1840 and 1850 United States census returns for New Jersey were important sources of information for age, occupation, and wealth.

2. Lee Benson, *The Concept of Jacksonian Democracy: New York as a Test Case* (Princeton, New Jersey: Princeton University Press, 1961), pp. 165–215, 270–328; and Formisano, *The Birth of Mass Political Parties*, pp. 137–334, emphasize the importance of religious and ethnic affiliation in determining the voting behavior of the American public in the Jackson period. The methods they use to determine the religious preferences of people, however, reveal nothing about the intensity of an individual's religious beliefs or of his involvement in the affairs of his church or community. Richard L. McCormick, "Ethno-Cultural Interpretations of Nineteenth Century American Voting Behavior," *Political Science Quarterly* 89 (June 1974): 351–77, provides solid criticism of this approach to American politics. Insufficient data prohibited meaningful comparisons of these factors to be made for party legislators in New Jersey. Similar problems occur elsewhere. Grady McWhiney, "Were the Whigs a Class Party in Alabama?", *Journal of Southern History* 23 (November 1957): 510–22, could find religious affiliations for only 12.9% of Alabama state legislators.

3. For convenience, National Republican and Whig legislators are treated as a single group.

4. Data on artisans and doctors illustrate the problems of using percentages to represent differences in small groups of numbers. Although 66.7% of all artisans who were legislators were either Whigs or National Republicans, only two more members of these parties then Democrats were artisans. Viewed solely in terms of percentages, the difference between party in this case appears significant. The actual situation that produced these large percentages is not.

5. Occupational breakdown in each house for every legislative session was undertaken to see if, in any given house, in a given year, significant differences existed in the occupations engaged in by Democrats and by Whigs. In the Council, some differences were noticed. Two Whig councillors might be lawyers, while no Democratic councillors engaged in such an occupation. When differences occurred in Council, however, they were too small to have a measurable quantitative effect on legislative voting behavior. In the Assembly, even less of a contrast was found. The major exceptions included 1837, when there were six Whig lawyers versus no Democratic lawyers; 1840, when there were six Whigs as compared to one Democrat engaged in business; and 1841, when there were seven Whigs and no Democrats engaged in business. Certainly within a given session on a particular set of roll calls, occupational discrepancies such as these might have a measurable impact on voting behavior. Only roll-call analysis using occupation as a variable can indicate its influence. *See* chapters 5 and 6 and Appendix B for the results of such investigations.

6. Similar tables for all legislators and for councillors reveal similar patterns of distribution.

7. Twelve percent more Democratic councillors as compared to Democratic assemblymen were lawyers while seventeen percent more Whig councillors as compared to Whig assemblymen were lawyers. Twenty-four percent more Democratic assemblymen as compared to Democratic councillors were farmers while twenty percent more Whig assemblymen as compared to Whig councillors were farmers.

8. Douglas T. Miller, *The Birth of Modern America, 1820–1850* (New York: Western Publishing Co., 1970), p. 150.

9. Pessen, pp. 251–55, summarizes the recent literature on this subject and concludes that "despite the inevitable differences in viewpoint, its most amazing feature is the essential similarity it discloses in the occupations, wealth, and status of Whig and Jacksonian leaders."

10. The constitution of 1776 required prospective legislators to be freeholders and residents of the county they wished to represent for one year prior to their election. Councillors had to be worth at least £1,000 in real and personal estate held within their county of residence, while assemblymen needed only half that amount to be eligible (*Proceedings 1844*, p. 2). No legislator was challenged for not having met these requirements between 1829 and 1844. It would seem that the general level of wealth enjoyed by New Jersey's legislators was rather high. Property qualifications were dropped in the 1844 constitution. Unfortunately, data that were obtained give no indication whether the wealth was recently acquired or whether the legislator came from an established, wealthy-family background.

11. *N.J.L.*, 1829–1844. Although many of the individuals listed in these charters are also listed as being employed in business, not all are. There was no way of determining whether the appearance of an individual's name in a business charter meant that he made his livelihood in that manner or whether it was just a means of investing a part of his capital. Because of this, a distinction was made between a legislator's occupation and his business interests.

12. Data on the length of legislative service were drawn from the membership lists of the journals of both houses. The only exception to the comparable rates of turnover for Democratic and Whig legislators occurred in Monmouth county. Here, fourteen Whigs and twenty-seven Democrats occupied all of the Council and Assembly seats between 1829 and 1844. No Whig served more than a single term in office, while twenty-six of the twenty-seven Democrats held their posts for two or more years.

13. Election data were gathered from the *Newark Daily Advertiser*.

14. In Salem, for instance, Democratic slates won election to the legislature seven times. National Republican and Whig tickets won eight times. Only three men from each side ran for office four or more times. Of the thirty-six Democrats who contested for seats, thirty-two tried no more than twice; twenty-one of these running only once. Similar patterns existed for National Republicans and Whigs. In Essex, National Republicans and Whigs filled all Council and Assembly positions for fourteen of sixteen years and shared them with the Democrats

during the other two years. Of the fifty-seven Whigs who vied for these posts, fifty ran no more than twice. Again, in Hunterdon, a county that only elected Democrats to legislative office, thirty-two of the forty-one Democratic candidates between 1829 and 1844 competed no more than twice.

15. Of the forty-one men who ran four times, 49 percent were elected each time and 80.5 percent were elected at least three times. Of the seventeen men running five times, 49 percent were elected each time and 59 percent were elected at least four times. Finally, 38 percent of the thirteen men who ran six times were elected each time and 77 percent of this group achieved office at least five times.

16. Nelson W. Polsby, "The Institutionalization of the United States House of Representatives," *American Political Science Review* 62 (March 1968): 144–68, is the source for all data concerning Congress. Polsby argues that certain phenomena indicate that the House of Representatives, over the years, developed into a stable organization in which democratic, representative government could be pursued. Among the things that Polsby points to as indications of the institutionalization of the House were the stabilization of membership, indicated by long careers, professionalization of leadership positions, the growth of internal complexity (measured by the number and the responsibility of committees), general increase in the provision of various emoluments such as office space, salaries, and staff aid, development of seniority, less of an emphasis on partisan behavior on such things as disputed elections, and, in general, a formalization and stabilization of systems of procedure. Not until the twentieth century, according to Polsby, did the gradual process of institutionalization reach maturity. Congress, in the nineteenth century, inhabited by inexperienced representatives and insufficiently structured and organized, posed serious problems for the operation of government. As pointed out in this chapter, in many respects, the situation in New Jersey, in terms of the particular criteria cited by Polsby, paralleled the situation in Congress in the nineteenth century.

17. Ibid., p. 149.

18. Information on the appointments of legislators was obtained from the records of the Joint Meeting. They appear at the end of the Council journals for each session.

19. The constitution of 1776 prohibited legislators from holding any public office except that of justice of the peace while serving in the legislature.

20. Sorauf, *Political Parties in the American System,* p. 127.

4

Party Voting in the New Jersey Legislature: An Interpretation

Legislative roll-call analysis establishes the quantitative significance of selected variables as determinants of voting
behavior. It does not explain causal relationships. The ability to isolate opposing groups of legislators by differing
party affiliations on roll calls indicates the significance of
party identity in the formation of voting alignments. Only
investigation of other kinds of evidence, however, can
begin to explain why party is an important factor.
  Both the identification and the explanation of the voting

91

patterns of New Jersey's legislators are the chief concerns of the remainder of this study. This chapter examines the effect of party on the voting records of these men for virtually all roll calls recorded in Joint Meeting and in Assembly between 1829 and 1844 as a basis for presenting a general understanding of party behavior in the legislature. Subsequent chapters on particular categories of legislation offer further documentation of this interpretation as well as detailed explanations of a whole range of forces that affected legislative decisions and legislative party operation.

I

Selected in Joint Meeting were New Jersey's United States Senators, the governor, the secretary of state, the attorney general, the state treasurer, the general and field militia officers, the reporter, clerk, and justices of the state supreme court, the state librarian, the keeper and the inspectors of the state prison, and the state's representative on the board of directors of the largest transportation company in New Jersey. County and local appointments matched the number of state civil and judicial posts filled each year. Judges in the inferior courts of common pleas, county prosecutors, justices of the peace, court clerks, county surrogates, and commissioners to take acknowledgment and proof of deeds were all chosen in Joint Meeting.[1]

In many instances the salaries and tenure of Joint Meeting appointees were substantial. Members of the state supreme court, for instance, were appointed for seven-year terms at an annual salary of $1,100. Even county appointees fared well. One commissioner for the acknowledgment and proof of deeds noted that "his office ha[d] been the means of throwing in [his] way a very full share of conveyances thereby yielding [him] an income of something like $500 a year ... [of] considerable importance to one standing alone in the '*wide world.*' "[2]

More than any other activity engaged in by legislative parties, Joint Meeting appointments generated the highest and most consistent displays of partisan cohesion. As described by one observer of the New Jersey legislature in 1833, legislative parties, when given the opportunity to control these appointments, made the most of it.

> The legislature have been almost all day in Joint Meeting. There were a number of vacancies in the Counties, some of important appointments, such as Surrogates, Prosecutors of the pleas, &c, &c. Each party had their favorite candidates, and the principal officers were appointed by a trial of strength between the parties in the Legislature. ... Whether this principle in making appointments be correct it is now no longer necessary to inquire, for as the party in power in the Legislature for the three previous years have introduced and rigidly enforced this system, it becomes a duty of those at present dominant, to protect their friends by restoring them to the places from which they have been ejected. As usual the suffering party gave signals of distress, but the spirit of party is usually merciless, and entirely banishes the ordinary feelings of compassion in which a generous heart loves to indulge in.[3]

Party discipline on appointments was facilitated by the legislative party caucus. The New Jersey press offers numerous illustrations that in any given year the caucus of the majority party in the legislature controlled the appointing power. In 1833 National Republicans were accused of appointing only Clay supporters to state posts. The machinations of the "grand-guillotine caucus" were held responsible for this work.[4] The following year, with the Democrats in control of the legislature, the editor of the *New Jersey State Gazette* (Trenton) observed that only Jackson advocates received appointments. Even the offices in those counties which elected Whig legislators were given to Democrats. Although the correspondent felt "such proceedings a burlesque upon free government," he acknowledged that in the past the opposition had proceeded in a similar fashion.[5] By 1843 the use of the caucus to decide appointments was so accepted that one newspaper could simply state that "there will be a Joint Meeting . . . to sanction the caucus nominations of Treasurer, State Prison Keeper, Inspector", without bothering to denounce the scheduled session.[6]

The actual operation of the Joint Meeting demonstrates the ability of legislative parties to maintain discipline on appointments. Over 6,700 of the 7,146 appointments distributed between 1829 and 1844 did not occasion roll-call votes. Individuals named to these posts were simply acknowledged in Joint Meeting proceedings without any indication of whether other candidates had competed for them. A mean number of 447 appointments approved annually took no more than four daily Joint Meeting sessions.[7] If appointments had not been prearranged in caucus, if conflicting claims had not been mediated in advance, and if the minority party had not usually accepted the appointment of opposition candidates as automatic, it would have been difficult to make so many appointments in so short a time period.

Appointments that did occasion roll-call votes produced highly partisan responses. These appointments were not concerned with the performance of duties different from those that went unchallenged. The 435 Joint Meeting roll calls took one of two forms.[8] Indecision on the part of the majority party in selecting candidates or delaying actions by the minority party elicited votes on motions to postpone consideration of appointments. When both parties offered candidates, the names of the two individuals vying for the appointment were proposed and voted upon.

Table 15 summarizes the degree of party voting on all Joint Meeting roll calls for the 1829–1844 period. By cal-

TABLE 15

Party Voting in the Joint Meeting, 1829-1844 Inclusive

Year*	Maj.** Pty.	Maj.*** Pty. Adv.	No. Appts. Made	No. Roll Calls	Index of Likeness						Percent of Roll Calls with Index of Likeness between 0-10
					0-10	11-20	21-30	31-50	51-66	67-100	
1829	N.R.	9	442	8	3	--	2	1	--	2	37.5
1830	J.D.	29	376	32	--	7	9	5	11	--	0.0
1831	J.D.	30	339	7	1	4	1	1	--	--	14.3
1832	J.D.	4	330	72	42	10	10	5	3	2	58.3
1833	N.R.	8	517	33	18	9	3	2	1	--	54.6
1834	D.	42	476	15	6	3	--	3	2	1	40.0
1835	D.	6	418	41	38	1	1	1	--	--	92.7
1836	D.	22	353	4	2	1	--	1	--	--	50.0
1837	D.	10	112	38	30	6	--	--	2	--	78.9
1838	W.	21	831	27	24	2	--	1	--	--	88.8
1839	W.	16	364	42	37	3	1	1	--	--	88.1
1840	W.	16	294	43	42	1	--	--	--	--	97.6
1841	W.	37	331	23	20	1	1	1	--	--	86.9
1842	W.	12	87	15	13	2	--	--	--	--	86.6
1843	W.	10	817	26	25	--	--	--	--	1	96.1
1844	D.	18	1,059	9	--	8	1	--	--	--	0.0
TOTALS:			7,146	435	301	58	29	22	19	6	

*Legislative sessions began in October and continued through February or March of the following year. Thus, for example, 1829 refers to the session that began in October 1828 and concluded sometime in 1829.

**Refers to that party which had a majority in the Joint Meeting. W. stands for Whigs, D. stands for Democrats, J.D. stands for Jacksonian Democrats, and N.R. for National Republicans.

***Refers to the actual size of the majority in Joint Meeting enjoyed by the party mentioned in the preceding column.

culating the percentage of the voting membership of each party casting affirmative votes on each Joint Meeting roll call and by subtracting the arithmetic difference between the percentage of each group voting affirmatively from 100, a measure of party opposition and cohesion known as the index of likeness is produced. Its values range from zero to 100. The lower the values, the more cohesively opposed to each other the compared groups must be. An index of 40, for instance, on a given roll call, might indicate that 80% of each group voted as blocs and in opposition to each other. It might also describe a situation in which one group registered 100% cohesion and the other only 60% cohesion in opposition to the first. Indices of 20 and below mean that a minimum of 80% of the voting membership of each group were cohesively opposed.[9]

Employment of this measure indicates that New Jersey's legislative parties firmly opposed each other regarding appointments. Between 1834 and 1844, years in which the major parties in New Jersey identified themselves as Democratic and Whig, only two roll calls registered indices of likeness over 66. On 237 roll calls, or 83.7% of the 283 roll calls recorded in these years, party indices of likeness ranged between 10 and 0. Over 93% of the 283 roll calls produced indices under 20.

On roll calls registering indices of likeness over 10, no consistent deviation patterns emerged. Neither the Whigs nor the Democrats were more likely than the other to be less cohesive between 1834 and 1844. Nor did the relative strength of the parties in the legislature affect their cohesiveness. Whether a party was in the minority or the majority did not quantitatively relate to its ability to remain united.

With the exception of the 1834 session, no striking relationship between the number of defections in any given session and the size of the majority in the Joint Meeting was apparent. Even in 1834 when only six of fifteen roll calls produced indices of likeness between 0 and 10 and when the Democrats possessed a forty-two seat advantage in Joint Meeting, both parties displayed cohesive voting behavior. The mean relative indices of cohesion for Democratic and Whig legislators voting on Joint Meeting roll calls in this session were 86.2 and 88.6, respectively.[10]

Close competition between Democrats and Whigs allowed both parties to share equally the benefits of partisan control over the distribution of appointments. Some 3,463 Joint Meeting appointments were filled during years of Democratic legislative majorities, while 3,683 appointments were made during years of National Republican and Whig control. With only one exception, the greatest number of appointments for single legislative sessions were made in those years when the majority party had returned to power after having been in the minority for at least the four preceding sessions. In 1844 the Democrats regained the ascendancy in the legislature after six consecutive years of Whig majorities. Anxious to revitalize their party machinery, they approved 1,059 appointments during the four days of Joint Meetings. Only ten of these appointments occasioned roll-call votes. Democratic action in 1844 paralleled Whig behavior during the 1838 and 1843 sessions. Reaching power in 1838, after an absence of four years, the Whigs in Joint Meeting approved 831 appointments. In 1843, the last of six consecutive years of Whigs majorities, they nearly matched their 1838 output by appointing 817 individuals to office.

Although New Jersey's legislative parties remained generally unified in deciding Joint Meeting appointments, it is clear that their ability to maintain cohesion improved over time. The formal appearance of the Democratic and Whig parties in the state after the period of coalitional reshuffling and stabilization between 1829 and 1833 coincided with a marked increase in party cohesion on Joint Meeting roll calls. Between 1829 and 1833 the percentage of Joint Meeting roll calls recording indices of likeness under 10 in a single session reached a maximum of 58.3.

For the five sessions involved, this measure of party cohesion achieved a mean of 42.1. In contrast, between 1834 and 1844 a maximum measure of 97.6 was recorded, while the mean for these sessions equaled 73.1. Indeed if data for the 1836 and 1844 session are excluded because of exceptional circumstances, the mean for the remaining nine sessions becomes 84.1 (Table 15).[11]

The ability of legislative parties to overcome internal disagreement over the proper party choice for particular positions also illustrates that, as party alignments became better defined and as party organizations matured, party cohesion in the legislature on appointments improved. During the 1829 session, the National Republicans, although having a majority in Joint Meeting, found it extremely difficult to decide who should be selected to fill a vacant United States Senate seat. Twelve roll calls were taken on this question, with the appointment finally going to Mahlon Dickerson, a Morris County Democrat, who later served as Secretary of the Navy between 1834 and 1837.[12] One National Republican leader, Charles Ewing, blamed the selection of Dickerson on the West Jersey members of his party who were set upon choosing someone from their part of the state to the office. As Ewing described it, "the result [was] the election of an opposition man and from the Eastern part of the state—How mollifying must be the reflections of the administration men from West Jersey!"[13]

Two other contests occasioned similar responses in this year. The selection of the clerk of the common pleas for Middlesex County found eight candidates vying for the position. After fifteen roll calls, no choice had been made and so further consideration of the appointment was postponed. Seven individuals competed for the office of state attorney general. After two ballots the contest narrowed down to three candidates, Samuel L. Southard, Garret Wall, and Lucius Q. C. Elmer. After four more ballots, Southard, the National Republican, defeated Wall, the

Jacksonian Democrat; the legislators of both parties voted for the candidate of their own political persuasion.[14] Such instances of multiple candidates and multiple ballots hardly occurred after 1833.

II

Party division on Joint Meeting appointments paralleled somewhat voting behavior on other legislative questions. Although these matters did not consistently provoke the intense partisanship and cohesion always present with Joint Meeting appointments, voting on them reveals the gradual emergence of party as a decisive factor of legislative behavior.

Table 16 summarizes party voting in the Assembly on 1,648 cleavage roll calls voted upon between 1829 and 1844. It does not include an account of the 944 unanimous roll calls recorded during this period.[15] Each cleavage roll call found over 15% of those assemblymen voting opposed to the majority position. Any roll call on which 85% or more of the participating assemblymen voted together was characterized as unanimous.[16] Although not shown, similar tables for 870 cleavage and 1,129 unanimous Council roll calls were constructed. With the exception of roll calls concerning the enactment of the 555 acts involving divorces and trusts, these totals include virtually every roll-call vote recorded in the New Jersey legislature between 1829 and 1844.

All roll calls were sorted by content into one of thirty issue categories and into one of three time periods. Within each category for each time period, the mean index of likeness for all cleavage roll calls in terms of the variable of party was computed.[17] Indices of likeness were not calculated for unanimous votes, since these roll calls, by their very nature, could not reveal the presence of significant cohesive groups. Although Council cleavage roll calls were

THE BEHAVIOR OF STATE LEGISLATIVE PARTIES

TABLE 16
Party Voting in the Assembly, 1829-1844:
Distribution of Indices of Likeness

Period	Issue Categories With Mean Party Indices of Likeness Between		
	0-10	11-20	21-30
		Resolutions-national (15)*	Election Disputes (29)
1829-1832			
	Resolutions-national (6)	Printing (17)	
1833-1837			
1838-1844	Appt. of legislative officials (6) Election disputes (1) Resolutions-national (7)	Constitutional reform (14) Counties and townships (19) Special Privileges-communities (17) State Prison (19)	Election (21) House operation (30) Printing (22)

*Number in parentheses represents mean party index of likeness for all cleavage roll calls in each issue category for the designated time period. Appendix A details the number of roll calls in each category on which these indices are based.

31-50	51-66	67-100
pt. of legis- ve officials (43)		Banking-special (75) Business-special (88) Business-gov't. involvement (72) Business-general regulatory (78) Counties and townships (70) Election (78) Enclosures (79) House operation (75) Insurance (86) Joint Companies (78) Judicial (80) Military (74) Mining (85) Miscellaneous (76) Printing (68) Religion (83) Social (86) Specie (95) State Prison (86) Taxation (85) Transportation (77)
ınties and townships(40) ction (37) ıse operation (49) ıt Companies (45) ıgion (48) cie (49) te Prison (49)	Appt. of legis- lative officials (56) Banking-general (55) Miscellaneous (64) Social (65) Taxation (61)	Banking-special (69) Business-special (70) Business-gov't. involvement (70) Business-general regulatory (78) Enclosures (74) Insurance (83) Judicial (68) Military (79) Mining (84) Natural Resources (85) Resolutions-Procedural (72) Special privileges- communities (81) Surplus revenue (86) Transportation (75)
king-special (40) king-general (41) iness-special (41) ıt Companies (36) ing (36) ıgion (44) olutions-procedural (41) cie (32) ation (49)	Business-gov't. involvement (61) Insurance (54) Judicial (65) Miscellaneous (56) Natural Resources (65) Transportation (54)	Business-general regulatory (70) Enclosures (72) Military (77) Social (68)

analyzed, the chief focus of this presentation is Assembly voting behavior. Council membership never exceeded eighteen between 1829 and 1844. Percentage calculations, essential to the computation of indices of likeness, may be misleading when based on small numbers. Using indices based on small groups of councillors can distort the significance of actual voting patterns. Although party voting in Council generally followed Assembly patterns, the small size of that body dictates concentration on the lower house.

Simple classification of roll-call votes into categories of legislation along with the calculation of party indices of likeness for them makes it possible to distinguish the types of questions that engendered or disrupted party unity.[18] These procedures also indicate the timing of party cohesion in the legislature.

As with Joint Meeting appointments, the effect of party as a determinant of legislative voting behavior increased over time. Between 1829 and 1832 partisan responses other than on the appointment of Assembly officials, election disputes, and resolutions on national political issues were infrequent. Of the thirty categories of roll calls, only these three recorded mean indices under 44. The series of roll calls concerned with the public printing was the only other group to record a mean index under 70.

During the 1833–1837 period, substantially more groups reflected the impact of party. Fourteen categories of legislation yielded moderate to high levels of party voting. Decisions concerning general banking legislation, the appointment of Assembly officials, the operation of the Assembly, the Camden and Amboy Railroad and Delaware and Raritan Canal Company, certain miscellaneous proposals, religion, social legislation, regulation of the state's monetary system, the state prison, and taxation all elicited mean indices between 67 and 41. Even higher indices of party voting were produced by legislation involving the formation of counties and townships, election laws, the distribution of the public printing, and resolutions on national political issues.

Between 1838 and 1844 party influence was even greater. During these years all but four categories of roll calls revealed some indication of party voting. Twelve categories recorded mean party indices of likeness between 67 and 41, while fourteen recorded indices under 41. Cleavage roll calls concerned with the appointment of Assembly officials, state constitutional reform, the formation of counties and townships, election laws and election disputes, the distribution of the public printing, resolutions on national issues, the granting of special privileges to individual communities, and the state prison all produced mean indices under 25.

III

Certain observations are apparent from the voting data. Party influence as the key determinant of patronage decisions preceded the emergence of party as an important factor of legislative voting behavior. Even when partisan cohesion on matters other than appointments occurred, the highest levels of party unity between 1829 and 1844 were in response to Joint Meeting roll calls. Effectiveness in this area, although relatively consistent, increased noticeably after 1833 as did partisan cohesion on the entire range of questions voted upon by the legislature.

The desire to exert partisan control over appointments stimulated the mobilization of legislative parties. Early and consistent party responses to Joint Meeting appointments indicates that New Jersey's legislative parties were well aware of the needs of the larger party organizations of which they were integral parts. Patronage and its control was a critical link between legislative parties and state party organizations. Joint Meeting appointments at the disposal of the legislature were the principal source of patronage necessary to secure and maintain the loyalties of party activists. Legislative parties, organized in the caucus, controlled and dispensed this patronage.

The experience of New Jersey's parties indicates the importance of this function for maintaining party organizations. Parties developed originally in New Jersey in the late 1820s as agencies designed to elect men to office and to reward loyal party workers. The willingness of individuals to participate actively in election campaigns and to staff party organizations was not simply a factor of nontangible incentives such as attachment to party principles or admiration of particular leaders.[19] The devotion of party activists to their organizations was often determined by the ability of the party to materially reward these individuals for their efforts. Specifically, without the prospect of receiving appointment to some state or county office once victory at the polls had been achieved, partisans were not likely to tax their energies during election campaigns.[20] A letter received by Samuel Southard during his term as governor in 1833, for instance, informed him that the National Republican, later Whig, party to which he belonged had severely damaged its position in Somerset by refusing to respond to the patronage requests of the party's supporters in that county. "So disgusted and disheartened" were the delegates to the party's county convention upon hearing of the failure of the National Republican-controlled legislature to appoint partisans to the county's judicial and civil posts "that the Convention broke up without making any definite arrangements. . . ." Nor would "the delegates from the several townships . . . even carry tickets to their townships for the coming election."[21] Democrats as well experienced such problems. Failure of the legislature in 1834, one that contained an overwhelming Democratic majority, to appoint Cape May Democrats to office caused one partisan to note that the party's workers in that county had been "almost driven . . . to perfect neutrality."[22]

Whether successful in securing appointments or not, potential officeholders were well aware that their credentials as hard-working partisans were crucial prerequisites for any Joint Meeting appointment. Letters of recommendation such as one written in behalf of an office seeker to a Democratic legislator in 1834, invariably noted that the aspirant "was a good [party] man, and that the *interests of the party* would be *vastly benefitted* by his appointment."[23]

Recognition of a close relationship between the patronage needs of competitive state party organizations and the activities of legislative parties suggest an understanding of party in New Jersey as a distinct institution with its own loyalties, cognizant and capable of satisfying its own interests. Similar conceptions of party apparently existed elsewhere in ante-bellum America. Michael Wallace's study of the New York political experience between 1815 and 1828, for instance, details the emergence of modern concepts of party and of political competition capable of justifying the activities of the professional politician.[24] Fundamental to this new conception was the idea that the party was a social institution—the proper form of political organization in a democratic state. As such, the major responsibility of party did not involve the making of public policy or the defense of a particular ideology. Devotion to the preservation of party organization—the bulwark of the state—became an end in itself. In fulfilling this goal, party activists both in the electorate and in the legislature owed strict loyalty to the party.[25] Glorification of this "ethos of subordination" and concern with self-preservation manifested itself in the general acceptance of caucus doctrine and in the behavior of state legislators who, although not expected to unite on public issues, were required to exhibit cohesion on matters, such as appointments, that "in some fashion affected the fortune of the organization itself."[26] The desire of New Jersey's Democrats and Whigs to control legislative patronage, the stimulant this interest was to the organization of legislative parties, the high levels of partisan cohesion on appointment roll calls, the acceptance by both parties of the legislative caucus as a conventional means of securing party discipline, and the manner in which the closeness of party competition complemented the efforts of the legislative party caucuses in maintaining the vitality of state party organizations together defined a role for New Jersey's legislative parties that complemented such explanations of party behavior.

The conscious efforts of party legislators to serve the special interests of their party organizations, however decisive in stimulating the mobilization of legislative parties, does not mean that the impact of legislative parties was limited to deciding obvious party questions. Although the high percentage of unanimous votes suggests a basic consensus among legislators, increased partisan cohesion over time on the entire range of issues subject to roll-call votes suggests that its activities went beyond predictable reactions to organizational needs. Effective party dominance with respect to the legislature's decision-making structure made New Jersey's legislative parties convenient mechanisms for channeling individual and group demands and for enacting legislation. The summaries of partisan voting patterns on Assembly roll calls do not reveal whether legislative parties initiated legislation, reflected contrasting belief systems, or engaged in the activities of responsible policy-making parties. Indications of party voting could have been a manifestation of the convenience of logrolling among legislators with the same political affiliation; the result of ideological agreement on the nature of particular legislation; the product of issue management by party leaders aimed at affecting political advantage—or some combination of such possibilities. Whatever the motivation, the data suggest that as party organization in the legislature matured and as procedures became regularized, legislative parties developed a constituent role in the decision-making process. By virtue of their stable organizations and their control of legislative machinery, New

Jersey's legislative parties, whether intended or not, engaged in activities essential to the structure and operation of the state's government.[27]

An understanding of the party in office as a branch of party capable of satisfying partisan demands as well as performing certain constituent functions is different from the models usually employed to describe party behavior in the Jacksonian era. Legislative parties in New Jersey were not simply the vanguards of responsible parties intent on pursuing policies with particular ideological bents. Nor were they mere accessories of larger organizations concerned solely with obtaining the perquisites and preferments of political power. Moreover, the ability of New Jersey's legislative parties to serve party as an interest and to facilitate the operation of government posed no internal contradictions. Close competition between Democrats and Whigs compelled the mobilization of legislative parties capable of providing the patronage necessary to sustain the larger party organizations. The establishment of legislative parties for purely partisan purposes also generated the preconditions that enabled them to perform constituent functions. Clearly the competitive nature of New Jersey politics directly affected manifestations of party in the legislative arena.

This statement of party role in the New Jersey legislature is not based on a belief that a two-party system is essential to the governing of a democratic state. Legislative parties in New Jersey were the means by which that state's government organized and operated. Other experiences in the Western democratic tradition, however, indicate that the recruitment of political leadership and the government of a regime do not necessarily require a party framework.[28] Nor is any comment intended on the ability of the Democrats or the Whigs to perform responsible policy-making functions or to successfully meet the demands of all groups in society. Observation of manifestations of party behavior in the legislature defines the partisan and constituent activities of these legislative parties in a highly competitive party situation.

Based on an analysis of composite voting data in terms of the single variable of party, this general presentation of legislative party behavior requires elaboration and clarification. Definition of a constituent role for legislative parties, for instance, does not preclude conscious attempts on their part, for whatever the reasons, to shape the content of substantive legislation. Even cursory examination of Assembly voting behavior reveals that certain issues elicited greater partisan responses than others. Within each category of legislation, individual roll calls produced party indices of likeness as low as those generated by Joint Meeting roll calls. Does this varying intensity of party influence suggest that in certain areas legislative parties consciously pursued the enactment of particular legislation? If so, what do their efforts reveal about their own perception of their roles? If conscious partisan manipulation by legislative parties occurred in specific instances, what effect, if any, did it have on legislative voting behavior in general? If patronage and its control was the greatest stimulant to the organization of legislative parties, did the loss of patronage power diminish their effectiveness? What effects did variables other than party have on legislative voting behavior? What is the significance of the high percentage of unanimous roll calls? Careful examination of particular categories of legislation in terms of a variety of variables will provide the answers to these and other questions crucial to a precise understanding of New Jersey's legislative parties.

Notes

1. *J.N.J.L.C.*, 1829–1844. Joint Meeting proceedings as noted earlier appeared at the end of the Council journals.

2. *N.J.L.*, 53d sess., 1829, p. 11; Grange W. King to Samuel L. Southard, 19 November 1832, Southard Papers, P.U.L.

3. *Newark Daily Advertiser,* 25 January 1833.

4. *Emporium and True American* (Trenton), 9 March 1833.

5. *New Jersey State Gazette* (Trenton), 8 November 1834.

6. *Newark Daily Advertiser,* 9 November 1843. *See* the following concerning other references to the caucus and Joint Meeting appointments. *Emporium and True American,* 3 November 1832, 13 September 1839, 25 October 1842; *Newark Daily Advertiser,* 18 and 25 January 1833, 25 October 1833, 26 January 1839, 9 November 1843; *New Jersey State Gazette,* 1 March 1834. *Also see* Joseph Jackson to Mahlon Dickerson, 22 October 1834, Mahlon Dickerson Papers, N.J.H.S.; Garret Wall to William Emley, James Cook, William Jeffers, Stacy Potts, and Peter D. Vroom, Jr., 1829, Philhower Collection, R.U.L.; Stacy Potts to Garret Wall, 30 October 1829, Philhower Collection, R.U.L.; Isaac Southard to Samuel L. Southard, 15 November 1838, and Ephriam Marsh to Samuel L. Southard, 18 February 1841, Southard Papers, P.U.L.

7. The number 447 refers to the mean number of appointments filled in a single legislative session. In certain sessions, notably 1838 and 1842, only two Joint Meetings were held.

8. Excluded from this total are series of roll calls involving three appointments noted upon in the 1829 session. These appointments involved more than two candidates, thus making it inconvenient to employ indices of likeness. *See* note 12 for further information.

9. Stuart Rice, "The Behavior of Legislative Groups," *Political Science Quarterly* 40 (March 1925): 60–72; Lee F. Anderson, Meredith W. Watts, Jr., and Allen R. Wilcox, *Legislative Roll-Call Analysis* (Evanston, Illinois: Northwestern University Press 1966), pp. 44–45, both provide descriptions of this method. An I.B.M. System/360 Model 30 computer was employed in my study. Programming was done primarily by Mr. Neil Polo, with assistance from Mr. David Kantor of the Rutgers University Computer center. Computer time was secured at the Rutgers center as well as at installations used for administrative university purposes under the supervision of Mr. Ralph Lindauer.

10. Relative index of cohesion is the percentage of the votes cast by the majority of the members of a particular group who actually vote on a particular roll call. It differs from an absolute index of cohesion that is the percentage of the votes cast by the majority of all members of a particular group, whether they vote or not. When no indices of likeness under 10 were recorded, Democrats and Whigs were still highly cohesive. The mean relative indices of cohesion for legislators of these parties were 92.5 and 90.0, respectively.

11. In 1836 only four roll calls were taken on 353 appointments. In 1844, although 1,059 appointments were awarded, only nine roll calls were recorded. Eight of these nine produced indices of likeness between 20 and 11.

12. *J.N.L.C.,* 53d session, 1829, pp. 19–30, of the Joint Meeting Records.

13. Charles Ewing to Samuel L. Southard, 1 February 1829, Southard Papers, P.U.L. *See also* Lewis Condict to Samuel L. Southard, 24 January 1829, Southard Papers, P.U.L.

14. *J.N.J.L.C.*, 53d session, 1829, pp. 33–46, 50–55, of the Joint Meeting records.

15. Appendix A includes descriptions of the categories employed in Table 16, as well as the specific number of cleavage and unanimous roll calls for each time period. Levine, "Party-in-the Legislature," on file at the Rutgers University Library, contains descriptions of all Assembly roll calls that are specifically referred to in this study.

16. The decision to classify roll-call votes as unanimous or cleavage on the basis of an 85%–15% majority-minority split was based on the size of the two houses of the New Jersey legislature. Membership in the Council never exceeded eighteen, while membership in the Assembly never exceeded fifty-eight, and in all but three years remained under fifty-four. Given the maximum participation of the legislators on every roll call in those years where the membership in the two houses was at its highest, this procedure permitted computer techniques to be applied to all Council roll calls where three or more members voted in the minority and to all Assembly roll calls where eight or more assemblymen voted in the minority. In reality, investigation of Council roll calls where only two members voted in the minority and of Assembly roll calls where as few as four assemblymen voted in the minority were undertaken when these votes constituted over 15% of the total ballots that were cast.

The underlying assumption of this classification system is that unanimous votes, by their very nature, can not reveal the presence of significant cohesive groups. Although the 85%-15% criterion takes some liberties with this assumption, its employment facilitated the examination of a large number of roll calls without seriously distorting the results that were obtained. The fact that almost every roll call that had two or more councillors or four or more assemblymen in the minority was included, virtually guaranteed that no significant cohesive group was excluded from analysis.

17. As noted in chapter 2, legislators felt that divorces and trusts were of little importance. They were usually decided by overwhelming majorities. This fact, along with the general disdain in which they were held, led me to eliminate them from analysis. Certain procedural roll calls whose significance could not be determined from the legislative journals were also omitted. These roll calls referred to motions to adjourn, which, given the time at which they appeared in the legislative records, apparently were not related to any strategic moves to postpone consideration of legislation. Their number did not exceed thirty for the period under study.

18. Jerome M. Clubb and Howard W. Allen, "Party Loyalty in the Progressive Years: The Senate, 1909–1915," in *Quantitative History: Selected Readings in the Quantitative Analysis of Historical Data*, ed. Don K. Rowney and James P. Graham, Jr. (Homewood, Illinois: The Dorsey Press, 1969), p. 445.

19. For an excellent discussion of incentives, *see* Sorauf, *Political Parties in the American System*, pp. 82–91.

20. Parties organized primarily as electoral mechanisms invariably produce

this pattern of loyalty. In other circumstances, however, party loyalty may exist for a variety of reasons. For instance, *see* Samuel H. Barnes, *Party Democracy: Politics in an Italian Socialist Federation* (New Haven, Connecticut: Yale University Press, 1967), pp. 112–96.

21. Isaac Southard to Samuel L. Southard, 4 November 1832, Southard Papers, P.U.L.

22. Robert P. Thompson to Peter D. Vroom, 13 April 1834, Vroom Papers, Columbia University Library.

23. *Newark Daily Advertiser*, 26 February 1834. The Southard Papers contain numerous examples of the necessity of partisan credentials.

24. Michael Wallace, "Changing Concepts of Party in the United States: New York, 1815–1828," *American Historical Review* 74 (December 1968): 453–91. *Also see* Perry M. Goldman, "Political Virtue in the Age of Jackson," *Political Science Quarterly* 77 (March 1972):46–62; Richard Hofstadter, *The Idea of a Party System: The Rise of Legitimate Oppositions in the United States, 1780–1840.* (Berkeley, California: University of California Press, 1969), pp. 212–72; and McCormick, *The Second American Party System,* pp. 353–55.

25. Wallace, "Changing Concepts of Party," pp. 453–91.

26. Ibid., pp. 463–65.

27. Lowi, pp. 238–76. My analysis rests largely on the constituent theory of party behavior presented in this essay.

28. McCormick, "Political Development and the Second Party System," pp. 92–93.

5
Legislative Voting Behavior: Banking and Currency

Throughout the 1830s and the 1840s legislators in New Jersey considered the demands of citizens eager for bank charters, deliberated over the need for state regulation of banks and currency, and debated the efficacy of the financial programs of national party leaders. Patterns of partisan voting behavior on all aspects of fiscal policy are clearly evident. Increased party cohesion and division over time defined a constituent function for legislative parties. The significance of this reaction, however, cannot be simply stated. Complex and sometimes contradictory forces determined legislative decisions. The pressure of party motivated by differences of opinion over the substance of legislation as well as by the exigencies of competitive state politics and the needs of party organizations affected legislative response. So, too, did the cross pressures of sectional, constituency, and personal interests.

I

Although the impact of a legislator's age, occupation, legislative experience, county residence, and party affiliation on roll-call voting were examined, description of results in this chapter and elsewhere primarily concern the relative impact of partisan, sectional, and county ties. No doubt the decisions of particular legislators on specific roll calls were affected by other factors. Analysis of aggregate data demonstrates, however, that age, experience, and occupation were not quantitatively significant variables. A legislator's age and experience had no measurable influence on voting.[1] In certain instances small voting blocs defined by occupation were noticeable (Table 17).[2] During the 1834 Assembly session, for instance, on seventeen banking and currency roll calls, legislators who were farmers and legislators who were lawyers disagreed more consistently than did legislators grouped by party identities. A similar situation occurred in 1843 when legislators who engaged in farming and those involved in commerce produced a mean index of likeness lower than that generated by party groupings. Generally, however, relative to party and section, this variable was not useful in identifying consistent and significant voting patterns.

All cleavage Assembly and Council banking and currency roll calls for the 1829–1844 period were scrutinized in order to determine the relative effect of different variables on voting. Although extremely low indices of likeness for particular variables demonstrated obvious group voting, the levels of intragroup cohesion and of intergroup cohesion necessary to assert bloc voting were not pre-

TABLE 17

Mean Indices of Likeness for Party and Occupational
Groups on Assembly Banking and Currency Legislation, 1829-18

Year (No. Roll Calls)	Democrats Vs National Republicans or Whigs	Farmers* Vs Lawyers	Farmers Vs Manufactur and Commer
1829 (3)	76.0	81.0	76.7
1830 (4)	74.5	84.8	91.2
1831 (5)	86.4	–––	–––
1832 (4)	81.0	–––	–––
1833 (12)	71.5	–––	–––
1834 (17)	79.2	77.6	–––
1835 (10)	16.7	81.2	81.8
1836 (34)	45.7	–––	85.5
1837 (76)	59.5	71.8	86.5
1838 (22)	27.9	70.4	–––
1839 (7)	26.9	–––	87.7
1840 (3)	61.3	–––	–––
1841 (10)	34.7	–––	75.2
1842 (18)	37.1	–––	85.8
1843 (5)	76.2	–––	76.4
1844 (0)			
Mean Indices	53.8	77.3	91.3

*The size of occupational groups varied greatly. The farmer group
contained a maximum of 29 in 1841 and a minimum of 22 in 1844.
Lawyer groups ranged between 9 and 6, commerce between 5 and 8,
manufacturing between 6 and 9, and the combined categories of
manufacturing and commerce between 8 and 16. Not all legislators in
these categories, however, voted on every roll call.

Lawyers Vs Manufacturing and Commerce	Farmers Vs Manufacturing	Farmers Vs Commerce	Lawyers Vs Commerce
85.0	---	---	---
89.0	---	---	---
---	89.6	---	---
---	---	---	---
---	---	---	---
---	---	---	---
70.9	---	---	---
---	---	78.5	---
67.1	---	---	67.5
---	---	---	---
---	---	87.7	---
---	---	74.0	---
---	---	73.2	---
---	---	91.3	---
---	78.4	75.2	---
76.6	84.0	80.0	67.5

determined. No fixed numbers designated significant cohesion. The ability of a variable group to maintain a high level of cohesion relative to other groups over a series of related roll calls served as the test of significance.[3]

Separate analysis of special and general banking and currency legislation and of legislative resolutions on national fiscal policy establishes the interplay of forces shaping the decision-making process.[4] Legislative banking and currency proposals appeared in three different forms. Up to 1850 all banks chartered in New Jersey were created by special legislative acts.[5] Between 1829 and 1844 sixteen banks received charters, numerous other requests were denied, and a variety of related legislation was acted upon. Much of this special legislation occupied legislators' time prior to the Panic of 1837. After that year, attention focused on general banking and currency proposals designed to improve the state's financial condition. In five different sessions during this sixteen-year span, the legislature also considered resolutions concerning federal fiscal policy.

Party influence varied inversely to the extent that banking and currency legislation affected local and special interests. Although National Republican and Whig legislators were more disposed than their Democratic counterparts to support special banking legislation, both sides were less distinguishable by their stands on these questions than by their positions on other aspects of fiscal legislation.

II

At the close of the 1837 legislative session, one Democratic newspaper editor exclaimed that "the Whig party . . . with almost the precision of party discipline," had passed nearly every bank charter before the legislature, thus "effectively settl[ing] the responsibility of creating more banks, so far as party [was] concerned."[6] During this session a greater proportion of Whigs than Democrats did support bank charter bills. The editor however neglected to remind his readers that in an Assembly that contained a ten-seat Democratic majority and in a Council evenly divided between the two parties, no bank charters could have been approved without substantial Democratic support. As it was in other sessions, constituency demands eroded cohesive party voting on special banking legislation. Up through 1844 voting behavior on special banking legislation was characterized by an absence of sectional division and by increased party voting after 1834, tempered always by the influence of particular local interests. Although Whig legislators were somewhat more friendly than Democrats to the enactment of probank legislation, party lines were not sharp enough to support traditional interpretations emphasizing polarized party position on banks.

Table 18 illustrates the tendency of New Jersey's legislators with the same party affiliations to vote together over time on special banking legislation. With one exception, in every year after 1834 at least two-thirds of the voting assemblymen of each party opposed each other on roll calls at all related to this subject.[7] In no single session, however, did party voting approach the extremes reached on Joint Meeting roll calls. Between 1829 and 1837, when all but three roll calls concerned specifically with charter bills were recorded and when all but 19 of the 129 special banking roll calls were decided, the mean index of likeness for individual sessions registered under 60 only three times. Prior to 1835 this measure of party influence never fell below .75. Moreover, fifteen of the sixteen bank charters granted in New Jersey between 1829 and 1844 were the product of legislatures containing Democratic majorities.

Examination of aggregated, county roll-call voting data suggests that factors other than party also shaped voting behavior. Table 19 summarizes the votes of the Assembly delegations from the fourteen counties that were in exis-

TABLE 18

Party Voting on Special Bank Legislation,
1829-1844 Assemblies

Year	No. RC	Mean Indices of Likeness
1829	4	76
1830	4	75
1831	3	76
1832	4	81
1833	10	88
1834	16	83
1835	1	31
1836	26	58
1837	42	65
1838	2	32
1839	4	31
1840	2	84
1841	7	33
1842	4	43
1843	–	–
1844	–	–
TOTAL:	129	

tence for the entire 1829–1844 period on bank-charter
passage and engrossment roll calls. Affirmative votes on
these roll calls clearly defined a probanking position. By
scaling the affirmative-percentage figures for each county,
the degree to which each county supported this legislation
is indicated.

Legislators from counties that had bank bills pending
tended to vote in favor of such legislation regardless of
their party identities. Greatest support for the incorporation of banks came from Essex. Located in the eastern part
of the state, this county was east New Jersey's commercial
and industrial center. Although Essex's rich soil yielded
valuable grain crops, many of its citizens were employed in
a variety of industrial trades and lived in developing urban
communities. Essex always returned Whigs to the legisla-

TABLE 19

County Voting on the Chartering of Banks,
1829-1844 Assemblies

County	Affirm. votes (Probank)	Neg. votes (Antibank)	Affirm. Percent.	No. Charter Bills for banks in each county
Essex	220	53	80	7
Warren	101	55	65	2
Middlesex	124	81	61	3
Sussex	97	63	61	1
Salem	88	68	57	--
Burlington	134	120	53	4
Morris	105	94	53	3
Bergen	80	73	52	1
Gloucester	101	110	48	--
Cape May	30	32	47	1
Somerset	74	87	46	--
Cumberland	61	91	40	--
Monmouth	75	131	36	1
Hunterdon	76	167	31	3

ture. Legislative consideration of charter bills for seven different Essex banks no doubt contributed to the county's strong support of charter legislation.

Of the other counties that gave more than sixty percent of their votes to the banking cause, Warren and Sussex invariably elected Democrats to represent them, while Middlesex was somewhat of a Whig stronghold.[8] Located in the northwestern corner of the state, Warren and Sussex were important agricultural centers for the production of wheat, corn, and rye. Although agriculture was the chief business in Middlesex, the location of the Camden and Amboy Railroad through its center encouraged considerable trade there.

Of the four counties that most consistently supported

banks, party strength was relatively even. This same general pattern existed for the remaining counties that recorded affirmative percentages over fifty. Between 1829 and 1844 Salem was represented equally by both parties in the legislature, the Whigs controlling the county's delegations for eight years and the Democrats for seven years. Morris and Bergen, the two counties along with Essex that carried on extensive commercial and industrial activities, were most often represented by Democrats in the legislature. Whigs usually served as delegates from Burlington.[9]

Although neither sectional nor party polarization is defined by this analysis, it is clear that the desire to establish local banking facilities influenced decisions. Except for Essex and Hunterdon, twelve counties produced affirmative percentages ranging between 65 and 36. Ten of these twelve counties scored between 61 and 40. Although the top four counties were all in the northern part of the state, they were not contiguous. Similarly, the four counties at the bottom of the scale, two primarily Whig and two Democratic, were geographically scattered throughout the state. Except for Salem and Middlesex, all eight counties that registered affirmative percentages over fifty had at least two charter bills for banks in their domain before the legislature between 1829 and 1844.

Voting behavior in individual legislative sessions approximates the general patterns revealed by the aggregate data. The lack of consistent sectional voting on special banking legislation is evident in the 1834, 1836, and 1837 sessions. During these three sessions, twenty-three bank charters were proposed and ten were approved. Table 20 records the attitudes of each county on the sixty-four Assembly, cleavage roll calls voted upon in these sessions that clearly defined either a probank or antibank position.[10] With no county scoring above 67 and with twelve of the fourteen counties scoring between 67 and 43, no significant breaks occurred that denote cohesive sectional groups for or against banking proposals. In terms of party

TABLE 20*

County Voting on Special Bank Legislation,
1834, 1836, 1837 Assemblies

County	Probank Votes	Antibank Votes	Probank Percent
Essex	114	56	67
Middlesex	134	66	67
Sussex	106	65	62
Warren	100	64	61
Salem	97	69	58
Bergen	84	70	55
Burlington	120	101	54
Cumberland	84	75	53
Cape May	29	28	51
Morris	91	103	47
Somerset	81	97	45
Gloucester	94	127	43
Monmouth	82	136	38
Hunterdon	38	191	17

*Roll calls pertaining to banks in particular counties were not included in the calculations for those counties. The table thus represents delegation attitudes toward banks other than those in their own bailiwicks.

cohesion, voting in these same sessions indicates that although Whig support and Democratic opposition to the expansion of banks increased after 1834, the split was not sharp enough to distinguish firm party positions.

The trend toward increased party voting is clearly illustrated in Fig. 1. In 1834, on sixteen roll calls concerned with the passage of seven bank charters, party lines were almost nonexistent. By 1836 division is evident. In this year, of the twenty-six roll calls concerned with special banking legislation, five recorded party indices of likeness between 35 and 20, while eleven fell between 60 and 36.

ROLL CALL NUMBERS

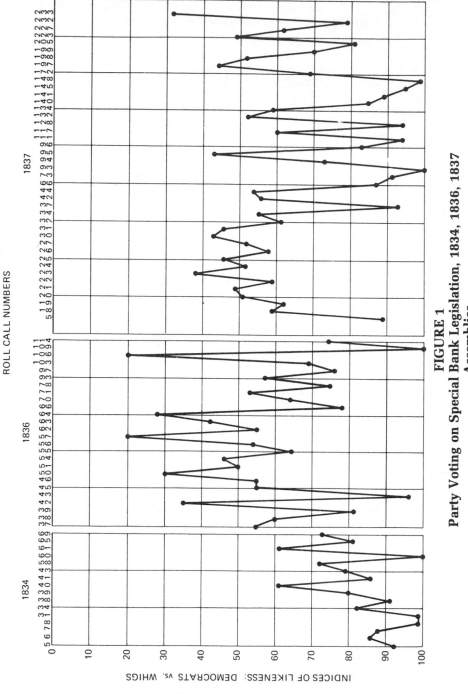

FIGURE 1

Party Voting on Special Bank Legislation, 1834, 1836, 1837
Assemblies

Whig legislators were particularly cohesive. The mean-relative index of cohesion for Whig assemblymen on these roll calls was 86. Only four times did less than 70% of those Whigs voting on a particular measure cast their ballots together. Instances of Democratic bloc voting were less frequent. Only three times did the majority party find more than 80% of its membership in the Assembly in agreement. The mean level of relative cohesion for Democratic assemblymen was 64.

As defined by their votes, the Whigs in 1836, were in favor of all seven proposed bank charters, for increasing the capital stock of other banks, and against provisions making stockholders individually responsible for the debts of their banks. Democrats strongly supported only the Morris bank (roll call 43, Democratic vote 21–10), were less committed to increasing the capital stock of others, and were more disposed to imposing liability on bank stockholders (roll call 46, Democratic vote 17–13).[11]

Similar positions were taken by both parties during the 1837 session. On twenty-two of forty-two banking roll calls voted upon in this year, party indices of likeness of 60 or under were recorded. On the fifteen roll calls calling for the enactment of bank-charter bills, the mean relative index of cohesion for Whig assemblymen was 72, while that of their Democratic counterparts was 65.

The tendency for party legislators, especially Whigs, to vote together on special banking legislation does not preclude the effects of constituency and personal interests on legislators' decisions. Often representatives traded votes in order to insure passage of proposals vital to their constituents. Table 21, for instance, records the probank attitudes of county delegations in the 1836 Assembly.[12] With the exception of Middlesex, counties that had the most at stake gave the greatest support to special banking questions. The three counties that had bank bills pending before the legislature—Essex represented by Whigs and Morris and Burlington represented by Democrats—gave a

TABLE 21

County Voting on Special Bank Legislation,
1836 Assembly

County	Probank Votes	Antibank Votes	Probank Percent
Essex	77	15	84
Middlesex	62	13	82
Morris	53	17	76
Burlington	68	29	70
Salem	36	19	65
Cape May	13	7	65
Cumberland	35	21	63
Sussex	31	26	54
Bergen	28	28	50
Monmouth	25	35	42
Warren	20	32	38
Somerset	20	35	36
Gloucester	23	51	31
Hunterdon	21	72	23

great deal of support to each other's proposals. Of twenty-five Essex delegation votes on the eight passage-and-engrossment roll calls involving bank bills for Morris and Burlington, twenty-one votes were in the affirmative. Similarly, Morris assemblymen supported those bills involving banks in Essex and Burlington, as did the Burlington representatives for bills concerning Morris and Essex institutions.[13] It is not surprising that none of the bottom seven counties on the scale, those most opposed to probank legislation, were directly involved in any of the measures before the Assembly.[14]

Obviously logrolling on banking proposals was not limited to situations in which only such measures were involved.[15] It is also likely that the desire of individual legislators to satisfy their own business aims or those of their colleagues affected decisions. Legislators were among the incorporators of fourteen of the sixteen banks that were granted charters by the legislature between 1829 and 1844. Nine charters were authorized in the very sessions in which involved legislators were serving. That some legislators used their office for personal benefit was suggested more than once between 1829 and 1844. As one newspaper editor stated commenting on the bank legislation enacted during the 1837 session, certain unmentioned lawmakers had "prostitut[ed] their station, and abus[ed] their 'brief authority' for the accomplishment of private objects and personal profit."[16]

Analysis of special banking legislation, while not disclosing the existence of disciplined party voting, indicates a noticeable tendency after 1834 for Democrats to be less disposed than Whigs toward such legislation. Substantial support from Democratic legislators, however, was required to approve banking proposals. Although no sectional voting patterns emerged, it appears that local demands and the interests of involved legislators influenced decisions.

It might be argued that the small number of bank charters that were allowed is proof enough of Democratic opposition to banks. Massachusetts, for example, incorporated seventy-two banks between 1830 and 1837, while New Jersey incorporated only sixteen of some thirty-six that were proposed between 1829 and 1844. This conservative response, however, was not a factor of party policy but rather a result of the state's unique geographic position. Situated between Philadelphia and New York, with the economies of the western and eastern parts of the state respectively dependent on these great trade centers, New Jersey did not require as large a number of its own banking facilities as did other states.[17] Where needs did exist, individual citizens, with the support of their communities, petitioned the legislature for charters.[18] Democratic and Whig legislators responded to the will of their constituents by using their votes to secure the passage of these charter bills. As the most convenient channels through which to engage support for legislation, legislative parties, by virtue of their presence less than by design, served important constituent functions in relation to special banking legislation.

III

Deliberations over general fiscal legislation engendered more conscious and meaningful roles for legislative parties than did special banking proposals. Patterns of party involvement in the enactment of general banking and currency bills were quite similar for both Democratic and Whig legislators. On both sides the tendency to vote as cohesive groups on special banking proposals increased. Party voting on general legislation was noticed first in 1835. The suspension of specie payments by the state's banks in 1837 coincided with increased party action and party solidarity in the legislature. Although neither party had taken the initiative to offer a comprehensive fiscal policy prior to the Panic of 1837, Democrats and Whigs in their election campaigns both presented their own contrasting programs for state action and supported them by their votes in the legislature. Both parties, in analyzing the causes of the economic crisis and in proposing remedies for it, sought to preserve their identity with their national party organizations. The Democrats denied the possibility that the Panic of 1837 had been the result of the policies of Andrew Jackson and Martin Van Buren and urged for reform of the currency and for immediate resumption of specie payments. The Whigs, for their part, placed all blame on Van Buren and Jackson. Their legislative proposals recognized the right of state banks to suspend specie payments, while opposing Democratic plans for a specie currency. Although constituency demands occasionally eroded party unity, what is most striking about party activity in the determination of general banking and currency legislation is the cohesion displayed by both Democrats and Whigs.

Assembly voting behavior during the 1838, 1841, 1842, and 1843 legislative sessions illustrates the preponderant influence of party on general fiscal legislation. The suspension of specie payments by New York and Philadelphia banks precipitated a financial crisis in New Jersey. New Jersey's banks responded in kind, even though such action was cause for the revocation of their charters. The 1837 legislature was the first to consider this problem. Although legislators of both parties opposed each other in consistent fashion on roll calls concerning bank relief, resolution of this question awaited the 1838 session.[19]

Both the 1838 legislative elections and the subsequent deliberations of the 1838 legislative session reveal an intensification of partisan division over banking policy. In July 1837, the Democratic *Emporium and True American,* after acknowledging that "certain differences" existed between the two parties, pledged the enactment of a threefold fiscal program if Democrats were elected to the legislature in the fall. This program included the resumption of specie payments by the state's banks, the prohibition of all bank notes under the value of twenty dollars, and the imposition of stockholder liability for all bank debts.[20] Although Whig majorities were elected to both the Council and the Assembly in the elections, the first of six consecutive legislative election victories for that party, the Democrats held to their campaign proposals. At the same time, Whig legislators articulated and supported their own analysis of the situation and their own remedies for it.

Early in the first sitting of the 1838 session, a special committee concerned with that part of the governor's message relating to the banking system and the "embarrassed condition of the country" issued its report. Majority and minority positions represented, respectively, the views of the Whig and the Democratic members of the committee. The minority report supported the opinions expressed in the message of the outgoing Democratic governor, Philemon Dickerson. Blame for the financial crisis was attributed to the suspension of specie payments by the banks and to the circulation of low denominations of paper currency. The effects of this crisis on the economy of the state were considered to be limited to the banking community and to "those branches of mercantile and mechanical employments, which depend[ed] upon bank accommodations." The resumption of specie payments by all banks and the prohibition of small bank notes were offered as remedies. It was further argued that no bill should be enacted to protect banks that had illegally suspended specie payments. The majority stand of the Whigs was also criticized for blaming the depression on the policies of Andrew Jackson and Martin Van Buren.[21]

The report of the Whig members of the committee did focus on the policies of these Democratic presidents. The removal of the federal government's funds from the Bank of the United States, their subsequent deposit into state banks, federal policy that encouraged overspeculation and overinvestment, and the Specie Circular were held responsible for a "disordered currency" and for the country's financial woes. According to the Whigs, only a new national policy toward banks and currency could alleviate the situation. Meanwhile New Jersey's banks were not to be abandoned. Their suspension of specie payments was condoned. While calling for a better system of regulation, no punitive measures against banks or their officers were suggested. The report further recommended continued circulation of low denomination bank notes.[22]

The contrast between the positions of the two parties was reflected by voting on Assembly roll calls dealing with matters contained in these reports. Five days after their presentation, George Molleson, a Whig representative from Middlesex, introduced a series of resolutions embodying the Whig analysis. These resolutions received approval by a party vote. All nineteen Democrats voted against passage, while thirty-one of the thirty-two Whigs who cast ballots voted in the affirmative (roll call 12).

Party voting on twenty-one other Assembly roll calls dealing with bank and specie legislation also was high (Figure 2). Of these roll calls, only one recorded an index of likeness over 60, while twelve recorded differences of 23 or under. As defined by their votes, Whigs successfully resisted attempts to have specific charters repealed; allowed banks, in violation of their charters, to continue to suspend specie payments; and supported the circulation of responsible paper currency of all denominations. In every instance the Democratic minority voted in firm opposition.

Four roll calls involved a bill calling for the repeal of specific bank charters (roll calls 22, 51, 52, and 53). Whigs were quite cohesive against engrossing the bill, voting 1–32 in opposition to that motion (roll call 53). Although party was the most important quantitative factor on these roll calls, a certain amount of sectional voting was apparent. Roll call 52, for instance, amended the bill to include the Medford Bank in Burlington. This amendment was defeated 11–37. The Democratic vote was 4–11 and the Whig vote was 7–26. Counties in the western part of the state— Cumberland, represented by Democrats, and Burlington, Salem, Gloucester, and Cape May, represented by Whigs voted 0–16 against the amendment. The fact that a Burlington bank was involved no doubt accounted for this vote.

Roll calls 9 and 102 included in two separate measures what first had been proposed in the general bank-relief bills of 1837. The first allowed the state's banks to continue the suspension of specie payments until fifteen days after New York and Philadelphia banks resumed payments. The second demanded that banks make reports of their operations to the state treasurer every month. All provisions of law imposing penalties and forfeiture of charters or liability because of failure to redeem notes in specie

ROLL CALL NUMBERS

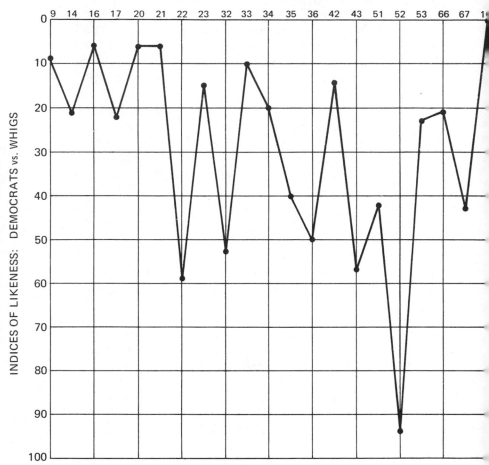

FIGURE 2
General Banking and Specie Legislation, 1838 Assembly

were suspended at least until the 1839 legislative session. Party indices of likeness on these two roll calls were 9 and 0, respectively. The Whig majority voted in favor of both bills.[23]

The attempts of both legislative parties to enact legislation cognizant with stated party positions on banks and resumption of specie payments paralleled similar efforts in regards to currency legislation. Again, the results were the same: Whig-sponsored legislation won approval, while Democratic proposals floundered.

Whig legislators were in favor of the circulation of responsible paper currency of all denominations. Democrats particularly opposed the circulation of low denomination notes. Three different bills related to this problem were presented before the 1838 legislature. Only one became law; a measure to repeal parts of certain acts approved in 1835 and 1836 that had prohibited the issue and circulation of bank notes under the denomination of five dollars.

The legislation enacted in 1835 and 1836 by Democratically controlled legislatures had evoked clear partisan responses, particularly on the part of the Democrats.[24] By 1838, party voting on similar legislation had increased greatly. Four Assembly roll calls were recorded on the bill to repeal the legislation approved in 1835 and 1836 (roll calls 20, 21, 23, and 42). Party indices of likeness on these roll calls were 6, 6, 15, and 14, respectively. Commenting on the bill's enactment, the *Emporium and True American* lamented that "the Small Note Bill is a law. All the Banks ... are permitted to issue these corporation shinplasters, so we shall soon have them as thick as locusts of Egypt. It passed by a strict party Vote: the Federalists [Whigs] for, the Republicans [Democrats] against."[25]

Although no general banking or currency legislation was enacted in 1841, voting patterns in the Whig-controlled Assembly indicate the same trends apparent in the determination of fiscal legislation throughout the 1830s and 1840s—where general legislation was concerned, both parties remained cohesive; where specific interests were involved, local and sectional pressures eroded party unity.

Seven 1841 roll calls concerned the requests of two banks for extension of their charters. Both bills received approval. A mean party index of likeness of 33 was recorded on these roll calls. The most interesting roll call and the one that elicited the greatest partisan division involved a question of public policy. Roll call 10 called for making the stockholders of the Paterson bank in Essex personally liable for the debts of that bank. The *Emporium and True American* urged the enactment of this amendment so as to protect the public from fraud.[26] In contrast, the Whig *Newark Daily Advertiser* argued that the imposition of liability would only drive from management the more responsible men of the community.[27] In line with the advice of their parties' newspapers, the Democrats voted 11–1 in favor of the liability clause, while the Whigs voted 0–33 against it. Party positions on this question paralleled those taken in 1837 when the question of bank liability legislation had also been discussed by the legislature.[28]

Also considered in 1841 was a resolution calling for the resumption of specie payments by all banks in the state. As of 1 January 1841 seventeen of the state's twenty-five banks had resumed payments. Of the eight banks that had not, three were located in Burlington and one each was located in Cumberland, Gloucester, Salem, Mercer, and Hunterdon. These banks, all located in western counties enjoyed an advantage over those banks that were paying specie.[29]

The fact that all of those counties in which banks had not resumed specie payment, with the exception of Hunterdon, were represented by Whigs in the legislature posed a serious problem for that party. Not to demand resumption would offend Whig supporters in eastern counties whose banks were already paying specie, while enactment of legislation that compelled all banks to resume specie payments would hurt the party in the western part of the state. In an attempt to avoid making a decision, a postponement of the question was sought. Roll calls 44, 52, and 53 each concerned motions to postpone consideration of the banking resolution. The twelve Democratic assemblymen voted 0–10, 0–12, and 0–12 not to postpone the resolution; no doubt a reflection of their hard-money views as well as their desire to embarrass the Whigs politically. Although the Whigs were able to secure postponement, they were far from cohesive on this subject, voting 27–10, 14–21, and 24–11. Whig votes against postponement came primarily from eastern counties. On roll call 44, eight of the ten Whig votes against postponement were from Essex, Morris, Somerset, and Hudson; on roll call 52, eighteen of the twenty-one Whig negative notes came from Essex, Morris, Monmouth, Middlesex, Somerset, and Passaic; while on roll call 53, eight of the eleven Whig votes against postponement came from Essex, Morris, Somerset, and Hudson. Although not totally cohesive, counties in which banks were paying specie provided most of the deviant Whig votes, while counties whose banks were not paying, voted against the resolution.[30]

By the 1842 session the Whigs resolved their dilemma by uniting behind a proposal that gave all banks until 15 August 1843 to resume specie payments. Failure to comply by that date was to result in the immediate revocation of all banking privileges.[31] Although the final passage of this bill received overwhelming bipartisan support, six roll calls, each concerned with the choice of a specific date by which resumption was to be reached, produced sharp party division. The mean index of party likeness on them was 14. In each case the Democratic minority favored immediate resumption, while the Whig majority favored a delay as a concession to the western part of the state.[32] The fact that the Whig majority of twenty-nine in the 1841 Assembly had slipped to only twelve in the 1842 Assembly and that four of the seats had been lost in Gloucester and Salem no doubt affected their course of action.

Democratic votes on these roll calls, though consistent

with the party's stand regarding specie, also illustrate the problems that arose when party policy and local interests came into conflict. On each of the six roll calls, the two Democratic representatives from Gloucester voted with the Whigs against immediate resumption and for the latest possible deadline in an effort to protect the interests of the bank in Gloucester, which had not as yet resumed specie payments.

Voting on fiscal legislation in 1842 and 1843 confirms the central tendency of New Jersey's legislative parties after 1837 to vote as blocs on general banking and currency proposals except when local and sectional demands were felt. Only one other aspect of the legislature's involvement with fiscal matters, the enactment of resolutions concerning national fiscal policy, produced greater displays of party solidarity. Resolutions on national policy were considered in five legislative sessions. In 1833, the National Republican-controlled Assembly approved a resolution calling for the rechartering of the Bank of the United States.[33] Democratic ascendancy in the legislature in 1834, 1835, and 1836 resulted in the passage of resolutions in each of these sessions that condemned the Bank, while lauding the achievement of Andrew Jackson in destroying it. The resolutions in 1834 specifically commended the course of action of Secretary of the Treasury Roger B. Taney for his removal of the deposits of the national government from the Bank of the United States. It also "instructed" New Jersey's United States Senators and "requested" the state's Congressmen, "to sustain by their votes and influence," Taney's removal policies.[34] In 1835 and 1836 resolutions were approved that praised Andrew Jackson for his diligent attack on the Bank of the United States. Finally, in 1838, with the legislature once again controlled by the Whigs, a series of twelve resolutions were enacted that blamed all of the financial woes of the nation on the destructive and irresponsible fiscal policies of Andrew Jackson and Martin Van Buren.[35]

A total of eighteen Assembly cleavage roll calls were voted upon in these five sessions to pass these resolutions. The mean party index of likeness on these votes was 3. In twelve instances indices of 0 were recorded. As might be expected, Democrats always supported and defended the policies of the national Democratic administration, while the opposition always attacked them. Invariably, both parties composed these resolutions and agreed upon them in caucus.[36]

No other group of roll calls concerned with any aspect of fiscal legislation voted upon in the New Jersey legislature between 1829 and 1844 registered such high indices of party cohesion. Figure 3 illustrates this fact. Summarized in this graph are the mean party indices of likeness for each category of banking and currency legislation by session for the 1829–1844 period. Clearly, partisan division was strongest on questions of national policy, fell off somewhat on general legislation, and was most erratic on special banking proposals.

IV

This examination of banking and currency legislation demonstrates the significant impact of party on legislative voting behavior. Party influence depended upon the nature of the specific legislation and the circumstances under which it was proposed. Only after Andrew Jackson commenced his assault on the Bank of the United States did banking and currency questions elicit partisan reactions from New Jersey's legislators. Although the responses of party legislators were not prearranged, after 1834, Whigs clearly gave more support than Democrats to special banking proposals. Without substantial corroboration by Democratic legislators, however, no bank charters could have been approved. The private interests of individual legislators and the special requests of constituency groups influenced deliberations.

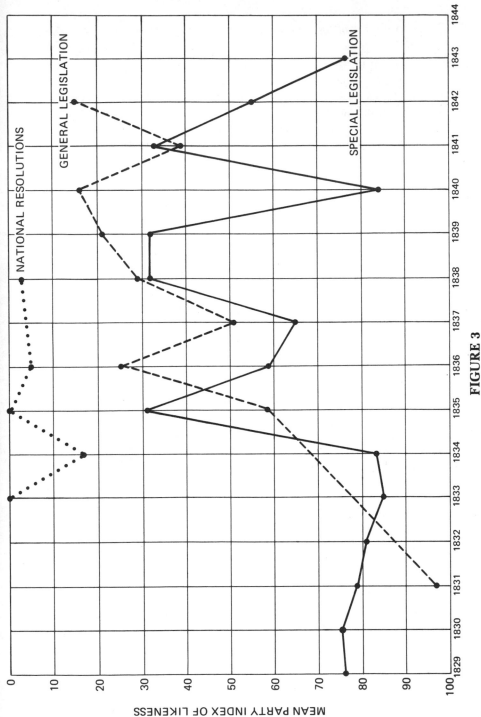

FIGURE 3
Party Voting on Banking and Currency Legislation,

More than special enactments, general banking and currency legislation were cause for organized partisan division. Both legislative parties devised their own explanations concerning the causes of the Panic of 1837, posited different programs for alleviating the financial difficulties of the state, and supported them by their votes in the legislature. Finally, the effect of party on legislative voting behavior was most apparent on resolutions concerning national fiscal policy.

Increased partisan division over time on all aspects of fiscal legislation confirms a constituent role for legislative parties. Roll-call analysis, however, provides no simple explanations of its meaning. Party control over legislative machinery, in the absence of other well-defined interest organizations capable of chaneling constituency demands, helps account for party influence. Nevertheless, voting particularly on general enactments and on national resolutions suggests that genuine differences of opinion existed between parties. It might even be argued, as has been done with similar evidence, that Democrats and Whigs in New Jersey stood ideologically opposed on questions that related to the development of American society.[37]

Such a thesis, however, fails to place party response in the legislature in the context of New Jersey society and politics. Democratic support for currency and bank reform in a state where banking was recognized and integrated into its economic life was hardly a sign of deep division over the future course of economic growth. As in other eastern states, reform not destruction of banks and of paper currency defined the objectives of New Jersey's Democratic politicians. Indeed in New York and in Pennsylvania artisans and entrepreneurs supported hard-money doctrine not out of any longing for fallen agrarian values, but in the belief that a specie currency would protect domestic manufacturing.[38] Moreover the similar occupational and business backgrounds of New

Jersey's legislators suggests that their disagreement over banking and currency policy were not reflective of contrasting belief systems. Although for individual legislators such arguments may be valid, the common desire of Democrats and Whigs to obtain political power must not be forgotten.

Politicians operating in a highly competitive two-party situation are likely to disagree on issues. For a variety of reasons, not the least of which concerns a need to present divergent appeals in order to compete for a mass electorate, party leaders and activists disagree more sharply than their followers. Personal stake in the outcome of elections compels them to define clearly the positions on which they base their chances for success. These distinctions may be sincerely grounded in different ideas about government and society. In situations where general consensus exists on basic social values and institutions, they may be the result of conscious manipulation by party leaders intent on offering the voter a recognizable choice. However formed, these party positions are designed to attract voters and to win elections.[39] Legislators in New Jersey, as loyal and active party members, were well aware of these needs. The nature and timing of legislative response in conjunction with the course of state electoral politics between 1829 and 1844 indicates that diverging party attitudes in the legislature on fiscal matters were closely related to perceptions of how best to achieve party identity and power in a competitive situation.

Formed essentially for the purpose of contesting the presidency, New Jersey's Democratic and Whig parties acquired their definition, their distinctive coloration, and their rhetoric by their identification with national party leaders and the stands of these leaders on substantive issues. In a situation where New Jerseyans were urged to vote even for state legislative candidates because they were "Jackson" supporters or "Clay" men, it is not surprising that when Jackson's assault on the Bank of the United

States became a national political issue, state party organizations, desirous of maintaining themselves and of competing for power, felt obliged to take sides. Although deterred occasionally by local and sectional demands, New Jersey's legislative parties, by their actions, recognized their obligations to their party organizations.

The politicizing of banking and currency questions in the New Jersey legislature coincided with Jackson's attack on the Bank of the United States, the emergence of fiscal policy as an important campaign issue, and the relative stabilization of the state Democratic and Whig parties. Jackson's veto of the Bank's recharter bill occurred in July 1832. The removal of federal deposits from the Bank's vaults commenced in the fall of 1833. Concurrently, the President's policies emerged as the major state campaign issue during the 1832 elections, while the legislature first considered resolutions concerning the Bank of the United States during the 1833 session.[40]

Between 1833 and 1836 additional legislative resolutions involving Jackson's Bank policy were enacted in partisan fashion by the Democratic-controlled legislature. These resolutions conformed to the campaign positions taken by Democratic state and county conventions.[41] Increased Democratic opposition to special banking proposals after 1834 and the enactment in 1835 and 1836 of legislation limiting the circulation of low denominations of paper currency corresponded to the suggestions offered by Democratic governor and party chieftain Peter D. Vroom in his annual messages to the legislature.[42] In contrast, Whig state conventions in 1834 and 1836 blasted Jackson's attempts to destroy the Bank and to impose a specie currency as "visionary and impracticable"— "madman's sport."[43]

Although the Bank of the United States became less important as a campaign issue after 1836, both state parties continued to emphasize related fiscal issues in order to appeal to the state's voters.[44] Following the Panic of 1837, the fiscal policies of Jackson and Van Buren and the executive authority displayed by Jackson in his veto and removal actions served as focal points for election campaigns in New Jersey. In October 1837, outgoing Democratic governor Philemon Dickerson, in line with President Van Buren's pronouncements, blamed the Panic of 1837, in part, on the unwarranted suspension of specie payments by state banks and on the lack of a specie-based currency.[45] His analysis of the Panic, his call for hard currency, and his plea not to recognize the right of state banks to suspend specie payments were echoed by state conventions in 1840 and 1842, by party newspapers during election campaigns, and by the voting records of Democratic legislators in the Council and the Assembly up through 1842.[46]

For their part the Whigs responded to the proposals of their own state conventions and of their governor William Pennington as announced in his legislative message during the 1838 session. Although no call for a new national bank emerged, the Panic was blamed on Democratic presidential leadership. Banking in general was defended and hard-money doctrine denounced. Whig election campaigns at every level focused on these appeals, while legislation concerning New Jersey's banks and currency enacted by Whig-controlled legislatures reflected them.[47] Indeed as late as September 1842, Whig newspapers urged the election of their candidates in New Jersey on the basis that their party was pledged to place restraints on the power of the President so that the repetition of the unjust actions taken by Jackson in his war on the Bank and by Van Buren in his defense of the subtreasury system could be avoided.[48]

The desire of New Jersey's legislative parties to serve their party organizations, then, best explains patterns of partisan behavior on banking and currency proposals. Resolutions on national fiscal policy always prompted the highest measures of party unity and the use of the legislative party caucus, because they most readily allowed the state parties to identify themselves with national party leaders in the minds of the voters. Partisan cohesion on general legislation also reflected the desires of Democrats and Whigs to align themselves with national leaders as well as to construct programs on which they could base their election campaigns. Although special banking proposals, concerned primarily with specific local needs, elicited the least partisan disagreement, party voting on them increased after 1834 as banks in general became a hot political issue. During the 1836 legislative session, for instance, the Democratic governor, Peter D. Vroom, opposed legislative approval of any bank charter for fear of "destroying the Administration Party [Democrats] in [the] State."[49]

The extent to which legislative parties catered to party organizational needs is underlined by the extraordinary happenings of the 1837 legislative session. Two months after the close of the second sitting, a special third sitting convened in Trenton to work out relief measures for the state's banks. This was the only instance that the legislature went into special session between 1829 and 1844. Called specifically to deal with serious matters of public policy, this sitting failed to enact any legislation because of party conflict over appointments.

During the regular second sitting, the Democratic majority in the legislature had been thwarted in their attempts to appoint partisans to Joint Meeting positions. Although enjoying a ten-seat advantage in the Assembly, the Democrats only controlled seven of the Council's fourteen seats. Seven Whig councilmen, joined by a maverick Democratic delegate from Hunterdon, prevented the holding of a Joint Meeting by voting against a resolution calling for such a session. When the third sitting convened, however, two Whig councillors failed to attend because of illness. Fearful that the Democrats would vote to go into Joint Meeting, the remaining five councillors refused to attend Council sessions. With the absence of a quorum no action was taken on

either the financial crisis nor on the matter of appointments.[50]

The Whig press blamed Democratic insistence over the
calling of a Joint Meeting for legislative inaction. "Upon
the Van Buren Councillors," declared the *Newark Daily
Advertiser,* "rests the responsibility of defeating the bill devised by the . . . Assembly for the relief of a suffering
community."[51] Clearly, however, the concerns of party
legislators on both sides over political perferment rather
than public welfare accounted for legislative behavior.

Although both parties sought to establish their identities
by underscoring their relationships with national party
positions and personalities, their specific approaches were
governed by New Jersey's own political exigencies. The
Whigs, more than the Democrats, were particularly affected by such considerations.

By 1834, banks had become extremely unpopular in
New Jersey. They were perceived by many as proof that
incorporated institutions "accumulate[d] power in the
hands of the wealthy at the expense of public right."[52]
Isaac Southard, in a letter to his brother Samuel, dated 1
January 1835, noted that "banking is unpopular with the
people." Concerning the Bank of the United States, he
commented that although he was "a decided friend of the
Institution . . . the least said on that subject by the minority
[Whigs] the better."[53] Although New Jersey Whigs sought
to define themselves in terms of their connections with
national party leaders, they were forced to vary their approach in light of this public animosity toward banks.

As demonstrated by the tone and the voting on the 1833
legislative resolution calling for the rechartering of the
Bank of the United States, Whig legislators initially identified themselves in opposition to Jackson's policies by
openly supporting that institution. By 1838, however, although they faulted the policies of Van Buren and Jackson
for bringing on the Panic of 1837, they were not quick to
offer a positive defense of the national bank nor to espouse publically any policy that might indicate their sup-

port of banks. One Whig partisan even proposed that the Whig-dominated 1839 legislature introduce legislation making it difficult to obtain a bank charter in order to do "away [with] the imputation of being the Bank Party in New Jersey."[54] The attack on the unjust use of powers by Jackson and Van Buren as late as 1842, divorced as it was from any defense of the Bank of the United States, is merely another indication of the ability of the Whigs to adapt national political issues to the circumstances of New Jersey politics.

The Whigs even took the offensive and tried to label the Democrats as the friends of banking. Their newspapers, for instance, pointed continually to the contradiction between Democratic pronouncements against all banks and the voting records of Democratic legislators on special banking legislation. As late as 1839, in response to Democratic attempts to brand all Whigs as *bankites*, one Whig correspondent denied the charge and accused leading "Van Burenmen" of being bank presidents and directors.[55]

Legislative deliberations over the resumption of specie payments in 1841 and 1842 reveals a similar awareness on both sides to conform actions to the realities of New Jersey's own political climate. The problem that faced the Whigs concerning the resumption of specie payments by banks in west Jersey was finally resolved in favor of that section in order to bolster the Whig cause in that region. The political implications of this decision were recognized not only by the Whigs but by the Democrats as well. One Whig newspaper editor went so far as to charge that lobbyists for the Democratic party were urging their legislators to vote for resumption "in order to be consistent with . . . democratic—specie—currency doctrine and professions," while *"still not let[ting]* the bill pass!" As the editor noted:

> thus if the bill passes, all dissatisfaction it creates in West Jersey is to be used to the disadvantage of the Whigs; and

on the other hand if it *does not pass,* in East Jersey all the blame will be thrown on the Whigs.[56]

In his perceptive study of Jacksonian finance, John McFaul notes that as the rechartering of the B.U.S. became less likely, "new symbols of party division" emerged in the fight over hard money. Support for or opposition to a specie currency became the new test of party loyalty. Although he argues that Democratic allegiance to hard money was not mere rhetoric, McFaul indicates that "the necessity of a new political battle cry was not overlooked either."[57] Clearly New Jersey's Democratic and Whig legislators recognized the need to differentiate their parties in the voter's mind. Although partisan policy differences on fiscal questions at no time reflected division over the basic structure and values of American liberal capitalism, after 1832 as national parties took distinctive colorations over their positions on fiscal policy, state parties in New Jersey attempted to maintain their identification, either positively or negatively, with their national counterparts in their efforts to establish identities and to win voter support. Responding to the needs of their organizations, party legislators opposed each other consistently on a variety of legislative proposals relating to fiscal policy. Even loss of legislative control failed effectively to diminish party cohesion.[58] Particularly after 1837, real differences of opinion among party legislators regarding banking and currency further increased the tendency toward party voting on these questions. In terms of fiscal legislation, more often than not, partisan affiliation provided a reliable index to a legislator's performance.

Notes

1. Appendix B contains tables comparing the voting behavior of legislators grouped by different categories of legislative experience and different age categories that illustrate this point.

2. Of the 340 assemblymen for whom information on occupation was obtained, 201 were farmers. The second-largest group, businessmen, included 73 legislators. In many years the number of assemblymen in the same occupational group serving simultaneously were too few to make meaningful evaluations of the quantitative significance of occupation as a variable of voting behavior. Table 17 represents comparisons in which the largest number of men were involved. A more comprehensive presentation of data on occupation appears in Peter D. Levine, "Party-in-the Legislature: New Jersey, 1829–1844," (Ph.D. dissertation, Dept. of History, Rutgers University, 1971), pp. 153–58. *Also see* Appendix B.

3. This approach differs somewhat from that of others who have employed some variation of Rice's index of likeness. For example, *see* Keefe, pp. 450–64.

4. Legislators also voted on a variety of taxation legislation. In every year but 1837, a state tax was levied on each county in New Jersey to provide revenue for state expenditures. Usually $40,000 was collected annually. Except in 1834 when invested capital was also taxed, the tax schedules included assessments on land, businesses, farm animals, and specified personal possessions. Except in 1831 and 1843, this general tax received unanimous approval in Council. On nine of the fifteen Assembly roll calls for passage between 1829 and 1844 similar support was given. On the six cleavage Assembly votes moderate to high levels of party voting were recorded with Whigs generally giving more support than Democrats. Taxation was one of few purely state issues that were discussed in election campaigns. Both party organizations charged each other with extravagant administration of state finances and for the most part legislative parties, in those few instances where cleavage voting occurred, reinforced by their voting the claims of party leaders. While the general tax did not generate sharp, consistent party division, proposals to tax invested capital found Whigs strongly opposed to such measures and Democrats generally divided. For a full description of voting behavior on taxation, *see* Levine, "Party-in-the Legislature," pp. 166–74.

5. Cadman, pp. 120–21. The first general incorporation act for banks in New Jersey was enacted in 1850.

6. *Emporium and True American* (Trenton), 14 April 1837.

7. Roll calls included votes on amendments to and enactment of charter bills, requests for charter extensions, relief measures for specific banks, and other related proposals. Roll-call numbers refer to numbers assigned to each roll call as it appeared chronologically in Council and Assembly journals. Different sets of numbers were assigned to cleavage and to unanimous roll calls. Numbers range from 1 to n for each house by legislative session for each category of roll call. The following references cover all roll calls summarized in Tables 18 and 19: 1829 Assembly, C.R.C. 26, p. 260; C.R.C. 33, p. 279; C.R.C. 38, p. 302. 1830 Assembly, C.R.C. 9, p. 110; C.R.C. 31, p. 151; C.R.C. 36, p. 160; C.R.C. 83, p. 257. 1831 Assembly, C.R.C. 16, p. 116; C.R.C. 33, p. 173; C.R.C. 39, p. 186. 1832 Assembly, C.R.C. 15, p. 149; C.R.C. 24, p. 181; C.R.C. 46, p. 218; C.R.C. 47, p. 218. 1833 Assembly, C.R.C. 12, p. 204; C.R.C. 21, p. 284; C.R.C. 24, p. 288; C.R.C. 33, p. 346; C.R.C. 44, p. 383; C.R.C. 45, p. 385; C.R.C. 46, p. 387; C.R.C. 50, p. 402; C.R.C. 58, p. 424; C.R.C. 69, p. 452. 1834 Assembly, C.R.C. 5–8, pp.

265–76; C.R.C. 31, p. 416; C.R.C. 34, p. 423; C.R.C. 38–41, pp. 430–43; C.R.C. 43, p. 446; C.R.C. 58, p. 518; C.R.C. 60, p. 520; C.R.C. 61, p. 521; C.R.C. 65, p. 528; C.R.C. 69, p. 540. 1835 Assembly, C.R.C. 3, p. 105. 1836 Assembly, C.R.C. 37–39, pp. 348–58; C.R.C. 42, p. 365; C.R.C. 43, p. 367; C.R.C. 45, p. 404; C.R.C. 46, p. 405; C.R.C. 50, p. 429; C.R.C. 51, p. 435; C.R.C. 54–56, pp. 440–44; C.R.C. 59, p. 469; C.R.C. 62, p. 476; C.R.C. 63, p. 477; C.R.C. 64, p. 478; C.R.C. 66, p. 484; C.R.C. 70, p. 512; C.R.C. 71, p. 513; C.R.C. 78, p. 529; C.R.C. 93, p. 567; C.R.C. 97, p. 560; C.R.C. 103, p. 602; C.R.C. 106, p. 606; C.R.C. 109, p. 614; C.R.C. 114, p. 624. 1837 Assembly, C.R.C. 5, p. 34; C.R.C. 18–27, pp. 78–202; C.R.C. 30–32, pp. 240–43; C.R.C. 34, p. 248; C.R.C. 37, p. 255; C.R.C. 42, p. 283; C.R.C. 44, p. 286; C.R.C. 66, p. 366; C.R.C. 73, p. 384; C.R.C. 93–96, pp. 466–78; C.R.C. 111, p. 526; C.R.C. 117, p. 537; C.R.C. 128, p. 580; C.R.C. 132, p. 587; C.R.C. 134, p. 592; C.R.C. 140, p. 601; C.R.C. 141, p. 602; C.R.C. 145, p. 606; C.R.C. 148, p. 614; C.R.C. 172, p. 681; C.R.C. 197–99, pp. 763–66; C.R.C. 205, p. 777; C.R.C. 223, p. 825; C.R.C. 227, p. 833; C.R.C. 232, p. 845; C.R.C. 233, p. 846. 1838 Assembly, C.R.C. 66, p. 515; C.R.C. 67, p. 516. 1839 Assembly, C.R.C. 38, p. 466; C.R.C. 45, p. 479; C.R.C. 63, p. 548; C.R.C. 73, p. 578. 1840 Assembly, C.R.C. 38, p. 282; C.R.C. 39, p. 283. 1841 Assembly, C.R.C. 9, p. 279; C.R.C. 10, p. 280; C.R.C. 18, p. 382; C.R.C. 19, p. 383; C.R.C. 22, p. 414; C.R.C. 45, p. 512; C.R.C. 46, p. 514. 1842 Assembly, C.R.C. 53, p. 485; C.R.C. 97–99, pp. 638–45.

8. Except in 1834 when one Whig was elected to the Assembly from Warren, Sussex and Warren elected only Democratic legislators. Whigs and National Republicans filled Middlesex legislative delegations in ten years and shared them in three others. Sixty-three of the eighty-four antibanking votes for this county were recorded in 1830, 1834, and 1837, years in which Democrats filled all but two of Middlesex's eleven Assembly seats.

9. Between 1829 and 1844 Democrats controlled Morris delegations in ten years and Bergen delegations in thirteen years. Burlington delegations were occupied by Whigs in eleven of sixteen sessions.

10. Excluded were roll calls on motions for postponement and votes on individual sections and amendments that did not clearly define an attitude toward banks. *See* note 7 for roll-call references.

11. *See* note 7 for roll-call references.

12. Table 21 is based on 21 of the 26 roll calls related to special banking legislation that clearly defined a position on such questions. Five roll calls—numbers 45, 55, 63, 66, and 78—were excluded because their contents were unclear. Note 7 contains references for all twenty-six roll calls.

13. The Morris delegation voted 22–13 on roll calls involving Essex and Burlington banks, while the Burlington delegation voted 27–15 on roll calls involving Morris and Essex banks. That these counties were in favor of bank legislation is further demonstrated by factoring out from the vote totals in Table 21, the votes for each county on roll calls involving banks in their own domain. The total for Essex becomes 31–15, for Morris, 41–17, and for Burlington, 49–21.

14. Similar situations occurred in 1834 and in 1837. *See* Levine, "Party-in-the Legislature," pp. 188–89.

15. *Proceedings 1844*, p. 354.

16. *Emporium and True American*, 3 February 1837, excerpted from the *Somerville Messenger*. Also see *Hunterdon Gazette* (Flemington), 2 November 1836, and *Newark Daily Advertiser*, 28 January 1833 and 2 November 1836.

17. *P.N.J.G.A.*, 66th sess., 1st sitting, 1842, p. 23. New Jersey's position was noted in Governor Pennington's address.

18. *Hunterdon Gazette*, 27 January 1830; *Newark Daily Advertiser*, 15 January 1834 and 22 January 1836.

19. Levine, "Party-in-the Legislature," pp. 192–94, describes voting behavior in 1837. On sixteen roll calls on bills to allow banks to suspend specie payments, the mean party index of likeness was 44. Peter Temin, *The Jacksonian Economy* (New York: W. W. Norton and Co., 1969), suggests that the crisis of the 1830s was not due to Jackson's policies but to overseas market conditions beyond the President's control. He also argues that economic conditions in the late 1830s and early 1840s were not as grave as some historians have argued. A survey of New Jersey newspapers between 1837 and 1844 suggests that regardless of what the true conditions were, the state's citizens were made to feel that a real crisis had developed.

20. *Emporium and True American*, 14 July 1837.

21. *J.N.J.L.C.*, 62d sess., 1st sitting, 1838, pp. 12–18; *P.N.J.G.A.*, 62d sess., 1st sitting, 1838, pp. 146–52. The quoted lines appear on page 146.

22. *P.N.J.G.A.*, 62d sess., 1st sitting, 1838, pp. 54–61.

23. The twenty-two 1838 Assembly cleavage roll calls on fiscal legislation included: C.R.C. 9, p. 164; C.R.C. 12, p. 181; C.R.C. 14, p. 316; C.R.C. 16, p. 333; C.R.C. 17, p. 346; C.R.C. 20–23, pp. 377–82; C.R.C. 32–36, pp. 414–17; C.R.C. 42, p. 426; C.R.C. 43, p. 427; C.R.C. 51–53, pp. 461–63; C.R.C. 66, p. 515; C.R.C. 67, p. 516; C.R.C. 102, p. 592. Voting in Council on banking measures also showed a high degree of party cohesion. Six roll calls, C.R.C. 4, p. 87; C.R.C. 5, p. 88; C.R.C. 10, p. 161; C.R.C. 12, p. 165; C.R.C. 41, p. 330; C.R.C. 44, p. 333, were taken on the bills relating to resumption and the regulation of banks. On four of these, nine of the ten Whig members and five of the six Democratic members opposed each other, just as their counterparts in the Assembly had done. Party indices of likeness were 0 each time. Two roll calls (41 and 44) concerned with the bill for the better regulation of banks scored indices of 33 but in each case only three Democrats cast votes. Assembly roll calls 66, 67, 14, 22, and 51 included on the graph were not individually discussed. The first two concerned the renewal of the charter of the Trenton Banking Company. This bill passed 31–13, Whigs voting 26–3 in favor. Roll call 14 concerned a resolution that 100 pages of bank statements be printed. This was defeated 14–30, the Whigs voting 2–28 against. Roll calls 22 and 51 concerned postponement of the act repealing bank charters. Although party indices of likeness of 59 and 42 were recorded, the content of these roll calls could not be determined.

24. Two Assembly roll calls were taken on a bill during the 1835 session aimed at preventing the circulation of small notes for the payment of money. Roll call 73, p. 460, a motion to postpone consideration was defeated, while roll call 74, p. 461, provided for the bill's enactment. Party indices of likeness of 55 and 64, respectively, were recorded on these roll calls. Democrats voted 2–24 against postponement, while 25–1 for passage. Whig votes were 10–9 for postponement and 12–8 for passage. The bill, as approved, prohibited the issuing of bank notes under the denomination of five dollars after July 1836. *N.J.L.*, 59th sess., 1835, p. 151. In 1836 one Assembly roll call, a passage vote on a bill to prevent the issuing and circulation of small notes, was recorded (roll call 116, p. 630). A party index of likeness of 30 was recorded. Democrats voted 29–0 for passage and the Whigs 3–7 against passage. In the Council the passage vote on the bill recorded a party index of likeness of 20, the Democrats unanimously voting for it, with the Whigs nearly as united in their opposition. 1836 Council, C.R.C. 58, p. 309. In 1837 a series of seven Assembly roll calls concerned a bill respecting the circulation of small notes. The bill was not approved and so its content remains unknown. On seven roll calls a mean party index of likeness of 27 was recorded. Whigs were particularly cohesive and apparently in favor of the bill. *See* C.R.C. 258, p. 902; C.R.C. 259, p. 903; C.R.C. 263, p. 917; C.R.C. 271, p. 928; C.R.C. 275, p. 932; C.R.C. 279, p. 937; C.R.C. 280, p. 940.

25. *Emporium and True American*, 2 February 1838. *See* note 23 for roll-call references.

26. Ibid., 5 February 1841.

27. *Newark Daily Advertiser*, 28 January 1841.

28. *See* note 7 for 1841 Assembly roll-call references. During the 1837 Assembly, five roll calls were taken on motions to make the presidents and directors of certain banks liable for all claims and debts of the banks that they operated (C.R.C. 20, p. 183; C.R.C. 23, p. 187; C.R.C. 26, p. 201; C.R.C. 73, p. 384; C.R.C. 95, p. 476). The votes of Whig assemblymen on these roll calls were 4–15, 2–17, 1–18, 10–9, and 1–12. All but once the Whigs were strongly opposed to the imposition of such restrictions. Democratic votes on these same roll calls provided 14 of 20, 10 of 14, 11 of 12, 19 of 29, and 9 of 12 of the affirmative votes on each roll call. Party indices of likeness roll calls were 51, 38, 58, 91, and 43.

29. *P.N.J.G.A.*, 65th sess., 2d sitting, 1841, p. 469.

30. 1841 Assembly, C.R.C. 44, p. 511; C.R.C. 52, p. 563; C.R.C. 53, p. 566. Two other roll calls (C.R.C. 4, p. 197; C.R.C. 5, p. 198) concerning a vote on a resolution making inquiries of banks relative to specie payments and the appointment of a committee of five to see if any alteration was needed in laws respecting banks, though not included in this discussion, recorded party indices of likeness of 81 and 40.

31. *N.J.L.*, 66th sess., 1842, p. 111. The bill also noted that no dividends were to be issued until resumption had commenced and that no banks were to issue notes other than their own.

32. 1842 Assembly, C.R.C. 16, p. 333; C.R.C. 30, p. 390; C.R.C. 31, p. 392;

C.R.C. 33, p. 395; C.R.C. 34, p. 398; C.R.C. 60, p. 506. *Newark Daily Advertiser,* 15 January 1842; *P.N.J.G.A.,* 66th sess., 1st sitting, 1842, p. 23.

33. A resolution concerning the tariff, internal improvements, and the re-chartering of the Bank of the United States was approved in the Assembly. Assembly roll call 5, p. 89, was on a motion to strike from the resolution the part that called for the rechartering of the Bank. It was defeated by a 16–30 margin and the resolution in its entirety was then approved by a 31–14 margin (roll call 6, p. 90). Party indices of likeness of 20 and 78 were recorded on these roll calls. In the Council only one roll call, on a motion to suspend the sixteenth rule so that the Assembly resolution could be read, was not approved. C.R.C. 2, p. 31, 1833 Council. All six Democratic councillors voted in favor of it. Although a party index of likeness of 12 was recorded, the negative vote of the Whig councillor from Cape May prevented the resolution from being considered.

34. *N.J.L.,* 58th sess., 1834, p. 177; Ershkowitz, "New Jersey Politics," p. 214.

35. *N.J.L.,* 59th sess., 1835, p. 12; *N.J.L.,* 60th sess., 1836, p. 29; *N.J.L.,* 62d sess., 1838, pp. 25–28.

36. *Newark Daily Advertiser,* 10 February 1834; Jeremiah Leaming to Samuel L. Southard, 11 January 1834, Southard Papers, P.U.L. Roll-call references for all eighteen roll calls on national resolutions include: 1833 Assembly, C.R.C. 5, p. 89; C.R.C. 6, p. 90. 1834 Assembly, C.R.C. 4, p. 225. 1835 Assembly, C.R.C. 4, p. 114; C.R.C. 9–13, pp. 121–28. 1836 Assembly, C.R.C. 3–9, pp. 96–109. 1838 Assembly, C.R.C. 12, p. 181; C.R.C. 14, p. 316.

37. Ershkowitz and Shade, "Consensus or Conflict?", 614–21; Sharp, pp. 321–22. In both cases, careful probing of the evidence presented by these authors indicates a gross overstatement of their positions.

38. Sharp, pp. 287, 318, 319.

39. McCloskey, Hoffman, and O'Hara, pp. 406–427. *Also see* Edelman.

40. *J.N.J.L.C.,* 57th sess., 1st sitting, 1833, p. 44; Ershkowitz, "New Jersey Politics," pp. 175–82. The address of the Democratic state convention of 1832 referred to the Bank of the United States as a "monstrous, aristocratic monopoly"; *see Emporium and True American,* 20 October 1832.

41. *Emporium and True American,* 13 September 1834 and 22 October 1836; *Address to the People of New Jersey on the Present Crisis, Reported to the Democratic State Convention by the Central Committee, 11 September 1834* (n.p., 1834).

42. *P.N.J.G.A.,* 59th sess., 1st sitting, 1835, pp. 13, 18; *J.N.J.L.C.,* 60th sess., 1st sitting, 1836, p. 17; *Newark Daily Advertiser,* 4 November 1836. *See also* Garret Wall to Peter D. Vroom, 17 January 1834, Garret Wall Papers, P.U.L.

43. *Newark Daily Advertiser,* 14 April and 12 September 1834 and 2 June and 30 September 1836.

44. John McFaul, "The Politics of Jacksonian Finance" (Ph.D. dissertation, Dept. of History, University of California at Berkeley, 1963), pp. 82–85.

45. *P.N.J.G.A.,* 62d sess., 1st sitting, 1838, pp. 12–18.

46. *Emporium and True American,* 14 July and 11 August 1837, 4 October 1839, 29 May 1840, 10 September 1841, and 9 September 1842. As late as 1840

Democrats referred to Whigs as the *Bank Aristocracy. See Emporium and True American,* 28 October 1840.

47. *P.N.J.G.A.,* 62d sess., 1st sitting, 1838, pp. 109–117; *Newark Daily Advertiser,* 6 September 1838, 14 November 1839, 21 August and 3 October 1840, 16 and 18 September and 1 October 1841, 15 September 1842, and 20 September 1843. Included in these references are accounts of state and county party conventions.

48. Ibid., 25 September 1842.

49. Joseph Jackson to Mahlon Dickerson, 8 February 1836, Mahlon Dickerson Papers, N.J.H.S.

50. *J.N.J.L.C.,* 61st sess., 2d sitting, 3d sitting, 1837, pp. 389–450. During the last three days of the third sitting, Whigs did attend Council meetings. Again joined by the Hunterdon delegate, they were able to match the six votes of the Democrats on a series of roll calls calling for a Joint Meeting.

51. *Newark Daily Advertiser,* 3 June 1837.

52. Ershkowitz, "New Jersey Politics," p. 225.

53. Isaac Southard to Samuel L. Southard, 1 January 1835, Southard Papers, P.U.L.

54. *Newark Daily Advertiser,* 21 October 1839. *See also* William Pennington to Samuel L. Southard, 18 November 1839, Southard Papers, P.U.L.

55. *Newark Daily Advertiser,* 26 February 1836 and 2 October 1839.

56. *Newark Daily Advertiser,* 25 January 1842.

57. McFaul, pp. 82–83.

58. This fact emerges implicitly in the narrative. Summary of the relative indices of cohesion for party on banking-and-currency roll calls underlines this phenomenon.

Mean Relative Index of Cohesion on
Banking-and-Currency Roll Calls
and National Resolutions

	1829–32	1833–37	1838–44
Democrats	70.7	73.8	85.5
National Republican-Whigs	65.1	79.8	77.6

Both parties show high and generally increased cohesion. Significantly minority parties appear more cohesive than majority parties. Thus between 1833 and 1837 when Democrats controlled the legislature in all but one session, National Republican-Whig cohesion was six points higher than Democratic cohesion. In the 1838–44 period, however, with Whigs in control in all years but 1844, Democratic cohesion is almost eight points higher than the Whigs.

6
Legislative Voting Behavior: Transportation, the Joint Companies, and Corporate Policy

Government participation in the expansion of New Jersey's economy primarily involved conferring corporate privileges to citizens who wished to engage in some type of business enterprise.[1] Even more than with fiscal measures, sectional and constituency pressures and legislators' personal interests eroded party cohesion on transportation and business legislation. Meaningful operation of legisla-

151

tive parties remained confined to those few questions that engendered public partisan controversy or that involved party needs.

I

The development of internal improvements in New Jersey proceeded differently than in neighboring states. Although retaining the right to inspect transportation company records, to receive transit duties, and to hold purchase options of privately owned works, New Jersey's lawmakers eschewed opportunities for the investment of state funds in favor of a laissez-faire policy that extended corporate rights to private citizens interested in building canals and railroads.[2]

General agreement among party leaders that such projects were in the public interest helps explain the lack of party disagreement in the legislature on such proposals.[3] Instead, the desire of legislators to satisfy constituency demands and at times to pursue their own material interests accounted for voting behavior.

Legislation involving transportation-charter bills usually received the Assembly's full support. Of eighty-three charters voted upon between 1829 and 1844, fifty-seven obtained approval in Assembly by unanimous consent (Table 22).[4]

Divisive voting behavior, when apparent, does not reveal consistent sectional tendencies. Summarized in Table 23 are county delegation voting patterns on the sixty-three Assembly, cleavage roll calls involving passage votes on transportation-charter and supplementary-charter bills. Only one county recorded an affirmative percentage under 50%, while ten counties registered percentages over 60% and seven counties over 70%.

Decided lack of disagreement among counties and sections corresponds to patterns of partisan response. Only in

TABLE 22

Roll-call Voting on Transportation Charters, 1829-1844 Assemblies

Year	No. Bills-Unanimous Roll Calls	No. Bills-Cleavage Roll Calls	No. Bills-Unanimous & Cleavage Roll Calls
1829	--	2	--
1830	--	4	--
1831	1	4	1
1832	2	3	2
1833	3	2	--
1834	2	3	1
1835	3	1	--
1836	13	3	2
1837	12	3	--
1838	3	--	--
1839	3	2	--
1840	1	--	--
1841	3	1	--
1842	2	2	--
1843	--	--	--
1844	3	1	--
TOTAL:	51	31*	6**

*Six charters were determined in the negative. These occurred one time each in 1829, 1830, 1832, 1834, 1837, and 1839.

**Final-passage roll calls on these six charters were approved unanimously.

TABLE 23

County Voting on the Chartering of Transportation
Companies, 1829-1844 Assemblies

County	Affirmative* Votes	Negative Votes	Affirmative Percentage
Middlesex	193	32	86
Essex	231	58	80
Bergen	120	40	75
Salem	124	42	75
Monmouth	155	56	74
Morris	157	62	72
Somerset	121	54	70
Burlington	186	84	69
Gloucester	152	75	67
Sussex	106	66	62
Hunterdon	142	106	57
Cumberland	97	78	55
Warren	88	74	54
Cape May	25	30	45

*Affirmative votes on roll calls included all indicated a
procorporation position.

1827, 1838, 1839, and 1841 did the mean indices of party
likeness on Assembly transportation roll calls fall under
65. In these some four sessions, six charter bills were decided by cleavage votes, while twenty-one received the Assembly's unanimous approval.[5]

Voting behavior during the 1836 and 1837 sessions illustrates the presence of a generally favorable attitude toward
transportation projects and the absence of party division
on them. Although no consistent sectional polarization occurred, as with special banking proposals, counties that
stood to benefit directly from proposed legislation offered
more support than others less advantageously affected.

The seventeen charters authorized in 1836 and the twelve charters approved in 1837 together accounted for 42% of the total number of transportation companies granted charters between 1829 and 1844. Only occasionally did these charter bills elicit divisive legislative voting. In fact, twenty-four of the twenty-nine charters received unanimous support in the Assembly.

Roll calls that produced disagreement failed to reveal the influence of party. Figure 4 records party voting on the thirty-two Assembly, cleavage roll calls on transportation legislation for the two sessions. These roll calls included ten passage votes on charter bills, eight passage votes on supplementary bills, six votes on procedural motions, and eight votes on amendments to various bills. On only six roll calls were party indices of likeness under 66 recorded.

Deliberations in 1837 on a bill incorporating the Hunterdon Railroad company indicate the nature of sectional response on transportation questions. Two groups of county delegations accounted for virtually all Assembly votes on five roll calls related to this bill.[6] Delegates from Hunterdon, Essex, Bergen, Monmouth, and Middlesex voted 20–0 in favor of the charter proposal, while assemblymen from Sussex, Warren, Burlington, Cumberland, Gloucester, Somerset, Cape May, and Salem voted 3–20 against it.[7] When tested on the remaining sixteen cleavage roll calls voted upon in 1837, however, these county alignments failed to maintain their cohesion.[8] Here and in other sessions, the enactment of transportation legislation involved vote-trading among county representatives with vested interests.[9] Indeed, the regularity with which logrolling tactics were employed on special legislation and on special incorporation bills in particular has been observed by economic historians as well as by contemporary observers of the New Jersey legislature.[10]

Aside from protecting county interests and securing the wants of particular constituents, legislators also voted to insure the enactment of charters for projects in which they themselves were involved. Legislators were among the in-

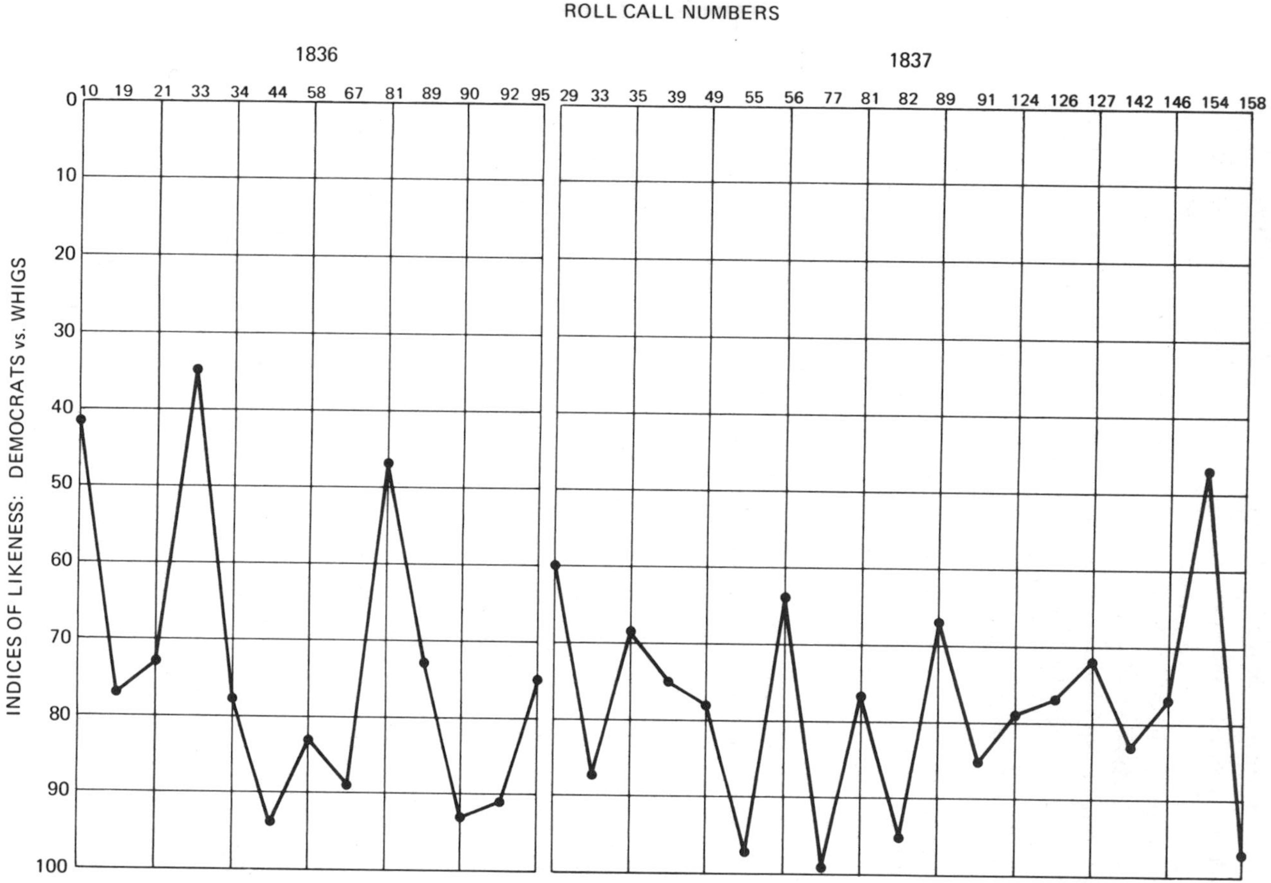

ROLL CALL NUMBERS

INDICES OF LIKENESS: DEMOCRATS vs. WHIGS

1836

1837

FIGURE 4

Transportation Legislation, 1836, 1837 Assemblies

corporators of forty-nine of the sixty-nine transportation companies that were granted charters between 1829 and 1844. Individuals who served in the legislature in these years were involved in thirteen of the seventeen charters approved in 1836 and all twelve of the charters granted in 1837. Five charters in 1836 and six in 1837 included as incorporators individuals who were in office during these sessions.[11] Although not possible to determine accurately, the ability of particular legislators to gain support for measures in which they had a personal interest doubtless affected voting alignments on transportation enactments.

Economic downturn in New Jersey after 1837 had the same effect on the rate of incorporation of transportation projects as it did on the incorporation of banks. A total of sixty-nine transportation companies were granted charters between 1829 and 1844. Fifty-five charters were approved by the 1838 session, while only fourteen companies received charters between 1838 and 1844. The trend toward increased party voting on special banking legislation, noticeable as early as 1835, however, never materialized as sharply on transportation enactments. Although the highest indices of party voting on transportation legislation were recorded after 1835, sixteen of the twenty-one charters voted upon between 1838 and 1844 won unanimous approval in the Assembly.[12]

A major exception to the pattern of nonpartisan behavior on transportation questions involved deliberations over the Delaware and Raritan Canal and Camden and Amboy Railroad and Transportation Company. Known as the Joint Companies, this enterprise was one of the largest corporations of any kind in the United States in the Jacksonian period. The Joint Companies were intimately tied to the state Democratic party. The party's five-member central committee appointed to prepare for the fall election in 1832 included three directors of the Joint Companies and Stacy Potts, the editor of the Democratic *Emporium and True American*.[13] Down through 1844, the

Joint Companies employed its financial resources to support the Democratic cause.[14] The chartering of the canal and railroad companies in 1830, their consolidation in 1831, and the extension of a legal monopoly to the Joint Companies over the transportation of all merchandise and passengers between New York and Philadelphia were granted by legislatures containing Democratic majorities. Although torn at times between protecting the economic interests of their county constituencies and fulfilling party needs, Democratic legislators worked actively to protect the Joint Companies. Opposition legislators, balancing the interests of their constituents, the attachment of certain party leaders to transportation companies concerned with challenging the Joint Companies, and their desire, as partisans, to gain political power, sought to use the relationship between the Democrats and the Joint Companies to political advantage. Legislative voting behavior reflects the interaction of these constituency and party pressures on the state's lawmakers.

Sectional attachments rather than party loyalties dominated legislators' initial responses to the Joint Companies. The granting of separate charters to the Camden and Amboy Railroad and Transportation Company and the Delaware and Raritan Canal Company, their consolidation into one company, and other related proposals engendered sectional voting clearly related to the proximity of counties to these canal and railroad facilities.

As proposed, the Camden and Amboy was to run through Middlesex, Burlington, and Gloucester counties connecting the cities of Camden and South Amboy. The Delaware and Raritan Canal was to connect the Delaware and Raritan rivers with terminals in Bordentown and New Brunswick. Not surprisingly the most consistent support for both projects came from Burlington, Cumberland, Gloucester, Salem, Cape May, Monmouth, and Middlesex delegations. The northern counties of Essex, Sussex,

Warren, Hunterdon, Bergen, and Somerset usually united in opposition. Their reliance on the Morris canal for trade and transportation best explains their position. As chartered in 1824, this canal, some 106 miles in length, coursed through Warren, Sussex, Morris, Essex, and Bergen and connected the Delaware and the Hudson rivers.[15]

Although sectional pressures continued to exert a real influence on legislative voting behavior, after 1831 interest in the Joint Companies took on an increasingly partisan flavor. Activity during the Democratically controlled 1832 legislative session illustrates this point.

In this session the Joint Companies gained a monopoly over all transportation between Philadelphia and New York by securing a veto power over the incorporation of any railroad or canal "intended . . . for the transportation of passengers or merchandise" between the two cities. As its consideration for this advantage, the corporation guaranteed the state 1,000 shares of stock and an annual revenue of $30,000 from transit duties and dividends.[16] At the suggestion of Governor Vroom, who had been active in the securing of the original charters for the Railroad and the Canal, the legislature also considered exercising the state's privilege to subscribe to one-quarter of the stock of the Joint Companies.[17]

Deliberations over the monopoly bill and the subscription proposal indicate that, while the votes of Democratic legislators were essential for the granting of exclusive privileges, constituency needs exerted a real influence on voting behavior. Two groups of assemblymen defined by membership in county delegations rather than by party affiliations were most cohesive on both measures (Figure 5). Representatives from Essex, Morris, Bergen, Cumberland, Middlesex, and Cape May—fifteen National Republicans and five Democrats—voted against both state subscription and the granting of monopoly privileges. Except for Middlesex, all

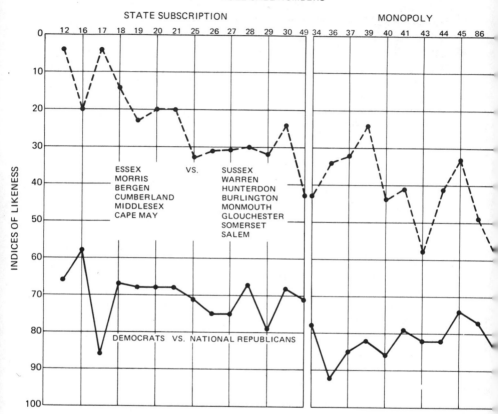

FIGURE 5
Joint Companies Legislation, 1832 Assembly

of these counties had voted against the chartering of either or both of the original companies. Opposing this group were representatives from Sussex, Warren, Hunterdon, Burlington, Monmouth, Gloucester, Somerset, and Salem. Composed of twenty-one Democrats and nine National Republicans (five from Burlington and four from Gloucester) all but three of these counties had always supported the Joint Companies. The addition of Sussex, Hunterdon, and Warren, all Democratic strongholds, underlines the strong ties between that party and the Joint Companies.

Despite the absence of total cohesion on the part of Democratic representatives in the legislature, National Republicans denounced the ties between the Joint Companies and the Democratic party. During the fall elections in 1832, the Joint Companies along with the Bank of the United States became the major campaign issues in the state. The National Republicans skillfully pictured the contradiction between Democratic opposition to the Bank of the United States as a monopoly and Democratic support for granting exclusive privileges to the Joint Companies. It was also charged that if the Democrats remained in control of the state legislature, they would use the power to invest state funds in the Joint Companies.[18]

Not all National Republican spokesmen were convinced that attacks on the Joint Companies were politically useful. In a letter to Samuel Southard, Abraham Brown, one of the incorporators of the Camden and Amboy Railroad, noted that continued denunciation of the Joint Companies in party newspapers would alienate voter support in west Jersey.[19] This concern, in line with voting behavior on Joint Company legislation, suggests the importance of party considerations and local economic needs in shaping reactions to such questions. Indeed, conflict over the next few years between the Joint Companies and a combination of corporations intent on challenging its monopoly rights indicates that, although partisan cohesion on Joint Company proposals increased over time, constituency pressures continually eroded party unity.

The four companies intent on competing with the Joint Companies for the trade between Philadelphia and New York included one Pennsylvania corporation—the Philadelphia and Trenton Railroad Company—and three New Jersey companies—the New Brunswick Bridge Company, the Trenton and New Brunswick Turnpike Company, and the New Jersey Railroad and Transportation Company. The president of the New Jersey Railroad was included among the leaders of the Whig party, while almost all of the directors of the company were Whigs.[20]

Together, these enterprises hoped to provide a continuous route from Philadelphia to Jersey City. All that was needed was permission from the New Jersey legislature to build a railroad from Trenton to New Brunswick, along the route of the Trenton and New Brunswick Turnpike Company.[21] Legislative action on this proposal first took place in 1835. Remonstrances signed by Robert L. Stevens and Robert F. Stockton, the presidents of the Joint Companies, accused their opponents of trying to obtain railroad privileges that were in direct violation of the Joint Companies' charter.[22] Two Assembly committees were formed to investigate this matter. One dealt directly with the request of the Trenton and New Brunswick Turnpike Company to lay rails on its road. The other considered a Council resolution concerned with the formulation of a general policy regarding the authorization of any railroad between New York and Philadelphia.

The majority report of the committee to which the turnpike proposal had been referred, although recommending that the company be allowed to increase its capital stock, expressed no opinion on its request to build a railroad.[23] The minority report, signed by the chairman of the committee, William D. Stewart, a Democrat from Somerset, expressly stated that the company should not be granted railroad privileges.[24] One roll call, to agree to the first section of the turnpike bill, was taken (roll call 48). It was defeated 9–38. The nine affirmative votes came from counties that had previously opposed the Joint Companies: Bergen, Essex, Middlesex, and Somerset. No further bill was reported out of Stewart's committee during the remainder of the session. The *Newark Daily Advertiser* charged that the original bill that had been voted upon called for a greater extension of powers than the Trenton and New Brunswick Company had requested. It implied that Stewart had allowed this bill to be reported out of committee, knowing that its defeat was certain. After recommittal, Stewart, according to the paper, upon the urgings of "the monopolists and their friends" pigeonholed the presentation of another version of the bill.[25]

The Council resolution concerning railroad policy was the subject of two roll calls. Roll call 78 was on a motion to lay on the table the majority report that supported the Joint Companies' charter rights. Roll call 79 was on a motion to agree with this opinion and to postpone further consideration of the resolution until the next session. Party indices of likeness on these roll calls were 53 and 41, respectively. Two county alignments, however, proved to be more significant. One group, composed of Essex, Morris, Middlesex, Salem, Bergen, and Cumberland voted 17–3 to lay the resolution on the table and 4–14 against accepting the committee's report. The remaining eight counties, virtually the same group that had supported the Joint Companies during 1832, voted 1–22 against laying the resolution on the table and 22–1 in favor of accepting the report. Indices of likeness for these groups on these roll calls were 19 and 26, respectively.[26] The group opposed to the committee report included seventeen Whigs and six Democrats. The group that favored protection of the monopoly privileges of the Joint Companies included twenty-one Democrats and six Whigs. Voting on these roll calls confirms again the pattern of partisan disagreement of enactments involving the Joint Companies. Yet, the six

Whigs and the six Democrats that failed to vote with their parties demonstrates that this division was not absolute. The six Democrats who voted with the majority of the Whigs in the Assembly were from Morris and Bergen. Representatives from these counties, regardless of their political affiliation, always opposed the Joint Companies. No doubt their attachment to protecting the interests of the Morris Canal had much to do with their stand. The six Whigs who voted with the majority of the Democrats were from Burlington and Cape May. Apparently the stake that these counties had in the major transportation facilities of their section were substantial enough to compel their representatives to support the Joint Companies.

During the 1836 session, the struggle between the Joint Companies and the combine led by the New Jersey Railroad Company subsided. After all of the commotion and debate in and out of the legislature, the money spent by both sides to secure newspaper support, legal opinions, and lobbyists, settlement came rather peacefully. In November 1835, the directors of the Joint Companies purchased the controlling interest in the Philadelphia and Trenton Railroad Company.[27]

Despite the companies' success in this venture, both Democratic leaders and company management remained aware of the intense criticism directed at the close ties between the party and the corporation. Writing to Garret Wall on 25 December 1835, Littleton Kirkpatrick, a leadng Democratic figure from Middlesex, noted that "the monopoly [Joint Companies] is looked upon as the creature of the Jackson Party" and that "it was formed by a Legislature having a Jackson majority." Having boasted of its creation, "the Jackson party," Kirkpatrick warned, "must now come in for a full share of the odium attached to the monopoly."[28] Only one week earlier, Robert F. Stockton, the president of the Camden and Amboy, expressed similar concern. In a letter to Democratic Governor Vroom, Stockton acknowledged that the Joint Companies "were the objects of the most bitter invective," and that "many political friends ha[d] urged [him] to offer to the state both the Canal and the Rail Road as the best if not the only means by which the above movement can be counteracted." He added that he did not feel "at liberty wholly to disregard [these views] because we are under great obligation to the Jackson Party."[29]

During the 1836 session both the Democratic party and the Companies sought to rehabilitate their public images in order to insure continued Democratic electoral success. Having gained control of the Philadelphia and Trenton Railroad, the Joint Companies offered to sell their entire works to the state for $7,650,000. If after purchase, the state desired a private corporation to manage the system, the companies proposed that the properties be leased to the Philadelphia and Trenton Railroad and the Trenton and New Brunswick Turnpike Companies for a minimum of thirty-six years at an annual rental equal to six percent of the purchase price.[30]

Although designed to stifle criticism of both the Joint Companies and the Democratic party, this proposal backfired. The sum asked for by the Companies for the sale of its works was $2,000,000 more than the corporation itself had invested in them. Moreover, the Companies' ownership of the Philadelphia and Trenton Railroad guaranteed its continued control over the entire operation. For these reasons, the Joint Companies' proposition was not well received. As one Whig legislative observer noted, "the feeling against . . . the State buying the canal and Railroad . . . is very great in all parts and if the Jackson party should pass on or take any active part to affect it, the party must be prostrated at the next election."[31]

Legislators also realized that Democratic support of the corporation's plan forboded disastrous political consequences for that party. During the 1836 legislative session, all fifteen roll calls related to the Joint Companies produced party indices of likeness between 60 and 16. The motion to dismiss from further consideration the Joint Companies' proposals was the most important of these votes (roll call 87). This motion was passed 27–17, thus preventing further discussion of the plan in the legislature. Democratic assemblymen voted 27–5 in favor of the motion, while the Whigs voted 0–12 against it, resulting in a party index of likeness of 16. The mean party index of likeness on nine other roll calls specifically dealing with the proposal to sell the corporations' works to the state was 33. On each of these measures, an average of 88% of all Whigs who voted opposed an average of 79% of all Democrats who voted. Democratic representatives from Somerset and Warren, two counties that had never maintained a consistent attitude toward the Joint Companies, most often voted with the Whigs on these measures.[32]

Whig votes on the motion to end debate on the Joint Companies' proposal, in light of the politics surrounding this situation, indicate an attempt to keep before the public an issue that could only hurt the Democratic cause. That these votes were cast by representatives from Essex, Middlesex, Cumberland, Salem, and Cape May adds another dimension to these affairs. All of these counties but Salem had originally opposed the granting of monopoly privileges to the Joint Companies in 1832. All five counties consistently voted against the Companies in 1835.

As for the Democrats and the Joint Companies, nothing had been lost by what had occurred. The Democrats, acting out of concern for their political well-being, were able to stifle further exposure of a proposal that apparently could do them no good. The Joint Companies continued on its prosperous course with its monopoly powers intact. Indeed, in terms of personal interest, the Joint Companies could not have lost, no matter what would have happened.[33]

Legislative response to the Joint Companies illustrates how partisan considerations could affect decisions on substantive issues. In part, Democratic electoral success in New Jersey depended upon the party's close ties to the Joint Companies. Whig efforts to expose this relationship were designed as well for maximum political advantage. Both parties endeavored to coordinate the behavior of their legislative representatives to satisfy these partisan objectives. Although the ability of legislative parties to maintain cohesion increased over time, the obligations of individual legislators to their constituencies prohibited absolute party unity. Indeed, on both the consolidation and the monopoly proposals, the legislator's sectional identity, determined primarily by his county's reliance on either the Joint Companies or the Morris Canal, most clearly shaped legislative decisions. Only after 1832, when legislation relevant to the Joint Companies' developed a heavy political emphasis, did voting behavior reflect clear-cut partisan division.

II

Legislative activity relevant to economic enterprise also focused on individual requests for business incorporations. Between 1829 and 1844 the New Jersey legislature granted corporate charters to ninety-six manufacturing companies, twelve mining companies, and twelve insurance companies; enacted some supplementary-charter bills; and approved a general business law authorizing limited partnerships.[34]

Requests for business charters met with the general approval of the state's legislators. All but five passage roll calls on 141 charter bills won Assembly approval. Ninety-three of these bills received the unanimous support of that body.

Only one aspect of this legislation, the incorporation of manufacturing companies, resulted in consistent, partisan voting behavior. Although sixty-two manufacturing charters did receive unanimous support in the Assembly, disagreement over manufacturing proposals after 1834 produced moderate to high levels of partisan cohesion. Table 24, a summary of party voting on all roll calls related to the enactment of these measures or to supplementary manufacturing charter bills whose contents defined a clear position on the expansion of corporate privilege, illustrates this point.[35] In eight of the ten legislative sessions between 1835 and 1844, bills that elicited divisive responses found an average of more than two-thirds of the legislative representatives of each party in the Assembly that voted opposed to each other.

TABLE 24

Party Voting on the Chartering of Manufacturing
Companies, 1829-1844 Assemblies

Year	No. Roll Calls	Mean Party Index of Likeness
1829	3	83
1830	2	85
1831	1	93
1832	--	--
1833	3	64
1834	4	85
1835	3	55
1836	11	55
1837	8	84
1838	6	19
1839	14	26
1840	7	85
1841	3	26
1842	5	50
1843	2	47
1844	3	66
TOTAL:	77	

Examination of voting patterns in these years and the political context in which they developed indicates that party voting on charter proposals coincided with the emergence of the subject of corporate privilege as an important campaign issue in New Jersey and in the nation. As it was with banking and currency legislation, practical political considerations, differences of opinion regarding the efficacy of incorporations, and constituency demands shaped legislative response.

Following the close of the 1835 legislative session, Stacy Potts declared in the *Emporium and True American* that "all incorporated companies are, more or less, Monopolies." After noting that the legislature should not violate the privileges already legally extended to particular companies (no doubt a comment aimed at protecting the Joint Companies in which he was so involved), Potts observed that it "ought cautiously to refrain from increasing the irresponsible power of any existing corporations, or of chartering new ones."[36]

This attack on corporate privilege by the leading Democratic newspaper in New Jersey intensified during the spring and summer of 1835 with the publication of ten articles on "Monopolies." The series noted that "amid the aristocratic features which are found in all incorporations, there seldom appears a redeeming trait. . . . To grasp all, and never voluntarily disgorge, are incident to their nature." The special favors extended to corporations were felt to create a "class of privileged, if not titled nobility—a nobility that will ever be reaching forward to higher emoluments, at the hazard of more deeply involving the rights of the public."[37] By October all corporations were identified as monopolies "clogging the impulse of private enterprise, and infusing the community with the heartless principles of aristocracy."[38]

The *Emporium's* anticorporation stance was directly related to Andrew Jackson's assault on the Bank of the United States as a privileged monopoly. In their attempt to

170 THE BEHAVIOR OF STATE LEGISLATIVE PARTIES

gain voter support, Democrats in New Jersey and elsewhere vocally protested the extension of corporate charters for groups engaged in pursuits that were in direct
competition with unincorporated enterprises.[39] Banks and
manufacturing companies bore the main force of this assault. During the state legislative election campaigns for the
1835 session, for instance, the Morris County Democratic
Convention guaranteed that its nominees for Council and
Assembly seats would vote against "all . . . incorporations,
whose tendency is to accumulate power in the hands of the
wealthy at the expense of public right," while during the
1836 campaign Democratic legislative candidates from
Sussex promised to work for the abolition of all chartered
corporations.[40] Addressing the legislature at the opening
of the 1836 session, Democratic Governor Vroom, in the
spirit of these pledges, noted that the "powers and privileges" given to corporations are those "which individuals
do not possess and cannot exercise. The contest between
the two is an unequal contest, and the result is always in
favor of the corporation." So, warned Vroom, not only
banks, but also "corporations of any description should be
sparingly created."[41]

Democratic defense of anticorporation policy in 1835
and 1836, however, correlates only slightly to legislative
voting behavior on manufacturing enactments in these
years. To be sure, the Whig minority in the Assembly was
particularly cohesive in supporting the granting of manufacturing charters. On fourteen cleavage, Assembly roll
calls involving the passage of nine charters, no more than
one Whig assemblyman on any one roll call voted in the
negative. The mean relative index of cohesion for Whig
assemblymen on these roll calls was 97. On nine occasions
it reached 100. Democratic voting was not as cohesive. The
mean party index of likeness on these roll calls was 55.
Democrats did not oppose every manufacturing charter,
but their support was not overwhelming.[42]

Although the variable of party consistently produced

the most cohesive alignments on these roll calls, clear-cut partisan division did not emerge on the incorporation issue in these sessions. All charters that were the subject of cleavage roll calls received approval in the Assembly. Thirteen manufacturing charter proposals voted upon in the Assembly and twelve voted upon in the Council received unanimous approval in each house. No charters could have been granted without substantial Democratic support, since that party maintained majorities in both houses of the legislature in 1835 and in 1836. The total absence of party voting during the 1837 session when twenty-three of the twenty-five manufacturing charters voted upon in the Assembly were passed by unanimous votes further indicates the lack of strong partisan disagreement in spite of Democratic pronouncements to the contrary.

Clearly factors other than party influenced voting behavior. During the 1836 session, for instance, individuals from ten different counties had charter bills before the legislature. Five of these counties were represented by Democrats. Moreover, legislators serving in 1836 were among the incorporators of four enterprises seeking charters. These circumstances help explain the overwhelming support given to charter legislation by a Democratically controlled legislature. As with transportation incorporation charters, vote-trading among legislators desirous of satisfying personal and constituency interests affected deliberations over manufacturing incorporation charters.[43]

A similar lack of consistency marked deliberations over a general law authorizing limited partnerships. During the 1836 session, the Democratic speaker of the Assembly, Daniel Ryall, spoke out against the bill as granting powers "too much like a corporation." As he saw it, "there was a strong prejudice in the public mind against corporations of every description."[44] Ryall, himself, one of a group of Democratic legislators who received a charter for a silk company during this session, along with a majority of Democratic assemblymen, voted down a proposal to engross the bill. A party index of likeness of 26 was recorded on the motion; Whig assemblymen voting 15–0 in favor of engrossment and Democrats voting 8–23 against it (roll call 60).

In 1837, with the Democrats still in control of the legislature, Democratic governor Philemon Dickerson urged the enactment of this legislation.[45] Accordingly, the measure was approved by the unanimous consent of the Council and by a 36–7 margin in the Assembly.[46] The seven negative votes in the Assembly were cast by five Democrats and two Whigs representing six different counties.[47] As enacted, this bill authorized the formation of partnerships by two or more individuals to conduct any "mercantile, mechanical, or manufacturing business" other than "for the purpose of banking or making insurance." By simply drawing up a certificate that included the names of those involved, the general nature of the business to be conducted, and the amount of money to be invested, and by having it authorized by an officer able to take acknowledgment and proof of deeds, interested individuals thus could obtain limited liability protection, while engaging in a business enterprise.[48]

After 1837 in spirit with the Locofoco rhetoric of the national Democratic party, New Jersey's Democrats continued their attack on the extension of corporate privilege.[49] Prior to the fall elections of 1838, the *Emporium* defined a Whig as "one who eats, drinks, and sleeps upon *special privileges* and swears by some corporations."[50] One year later, a writer for the same paper claimed that "the Democrats [were] opposed to all monopolies and exclusive privileges, [while] the Whigs [were] for them."[51] During the 1841 election campaign, the *Emporium* pledged that if the Democrats were elected to the legislature "no monopolies [would] be chartered where the interests of the few are advanced to the injury and the oppression of the many."[52] Although such appeals failed to give the party a single legislative majority between 1838 and 1843, the voting behavior of Democratic legislators in these years generally supported party rhetoric.

Only twenty-nine manufacturing-charter bills were voted upon in the Assembly between 1838 and 1844. Of these bills, twenty-six received Assembly approval and twenty-three eventually became law. All but five bills were the subject of cleavage votes. Voting in 1838 and 1839 illustrates that after 1837, legislators' political affiliations were key determinants in the decision-making process.[53]

In each of these sessions, the Whig majority in the Assembly—seventeen in 1838 and thirteen in 1839—supported the incorporation of new businesses, while the Democratic minority offered consistent opposition. During the 1838 Assembly, a mean of 92% of all Democrats who voted opposed a mean of 89% of all Whigs who voted on fifteen cleavage roll calls concerned with business incorporations.[54] As defined by their votes, Democrats opposed all measures involving the extension of corporate privilege, while Whigs invariably supported them. Similar positions were maintained in 1839 when on each of fourteen Assembly, cleavage roll calls concerned with the granting of nine business charters, an average of 87% of all Democrats that cast ballots opposed an average of 89% of all Whigs that voted.[55]

Although few manufacturing incorporation charters granted between 1829 and 1844 included provisions for stockholder or management liability, after 1837 proposals to impose such restrictions generally engendered partisan voting behavior.[56] Like similar legislation involving banks, Democratic legislators fostered these measures, while Whigs opposed them. During the 1841 Assembly, for instance, a bill to make the directors of a particular manufacturing corporation liable for all company debts was defeated by a 13–30 margin (roll call 31). Whig assemblymen voted 5–29 against the proposal, while the Democrats favored passage by an 8–1 margin. A party index of likeness of 16 was recorded on this roll call. Again in 1842, liability legislation involving another corporation produced comparable results. Three separate proposals, each of which indicated a preference for restrictive control over the company's activities, were supported by the Democratic minority and rejected by the Whig majority. Party indices of likeness on three roll calls involving this legislation were 38, 11, and 18, respectively. The composite Democratic vote for all three votes was 37–4, while that of the Whigs was 10–74. After defeating each of these amendments, the Whig majority approved the corporation's charter bill by providing twenty-seven of the twenty-eight affirmative votes on the passage. The Democrats voted 1–20, providing all of the negative votes on this measure.[57]

Attempts to impose liability restrictions met with greater success with the return of the Democrats to power in 1844. Three charters were enacted that made company officials and stockholders liable if the debts of their companies exceeded the paid-in capital, if any dividend that was declared made the companies insolvent, if any capital was refunded when debts were outstanding, or if the directors did not submit to the stockholders an annual statement of the amount of capital paid in and of debts outstanding. In addition, a supplementary act to increase the capital of an existing manufacturing company included identical personal liability provisions for its officials and stockholders.

Party voting on these measures, unlike the situation in other years, was hardly apparent. All of these proposals received unanimous approval.[58] Moreover, a motion concerned with a second supplementary-charter bill that called for recommitting the bill so as to amend it by making stockholders and directors liable received more support from Whigs than Democrats.[59]

After 1834, then, the granting of special acts of incorporation to manufacturing companies increasingly became the object of partisan conflict within the legislature. Democratic legislators' opposition to such enactments and their support of restrictive liability provisions coincided with the emergence of a clear Democratic bias against the extension of corporate privilege. Although by 1838 even New Jersey's Whigs campaigned for office by opposing "a further increase of useless and pernicious acts of incorporation," the tendency of Democratic and Whig legislators to oppose each other on banking and manufacturing-company incorporation proposals were focused upon by the Democrats in their efforts to gain voter support in the state.[60]

Enactment of legislation involving the expansion of business enterprises and the development of transportation facilities compelled legislators to balance the demands of a variety of interests. Although not felt on every decision, the legislator's own interests and beliefs, constituency demands, sectional considerations, and party needs all affected the decision-making process.

Legislation concerned with the development of internal improvements and the incorporation of mining and insurance companies rarely elicited divisive voting behavior. When legislators disagreed on such questions, their partisan identities failed to correlate with the voting patterns that emerged. Instead, vote trading among legislators out to protect their own interests or those of their constituents usually accounted for decisions.

Only questions that in some way involved party interests engendered partisan responses in the legislature. The close relationship between the Joint Companies and the Democratic party as well as the involvement of Whig leaders with the New Jersey Railroad Company accounted for the relatively high levels of party voting on legislation concerning the Joint Companies. Specifically, Democratic reliance on the financial support of the corporation and the importance of the Companies' powers as a major, state-campaign issue explain the activities of legislative parties with respect to the Joint Companies.

The tendency for manufacturing incorporation proposals and restrictive liability legislation to provoke partisan voting behavior coincided with the efforts of Democratic legislators to conform to the party's antimonopoly campaign rhetoric. As it was with party influence on fiscal enactments, increased party voting on these matters as well as on proposals involving the Joint Companies emerged after 1834, following the relative stabilization of party alignments in the state.

Beginning with Jackson's assault on the Bank of the United States and particularly after 1837, party legislators in New Jersey were distinguished by their reactions to the issue of corporate privilege. Consistent Whig support for the incorporation of manufacturing companies and their opposition to harsh liability requirements for banks and other corporations increasingly contrast over time to Democratic positions on these questions. Similarly, partisan division in and out of the legislature over the B.U.S. and over general fiscal policy, despite some deviations, appears consistent with the differing images of Democrats and Whigs that emerged over manufacturing-charter legislation.

Even on these questions, however, absolute party unity was rarely achieved. Legislators' involvement in manufacturing companies, for instance, as well as the demands made on them by concerned constituents worked against cohesive partisan responses. For the most part, the ability of legislative parties to control the lawmaking process was greater when concerned with such matters as national fiscal resolutions or with general banking and currency proposals than it was when dealing with special acts of incorporation for banks or manufacturing companies. The different nature of these enactments helps account for the pattern. General fiscal legislation and particularly resolutions on national fiscal policy was devised by Democrats and Whigs primarily to serve as means of identifying themselves with national party policies and personalities. Charter legislation, however, was advanced by individual citizens in various parts of the state to satisfy local and

personal interests. Legislators, except when seeking charters for their own enterprises, did not initiate special
incorporation bills; they merely acted on the individual
requests presented before them. Thus, although concerned with adhering to announced party positions, the
legislator also had to be aware of how his behavior might
affect his own interests and those of his friends.

Although voting behavior on business legislation indicates the existence of real differences of opinion among
Democratic and Whig legislators, particularly after 1837,
neither party exhibited the ideological zeal on economic
questions that the most extreme interpretations of Jacksonian politics describe. Democratic legislators might have
voted against the few charter proposals offered between
1838 and 1844, but in no way did their behavior indicate a
criticism of capitalism or a desire to check its development.[61]

Inconsistencies in the responses of Democrats and
Whigs suggest the limits of party conflict over economic
issues. Strong Whig support for corporate enterprise, for
instance, contrasts sharply with that party's opposition to
the Joint Companies and with its attempts in the late 1830s
to campaign for office on the basis of its opposition to
privileged corporations. At the same time, as New Jersey's
Whigs were quick to point out, the union of the Democratic party with the Joint Companies, one of the most
powerful monopolies in the United States, was hardly consistent with that party's announced stand against special
privilege.[62]

Only by viewing the activities of both parties in terms of
the struggle for political power in New Jersey can any
sense be made of these discrepancies. Partisan responses
on substantive economic questions, in large part, were
predicated on the parties' perceptions of how their behavior might affect their ability to successfully gain dominance. Organized operation of legislative parties, tempered always by the demands of a variety of interests, was

most apparent on questions deemed significant within this context.

Notes

1. Certain regulatory legislation was also enacted by the legislature. Liability proposals, a general incorporation law for limited partnerships will be discussed in due course. Between 1829 and 1844 some 138 Assembly cleavage roll calls and 57 unanimous Assembly roll calls were recorded that were concerned primarily with regulating particular economic activities in the state. Among the topics of legislation were acts regulating inns and taverns, horseracing, oyster beds, medical societies, fishing grounds, and the maintenance of fences. The mean party index of likeness on these cleavage roll calls was 74. No consistent party positions emerged on these various regulatory proposals, nor did the state's newspapers deal with this type of legislation. Tables in Appendix B contain a summary of voting on these roll calls.

2. Cadman, pp. 48–53, 398.

3. Bipartisan support is demonstrated by the absence of the incorporation of transportation charters as a campaign issue and by the positive statements from both parties referring to the benefits derived from the granting of such charters. For instance, see *Emporium and True American* (Trenton), 3 January 1835; *Newark Daily Advertiser*, 7 February 1833; *P.N.J.G.A.*, 61st sess., 1st sitting, 1837, pp. 121–29. Only with respect to the Joint Companies was partisan disagreement noticeable. Roll calls involving the Joint Companies will be dealt with separately in this chapter.

4. All cleavage roll calls summarized in Table 22 are included in Table 23.

5. 1829 Assembly, C.R.C. 4, p. 124; C.R.C. 35, p. 292. 1830 Assembly, C.R.C. 12, p. 122; C.R.C. 61, p. 217; C.R.C. 68, p. 225. 1831 Assembly, C.R.C. 11, p. 94; C.R.C. 13, p. 106; C.R.C. 23, p. 146; C.R.C. 25, p. 151; C.R.C. 30, p. 163; C.R.C. 35, p. 179; C.R.C. 49, p. 200. 1832 Assembly, C.R.C. 7, p. 87; C.R.C. 22, 174; C.R.C. 32, p. 199; C.R.C. 35, p. 204; C.R.C. 51, p. 225; C.R.C. 68, p. 276; C.R.C. 74, p. 296; C.R.C. 77, p. 304. 1833 Assembly, C.R.C. 8, p. 172; C.R.C. 19, p. 283; C.R.C. 29, p. 316; C.R.C. 38, p. 360; C.R.C. 47, p. 389. 1834 Assembly, C.R.C. 14, p. 307; C.R.C. 16, p. 332; C.R.C. 17, p. 340, C.R.C. 29, p. 405; C.R.C. 53, p. 511. 1835 Assembly, C.R.C. 23, p. 241; C.R.C. 36, p. 323; C.R.C. 66, p. 447; C.R.C. 80, p. 477. 1836 Assembly, C.R.C. 10, p. 111; C.R.C. 19, p. 223; C.R.C. 21, p. 264; C.R.C. 44, p. 372; C.R.C. 58, p. 465; C.R.C. 81, p. 538. 1837 Assembly, C.R.C. 29, p. 237; C.R.C. 35, p. 249; C.R.C. 81, p. 421; C.R.C. 91, p. 461; C.R.C. 124, p. 572; C.R.C. 142, p. 603; C.R.C. 154, p. 629. 1838 Assembly, C.R.C. 39, p. 421; C.R.C. 55, p. 467; C.R.C. 56, p. 484; C.R.C. 63, p. 512; C.R.C. 91, p. 558. 1839 Assembly, C.R.C. 49, p. 513; C.R.C. 57, p. 528; C.R.C. 92, p. 625. 1840 Assembly, C.R.C. 27, p. 483. 1841 Assembly, C.R.C. 60, p. 619. 1842

Assembly, C.R.C. 39, p. 443; C.R.C. 45, p. 465; C.R.C. 80, p. 584; C.R.C. 26, p. 421; C.R.C. 75, p. 595. Analysis of voting behavior on transportation roll calls by occupation revealed no significant patterns. Neither a legislator's occupational identity nor his political affiliation distinguished cohesive voting groups on legislation that generally occasioned little opposition. *See* Appendix B.

6. Roll calls 33, 39, 81, 82, and 89 on this bill are graphed in Table 22. Roll-call references for all roll calls in Table 22 can be found in note 5 with the following additions: 1836 Assembly, C.R.C. 33, p. 314; C.R.C. 34, p. 314; C.R.C. 67, p. 491; C.R.C. 89, p. 557; C.R.C. 90, p. 563; C.R.C. 92, p. 566; C.R.C. 95, p. 583. 1837 Assembly, C.R.C. 33, p. 247; C.R.C. 39, p. 265; C.R.C. 49, p. 306; C.R.C. 55, p. 321; C.R.C. 56, p. 322; C.R.C. 77, p. 398; C.R.C. 126, p. 574; C.R.C. 127, p. 577; C.R.C. 146, p. 607; C.R.C. 158, p. 645.

7. Morris was omitted, as on roll call 81—the passage vote—its delegation split 2–2. Since this roll call was used as the key to the organization of the two groups, the lack of commitment as a delegation forced its omission. The indices of likeness for these groups on the five roll calls were 74, 41, 13, 32, and 68, respectively. The mean party index of likeness for these same five roll calls was 80.

8. Indices of likeness for these groups on two other roll calls, for example, were 82 on roll call 29 and 85 on roll call 35.

9. In 1832, for example, in an Assembly containing twenty-six Democrats and twenty-four Whigs, the mean party index of likeness on ten roll calls calling for the creation of six transportation companies and for the right of two railroads to expand their facilities was 85. Delegations from counties that stood to benefit directly from proposed legislation generally supported these transportation proposals, while delegations from counties far removed from likely benefit, opposed it. *See* Levine, "Party-in-the Legislature," pp. 263, 266, 267.

10.Cadman, p. 11; *Proceedings 1844,* pp. 179, 354. *Also see Newark Daily Advertiser,* 28 January 1833 and 3 March 1837. It is clear that logrolling could involve virtually any combination of bills that legislators, for whatever the reasons, may have had a particular interest in.

11. *See* chapter 3 for a full presentation of this data. Sitgreaves, in his *Manual of Legislative Practice,* noted the following rule governing the behavior in the Assembly when the private interests of the legislator were involved. "When the private interests of a member are concerned in a bill or questions, he is to withdraw. And when such an interest has appeared, his voice has been disallowed even after a division."

12. The lowest mean party indices of likeness on charter bills were 22 in 1838 (based on two cleavage roll calls) and 33 in 1841 (based on one cleavage roll call). Voting during the 1842 Assembly session illustrates what occurred between 1839 and 1844. Six roll calls of the cleavage variety were considered. Three, including two passage votes, involved authorizing the board of freeholders of Salem to build a bridge over Salem Creek (C.R.C. 39, p. 443; C.R.C. 43, p. 460; C.R.C. 45, p. 542). Roll call 80 was on a motion to grant a corporation charter to the Trenton City Bridge Company. The remaining two roll calls involved a resolu-

tion concerning transit duties owed to the state by the New Jersey Railroad Company (C.R.C. 68, p. 542; C.R.C. 69, p. 549). The mean party index of likeness on these six roll calls was 90. The vote totals on the three roll calls calling for the enactment of the two charter bills were 40–9, 30–15, and 38–11 (roll calls 39, 45, 80). Negative votes on these roll calls were cast by delegates from nine, eleven, and four counties, respectively.

13. McCormick, "Party Formation," p. 169. The best accounts of the Joint Companies and their relation to New Jersey politics are Robert T. Thompson, *Colonel James Neilson, A Business Man of the Early Machine Age in New Jersey, 1784–1862* (New Brunswick, New Jersey: Rutgers University Press, 1940), pp. 157–213; idem, "Transportation Combines and Pressure Politics in New Jersey: 1833–1836"; Wheaton J. Lane, *From Indian Trail to Iron Horse, Travel and Transportation in New Jesey, 1620–1860* (Princeton, New Jersey: Princeton University Press, 1939), pp. 279–413.

14. Ershkowitz, "New Jersey Politics," p. 164.

15. Levine, "Party-in-the Legislature," pp. 276–82, details fully legislative response to the Joint Companies prior to 1832. Individual charters for the railroad and the canal were approved in 1830. During the 1831 session consolidation of the two companies took place. A supplementary charter bill also approved in this session authorized the transfer of 1,000 shares of Camden and Amboy stock to the state on condition that no other company be given permission to construct a railroad between New York and Philadelphia. If such permission was granted, the 1,000 shares of stock would revert back to the Camden and Amboy. *N.J.L.,* 55th sess., 1831, p. 73.

16. *N.J.L.,* 56th sess., 1832, pp. 79–81.

17. Ershkowitz, "New Jersey Politics," pp. 164, 169–170.

18. *Newark Daily Advertiser,* 6 and 7 September and 8 and 9 October 1832. *Also see* Ershkowitz, "New Jersey Politics," p. 174. Roll-call references for figure 5 are: 1832 Assembly, C.R.C. 12, p. 136; C.R.C. 16–21, pp. 151–62; C.R.C. 25–30, pp. 181–87; C.R.C. 34, p. 202; C.R.C. 36, p. 205; C.R.C. 37, p. 206; C.R.C. 39, p. 209; C.R.C. 40, p. 210; C.R.C. 41, p. 210; C.R.C. 43–45; pp. 215–216; C.R.C. 49, p. 220; C.R.C. 86, p. 317; C.R.C. 87, p. 319.

19. Abraham Brown to Samuel L. Southard, 12 September 1832, Southard Papers, P.U.L.

20. McCormick, "Party Formation," p. 169.

21. Robert T. Thompson, "Transportation Combines and Pressure Politics in New Jersey: 1833–1836," p. 3.

22. *P.N.J.G.A.,* 59th sess., 2d sitting, 1835, p. 145.

23. Ibid., pp. 219, 366, 470.

24. Ibid., p. 223.

25. 1835 Assembly, C.R.C. 48, p. 377; *Newark Daily Advertiser,* 30 January 1835.

26. 1835 Assembly, C.R.C. 78, p. 471; C.R.C. 79, p. 472. One unexplainable exception concerning sectional voting on the Joint Companies occurred during the 1835 Assembly. Roll call 37, p. 331, was on the passage of a bill that au-

thorized the Camden and Amboy Railroad to construct a lateral road to South River in Middlesex County. This bill was enacted by a 27–20 margin. Delegates from Essex, Morris, and Bergen voted 10–2 in favor of this measure. Since these counties had consistently opposed the Joint Companies in the past, their votes on this measure seemed out of place.

27. Robert T. Thompson, "Transportation Combines and Pressure Politics in New Jersey: 1833–1836"; Lane, p. 329.

28. Littleton Kirkpatrick to Garret Wall, 23 December 1835, Garret Wall Papers, P.U.L.

29. Robert F. Stockton to Peter D. Vroom, 15 December 1835, Vroom Papers, N.J.H.S.

30. Robert T. Thompson, "Transportation Combines and Pressure Politics in New Jersey: 1833–1836," pp. 84–85; *P.N.J.G.A.*, 60th sess., 2d sitting, 1836, pp. 279–82.

31. Lane, pp. 330–31; Thomas Perrine to Samuel L. Southard, 24 February 1836, Southard Papers, P.U.L.

32. 1836 Assembly, C.R.C. 11–13, pp. 114–18; C.R.C. 15, p. 125; C.R.C. 17, p. 133; C.R.C. 74–77, pp. 524–528; C.R.C. 83–87, pp. 542–548; C.R.C. 131, p. 663. Between 1829 and 1844, twenty-two of the sixty-six cleavage roll calls involving the Joint Companies produced party indices of likeness under 67. All fifteen roll calls voted upon in 1836 recorded indices under 67. The five 1836 roll calls not discussed in the text concerned the enactment of a supplementary bill to allow the Joint Companies to build a branch to Trenton (roll calls 11, 12, 13, 15, and 17). Party indices of likeness on these roll calls were 20, 13, 39, 52, and 42, respectively.

33. Events during the 1836 session marked the high point of legislative activity involving the Joint Companies during the Jackson period. A controversy arose in 1839 concerning the amount of transit duties to be paid by the Camden and Amboy. This conflict continued through 1841 with the Whig governor, William Pennington, using his influence against the railroad. Finally the Companies capitulated to the state's demands in 1842. *See* Lane, pp. 334–36. Lane and others have also pointed out that after 1836, the Joint Companies made a concerted effort to elect their own people to legislative office, most often working through the Democratic party.

34. Cadman, p. 206.

35. Roll-call references for roll calls included in Table 24 are: 1829 Assembly, C.R.C. 10, p. 208; C.R.C. 24, p. 259; C.R.C. 27, p. 261. 1830 Assembly, C.R.C. 49, p. 203; C.R.C. 81, p. 254. 1831 Assembly, C.R.C. 48, p. 199. 1833 Assembly, C.R.C. 27, p. 305; C.R.C. 42, p. 375; C.R.C. 52, p. 407. 1834 Assembly, C.R.C. 2, p. 200; C.R.C. 3, p. 205; C.R.C. 18, p. 349; C.R.C. 22, p. 372. 1835 Assembly, C.R.C. 7, p. 118; C.R.C. 25, p. 276; C.R.C. 53, p. 598. 1836 Assembly, C.R.C. 14, p. 123; C.R.C. 16, p. 130; C.R.C. 18, p. 193; C.R.C. 36, p. 345; C.R.C. 47, p. 412; C.R.C. 48, p. 417; C.R.C. 49, p. 426; C.R.C. 53, p. 438; C.R.C. 57, p. 445; C.R.C. 61, p. 475; C.R.C. 105, p. 605. 1837 Assembly, C.R.C. 36, p. 250; C.R.C. 38, p. 262; C.R.C. 45, p. 287; C.R.C. 79, p. 410; C.R.C. 110, p. 523; C.R.C. 125, p. 572;

C.R.C. 131, p. 586; C.R.C. 143, p. 603; C.R.C. 190, p. 706. 1838 Assembly, C.R.C. 19, p. 353; C.R.C. 58, p. 490; C.R.C. 104, p. 595; C.R.C. 106, p. 598; C.R.C. 111, p. 609; C.R.C. 118, p. 626. 1839 Assembly, C.R.C. 12, p. 324; C.R.C. 15, p. 372; C.R.C. 16, p. 376; C.R.C. 24, p. 408; C.R.C. 25, p. 409; C.R.C. 32, p. 427; C.R.C. 33, p. 444; C.R.C. 34, p. 451; C.R.C. 42, p. 472; C.R.C. 43, p. 478; C.R.C. 52, p. 520; C.R.C. 62, p. 547; C.R.C. 74, p. 580; C.R.C. 80, p. 593. 1840 Assembly, C.R.C. 36, p. 279; C.R.C. 37, p. 280; C.R.C. 42, p. 307; C.R.C. 59, p. 361; C.R.C. 65, p. 415; C.R.C. 66, p. 422; C.R.C. 76, p. 478. 1841 Assembly, C.R.C. 32, p. 440; C.R.C. 33, p. 441; C.R.C. 72, p. 647. 1842 Assembly, C.R.C. 6, p. 187; C.R.C. 36, p. 360; C.R.C. 59, p. 504; C.R.C. 72, p. 564; C.R.C. 94, p. 635. 1843 Assembly, C.R.C. 19, p. 336; C.R.C. 61, p. 475. 1844 Assembly, C.R.C. 20, p. 356; C.R.C. 43, p. 506; C.R.C. 106, p. 655.

36. *Emporium and True American*, 25 April 1835.

37. Ibid., 18 July 1835.

38. Ibid., 3 October 1835. The quotation is from an excerpt from the *Somerville Messenger*.

39. Cadman, pp. 75, 429.

40. Ershkowitz, "New Jersey Politics," p. 225. The combined vote of the Democratic Assembly delegation from Morris in 1835 on three charter roll calls was 3–6. The Democratic delegation from Sussex in 1836 collectively voted 17–16 on twelve charter roll calls. Nine of the sixteen negative votes came on roll calls 14, 16, and 18. These three roll calls involved Essex county corporations.

41. *J.N.J.L.C.*, 60th sess., 1st sitting, 1836, p. 17.

42. *See* note thirty-five for roll-call references. Analysis of twenty Council roll calls in these same sessions reveals a similar pattern. Affirmative votes on twenty of these roll calls defined a procorporation attitude. The total Whig vote on them was 81–10. Eight of the ten negative votes were on two roll calls calling for approval of a manufacturing company in Sussex, a Democratic stronghold (1836 Council, C.R.C. 60, 70). The total Democratic vote on these same twenty roll calls was 88–63. Roll calls were as follows: 1835 Council, C.R.C. 6, p. 116; C.R.C. 20, p. 192. 1836 Council, C.R.C. 9, p. 125; C.R.C. 13, p. 143; C.R.C. 19, p. 171; C.R.C. 20, p. 173; C.R.C. 21, p. 175; C.R.C. 22, p. 181; C.R.C. 24, p. 191; C.R.C. 31, p. 224; C.R.C. 37, p. 251; C.R.C. 39, p. 253; C.R.C. 47, p. 271; C.R.C. 51, p. 289; C.R.C. 52, p. 290; C.R.C. 57, p. 309; C.R.C. 59, p. 310; C.R.C. 60, p. 311; C.R.C. 61, p. 314; C.R.C. 70, p. 329. One other roll call was a motion to make the stockholders and directors of the Newark Malleable Iron Company liable for the company's debts. Democrats supported this motion (6–3), while the Whigs voted unanimously against it (0–5); 1836 Council, C.R.C. 16, p. 159.

43. Of the ninety-six charters granted between 1829 and 1844, thirty-six contained legislators as incorporators.

44. *Newark Daily Advertiser,* 23 June 1836.

45. *P.N.J.G.A.,* 61st sess., 1st sitting, 1837, pp. 121–29.

46. 1836 Assembly, C.R.C. 60, p. 471; 1837 Assembly, U.R.C. 47, p. 349; 1837 Council, U.R.C. 33, p. 159.

47. Two delegates from Burlington and one each from Monmouth, Salem, Gloucester, Hunterdon, and Warren voted in the negative.

48. *N.J.L.*, 61st sess., 1837, pp. 121–25.

49. Cadman, pp. 79–82.

50. *Emporium and True American,* 14 September 1838.

51. Ibid., 6 September 1839.

52. Ibid., 23 October 1840.

53. Levine, "Party-in-the Legislature," pp. 310–313, details voting in other years after 1839.

54. Roll-call references for roll calls other than those included in note 35 include: 1838 Assembly, C.R.C. 18, p. 352; C.R.C. 59, p. 491; C.R.C. 82, p. 540; C.R.C. 88, p. 550; C.R.C. 94, p. 563; C.R.C. 95, p. 563; C.R.C. 98, p. 577; C.R.C. 105, p. 597; C.R.C. 107, p. 600. Six roll calls involved the incorporation of the New Jersey Agricultural Company (roll calls 88, 94, 95, 105, 106, 118). All but one resulted in a party index of likeness under 11. As agreed upon, this act enabled the company to construct locks in the Hackensack River to reclaim marshland in Bergen County. The remaining nine roll calls involved the passage of two manufacturing charter bills and one supplementary charter bill. Particularly on the charter bills, both the Democratic minority and the Whig majority were quite cohesive. The party indices of likeness on the two final passage roll calls were 25 and 9 (roll calls 58, 111). In both instances the Whigs voted in favor of the charters, thus securing their approval in the Assembly.

55. *See* note 35 for roll-call references. Whig cohesion was not greater because of the voting record of the Cumberland delegation. Although elected as Whigs, these individuals consistently voted with the Democrats on incorporation questions. For example, on the seven charter-bill passage roll calls where party indices of likeness were under 20, the total number of anticorporation (negative) votes cast by Whig assemblymen was nineteen. The Cumberland delegation accounted for thirteen of these votes (roll calls 12, 16, 24, 25, 32, 43, 62). Democratic unity broke down on three occasions (roll calls 15, 33, 52). The first two roll calls involved the incorporation of the Plainfield Steam Power Association and the third called for the incorporation of the Whippany Manufacturing Company. Democratic votes on these passage roll calls were 6–7, 6–9, and 7–10. Assemblymen from Sussex, Warren, and Hunterdon provided five of the seven, seven of the nine, and eight of the ten negative votes that were cast.

56. Cadman, pp. 361–62.

57. 1841 Assembly, C.R.C. 31, p. 436; *P.N.J.G.A.,* 66th sess., 2d sitting, 1842, pp. 367–77. 1842 Assembly, C.R.C. 26, p. 367; C.R.C. 28, p. 375; C.R.C. 29, p. 377; C.R.C. 36, p. 430.

58. *N.J.L.,* 68th sess., 1844, pp. 55, 57, 155, 265. For a complete discussion of the institution of liability provisions, *see* Cadman, pp. 325–62. In the course of his discussion, Cadman notes that between 1834 and 1850 a movement originated among the members of the radical wing of the Democratic party to impose a large measure of personal liability on stockholders in business corporations.

Except for Jonathan Pickel, who served in 1838 and 1843, no individuals are specifically named. Moreover Pickel's role in this movement, as Cadman himself points out, was most noticeable between 1845 and 1850. As noted in my discussion, analysis of the legislative roll calls concerned with liability provisions voted upon between 1829 and 1844 failed to reveal the operation of any such group in the legislature. As Cadman points out on p. 361, the Democrats, again no name mentioned, until 1850 were "sponsoring a losing cause" in their attempts to secure stockholder liability.

59. The Democrats voted 14–18 against the motion, while the Whigs voted 14–7 in favor of it. 1844 Assembly, C.R.C. 18, p. 350.

60. *Newark Daily Advertiser,* 6 October 1838.

61. William G. Carleton, "Political Aspects of the Van Buren Era," *South Atlantic Quarterly* 50 (April 1951): 167–85.

62. *See* the discussion of the Joint Companies in this chapter. The 4 November 1835 issue of the *Newark Daily Advertiser* commented on Governor Vroom's remarks concerning the extension of corporate privilege as "conceived in the *ad captandum* spirit of party." Three years later, in the 25 January 1839 edition of the same paper, it was noted that Democrats were not principled and that their changing attitude toward corporate privilege was an indication that the "democratic creed changes with circumstances." Ershkowitz, "New Jersey Politics," pp. 221–49, attempts to show that a radical minority within the Democratic party "sought to destroy the power of all corporations" after the attack on the Bank of the United States in 1832. Yet he never names one individual by name nor does he bother to examine the impact of this force on legislative voting behavior. His discussion of the radical attack on the Joint Companies is also not supported by what transpired in the legislature. Also, in light of Kirkpatrick's and Stockton's letters concerning the Joint Companies, and the subsequent events in the legislature during the 1836 session, Ershkowitz's discussion of the Joint Companies role in offering to sell their properties to the state is not supported.

7
Legislative Voting Behavior: Social Legislation

The limited role of government in the development of New Jersey's economy was more than equaled by its lack of involvement in the social improvement of the state's citizens. Although the reform impulse was not entirely absent, there was an evident unwillingness to commit the state's resources to the cause of social betterment. Programs to provide a free, common-school education for all children, to care for the mentally retarded and the physically handicapped, to abolish imprisonment for debt, and to reduce the cost and to simplify the procedures for obtaining justice, although on the agenda of the legislature between 1829 and 1844, resulted in only temporary and incomplete solutions to real social problems.[1] The insignificance of legislative parties in dealing with these matters correlates with the reluctance of the major parties to oppose each other on social-reform questions. Although party leaders spoke out on the need for various changes, neither side was much concerned with establishing its identity by its stand on social issues.

I

The movement to institute a common-school system illustrates the lack of partisan behavior with respect to projects of social improvement. The campaign to provide a free, rudimentary education for all children was the best-organized and most persistent reform effort in New Jersey in the 1830s and the 1840s. Support for such a system, both in and out of the legislature, was completely bipartisan. Throughout these years, governors and legislators of both parties spoke eloquently about the need for such a system, emphasizing the importance of an adequate combination of state and local financial support and of a similar mixture of organization and supervision.[2]

The establishment of a School Fund by the legislature in 1816 provided the foundation for state aid to common schools, yet the actual amount drawn from this fund was not sufficient to establish an even level of educational facilities throughout the state.[3] The absence of an adequate financial base along with the wide disparity in the quality of teaching and in the organization of local school systems became the key issues around which school reformers in New Jersey rallied. Aligned against them were powerful private-school interests who sought to maintain their positions against potential rivals.[4] The struggle between these forces delayed the establishment of a state-supervised common-school system supported by compulsory local taxation and by appropriations from the School Fund until 1846. Although such strong division was not as noticeable in the legislature between 1829 and 1844, the twin issues of financing and supervision occupied what little attention legislators gave to the question of educational reform in these years.

Prior to and during the 1829 session, the advocates of the common school mounted a concerted drive to secure a public commitment to provide a uniform, free education for all children. Local and county protest meetings were held where reports of the inadequate and uneven educational facilities in the state were presented, essays on the need for state supervision and for sufficient funds were reprinted in many of the state's newspapers, and petitions were sent to the legislature demanding action.[5] Responding to this pressure, a joint legislative committee to which these appeals had been referred recommended that the state's School Fund be put to use "to realize the benefits which it was intended to yield, and to dispense its bounties in a way, which may at once satisfy the wants of the people."[6]

By votes of 11–1 in the Council and 28–6 in the Assembly, legislators followed the advice of their peers and enacted the state's first comprehensive school law.[7] The lack of disagreement indicated by the passage votes in both the Council and the Assembly reflected the rather limited nature of this act. For the first time since the School Fund's inception, its income was to go toward the establishment of common schools. The act authorized the trustees of the School Fund to apportion an annual amount of $20,000 among the state's counties. Each county was to receive a sum in direct proportion to the amount of state tax it paid each year. In turn, the board of chosen freeholders in each county was to apportion its share of the School Fund among its townships according to the taxes that they paid. In order for a township to receive its full share, its inhabitants, at their annual town meeting, had to agree to raise "an additional amount" of money by any means decided upon to be used to institute common schools. Parents who could afford the tuition costs were still required to pay them, because the funds that were to be provided by the state and the townships were not sufficient to provide a free education for all children. The act also authorized each township to elect school committees with the responsibilities of setting up school districts, examining and licensing teachers, and holding district meetings.[8]

Although this act authorized the use of state monies to improve educational facilities, it set no standard requirements for the qualification of teachers nor for the course of instruction. Moreover, its allotment of $20,000 hardly guaranteed that all children would receive even a minimal education. The basis for the division of these funds further complicated matters, for it provided the least amount of aid to the poorer, low-tax-paying counties in need of the most help. As individual townships only had to pledge additional support rather than a specified amount as a prerequisite for receiving state funds, there was no guarantee that enough money would be raised to establish free schools. "A dollar raised for the object [was] as effectual as one thousand" for a township to secure its share of the annual state appropriation.[9]

Only one aspect of the 1829 common-school bill, the question of township support, provoked real disagreement among legislators. Assemblymen from Warren, Burlington, Cumberland, Monmouth, and Cape May consistently opposed all provisions that involved compulsory local taxation as a prerequisite for receiving state aid. In contrast, representatives from Essex and Gloucester firmly approved such measures.[10]

Legislative activity during the 1830 session also focused on the question of local financing. An amendment to the supplementary-education bill of this year ordered each township to raise an amount equal to or greater than that part of the School Fund apportioned to it in order to receive its share of the fund. This amendment was defeated by a 9–28 margin (roll call 97). A party index of likeness of 99 was recorded on this roll call. Affirmative votes were cast by delegates from Essex, Middlesex, Sussex, Hunterdon, Bergen, and Somerset. Although the representatives from these counties combined to produce eleven negative votes, they supplied what support there was for compulsory local participation. Counties that had been either completely or partially opposed to this position in 1829 reiterated their stand in 1830. The west Jersey bloc, with Gloucester returning to the fold, and the representatives from Monmouth and Warren voted 0–17 against this amendment.

Division over the question of taxation did not prohibit agreement on the final version of the bill. Indeed, the bill supplementary to the common-school act of 1829 received the unanimous support of both houses of the legislature.[11] The terms of this measure dealt a serious setback to the common-school crusade. Repealed were those sections of the 1829 act that had required examination and licensing of teachers by the township school committees and that had demanded the contribution by each township of an unspecified sum of money as a prerequisite for receiving its full share of the School Fund.[12] The lack of disagreement on this measure as compared to the voting behavior on the taxation issue suggests that legislators were less concerned with the efficient supervision and the uniform statewide instruction of the young as they were with working out a formula by which to provide financially for a school system. The deliberations of the 1831 and the 1838 legislative sessions further illustrate this point.

The enactment of an act relative to common schools in 1831 effectively destroyed whatever gains had been made in 1829. Although the annual appropriation of $20,000 from the income of the School Fund was retained, the other provisions of the 1829 act were repealed. By the terms of the common-school act of 1831, private and parochial schools were permitted to share in this appropriation. It was left to the individual townships to disburse their share of the fund, with the stipulation that if this revenue was used only to educate pauper children, then nonpauper children would be required to pay tuition. No provision was made to compel the formation of school districts, to require the examination and licensing of teachers, or to provide for state supervision.[13]

No significant division over this measure occurred in the Council.[14] Assembly voting behavior revealed a disagreement similar to that engendered by the tax amendment to the 1830 measure. Western counties, joined by the voting members of the Morris delegation, voted 18–0 in favor of the bill, while the remaining eight counties voted 11–14 against it (roll call 63).[15] Of these eight counties, Sussex, Middlesex, and Somerset were most firm in their opposition, providing half of the negative votes and only one affirmative vote. Essex, though providing two negative votes, also cast three affirmative votes. Like other years, the significance of party in the determination of this legislation was scarcely felt.[16]

Voting during the 1838 session again illustrates that support for compulsory taxation centered in the north, while the most consistent opposition to it came from west Jersey. That this issue, rather than the conflict over the questions of supervision and licensing, was at the heart of legislative division on education legislation was clearly demonstrated in this session.

Responding to the demands of the New Jersey Convention on Popular Education held in Trenton in January, the Whig-dominated legislature passed a new common-school act that repealed the act of 1831.[17] Although the annual appropriation from the School Fund was increased to $30,000, the 1838 law made no provisions for either state supervision or compulsory local taxation. County boards of examiners, responsible for the examining and licensing of teachers, were established, but their prerogatives were limited by the inclusion of a provision that allowed the individual township school committees, if they so desired, to select their own instructors.[18]

The rather limited reforms of this measure account for the unanimous support it received in the Assembly.[19] Only on the question of taxation was significant division noticeable. Two amendments that called for each township to collect an amount equal to or greater than its share of the School Fund as a requirement for receiving state funds suffered overwhelming defeat (roll calls 69, 71).[20] Of the fifteen votes in support of these measures, all but three were from delegates from northern counties. Western counties remained consistent in their opposition to local taxation by voting 2–13 and 1–15, respectively, on these motions.

Attempts to establish an efficient, well-organized, adequately financed common-school system met with limited success in New Jersey between 1829 and 1844. The unwillingness of the state to commit its financial resources to public improvement projects retarded development in this area. The lack of party voting on education measures suggests that party legislators did not consider common-school reform worthy of unified action. Legislative parties were capable of serving as convenient channels to organize the business of the legislature and to focus support for particular projects. Their lack of involvement in this area only added to the problems of the common-school cause.[21]

The parsimonious attitudes of the state's lawmakers combined with a lack of party commitment to progressive social reform stifled other programs aimed at improving the lot of New Jersey's citizens. For instance, although the construction of an asylum for the mentally ill was begun in Trenton in 1845, the care of the physically and mentally handicapped received only the cursory attention of the state's lawmakers prior to that year. To be sure, annual appropriations in amounts under $2,000 were set aside for the deaf and dumb, and for the blind and the insane. These appropriations, called for by the state's governors and always granted with the unanimous consent of the legislature, were used to send a small fraction of the disabled to public institutions located in New York and Pennsylvania.[22] Those unfortunates who failed to obtain this aid were left at the mercy of local and private beneficence. Not until 1840 did the legislature even consider the possibility of building state institutions. In that year a legislative committee charged with reporting on the number and the condition of the state's insane called for the construction of a state asylum. Rather than proposing that the $20,000 estimated cost of the project be provided from public resources, the committee hoped "that some philanthropic gentlemen in the state, who have evinced a deep interest in behalf of the suffering insane, may contribute liberally" and thus defray the expense.[23]

Only when practical party considerations became tied to legislative proposals for state institutions did party legislators respond cohesively. During the 1842 session the Assembly recorded five roll calls on a resolution that called for the governor to appoint an investigating committee to choose a convenient location for an asylum.[24] Voting on these roll calls indicates partisan disagreement not over the necessity of the asylum, but over how the investigating committee was to be appointed. Democrats, in the minority, opposed proposals calling for either the legislature in Joint Meeting, or the governor, to appoint the members of the committee. Party indices of likeness on the two roll calls directly involved with these suggestions were 15 and 27, respectively (roll calls 22, 23). The resolution, itself, was approved by a 37–9 margin (roll call 96). All twenty-nine Whigs voted in the affirmative. Although nine Democrats voted in the negative, their responses appear to reflect their dislike for Whig control over the appointments to the investigating committee rather than of the project itself. This is borne out by the fact that in 1845 the legislature unanimously agreed to undertake the construction of the asylum.[25]

The chief obstacle to early construction of asylums for the deaf and dumb and for the mentally ill was the government's reluctance to finance such projects. Although men of all parties and from all parts of the state might agree that public institutions were necessary, they were quick to point out the dangerous economic consequences of the excessive investment of state funds. Even the construction of a new state prison in the 1830s, the only major public building project undertaken between 1829 and 1844, reveals the frugal attitude of the state government. Similar to other social-reform legislation, this venture occasioned little opposition except when the question of financing arose.

In his messages to the legislature in 1830, 1831, and 1832, Governor Vroom urged that a new state prison be constructed.[26] Although bills to that effect were introduced in each of these sessions, the legislature, in nonpartisan fashion, postponed action on them.[27] The request of Governor Southard in 1833 for similar legislation, however, met with greater success and a law calling for the erection of a new prison was enacted.

Commenting on legislative deliberations on the 1833 proposal, one writer for the *Newark Daily Advertiser* noted that general agreement existed both in and out of the legislature on the need for a new prison in spite of the fact that some legislators were hesitant, because they were "inclined to a parsimonious course, from mistaken notions of true economy."[28] Voting in the 1833 Assembly on the prison bill and on related legislation reveals the accuracy of these remarks. The prison bill itself was passed by a 30–14 margin (roll call 36).[29] The fourteen negative votes were scattered among eight counties. Hunterdon and Warren, both represented by Democrats and both in the northwestern part of the state, provided six of these votes, while Cumberland and Salem, both represented by National Republicans and both in west Jersey, accounted for five negative votes. The party index of likeness on this roll call was 88.

This act committed the state to build a facility capable of holding 150 prisoners in separate cells. It called for the appointment of commissioners to contract for the construction of the prison and to hire an architect. Initial expenses for the project were covered by a $30,000 appropriation from the treasury's accounts payable on warrants drawn by the governor, with no more than $12,000 to be used by November 1834. The bill did not include any provision for further funding of the project.[30]

Although the prison bill itself elicited little disagreement, two proposals concerning financing provoked partisan responses. The National Republican majority in the Assembly successfully defeated a bill that authorized the use of a lottery to raise funds for the building of the prison. The roll call on the motion to dismiss this bill from consideration produced a party index of likeness of 18.[31] The editor of one National Republican newspaper noted that the lottery bill had been "fostered by one of the leaders of the Jackson party" and was defeated "through the instrumentality of the National Republican party." By its actions, this correspondent concluded, the National Republicans had saved New Jersey "from the singular anomaly of building a prison by means eminently calculated to encourage crime, and engender subjects for its occupancy."[32]

A second proposal permitted the remaining $18,000 of the $30,000 originally appropriated for the construction of the prison to be used immediately, rather than waiting until November 1834. National Republicans voted in favor of laying the bill on the table, against striking out its first section, and for its passage, while the Democrats took the opposite position each time. Party indices of likeness on the three roll calls pertaining to these motions were 22, 36, and 53. As finally enacted, the bill authorized the governor to draw from the treasury the additional $18,000 from any unappropriated monies in the state. If not available from the treasury, the governor was further authorized to borrow the needed amount at no more than five percent annual interest.[33]

The desire to avoid identification with any financial scheme that smacked of extravagance and that might result in unfortunate political repercussions explains partisan division on these questions. National Republican legislators acted to avoid possible charges that they were irresponsible caretakers of the state's finances. In light of subsequent Democratic denunciations of "Whig extravagance" concerning the prison during election campaigns, their concern seems justified.[34]

The construction of the prison represents one of the few times that the state completed a project that bore some relation to social reform between 1829 and 1844. Although it was by far the largest expenditure by the state for any single object, even in this instance the final result was something less than the original intent. As first conceived, the prison was to consist of five blocks and 300 cells, each cell with its own small exercise yard, to be built at a cost of $150,000. By 1837, over $190,000 had been spent and only two of the five blocks and less than 200 cells had been completed. Individual exercise yards had been eliminated and instead of providing regular paid moral instruction, volunteer preaching was introduced.[35]

The government's limited response to serious social problems was not confined to situations that involved the expenditure of public funds. Legislative activity over the question of the abolition of imprisonment for debt is a case in point. It was not until the early 1840s that the debtor's prison was abolished in New Jersey. This achievement was less a measure of humanitarian zeal than an expression of the state's economic subservience to New York and Pennsylvania. Once these states had eliminated this practice, it became incumbent upon New Jersey, out of pure commercial expedience, to follow their lead.[36]

Whether viewed in economic or humanitarian terms it is clear that the state's lawmakers were not committed to the quick resolution of this problem. Between 1829 and 1841, almost no positive action toward the effective elimination of the debtor laws was achieved. During the 1830 session, the legislature did enact a law to abolish imprisonment for debt in certain cases. This measure provided that if a debtor could post bond equal to twice the amount that he owed, he could remain out of jail until his final hearing. Revolutionary-war veterans over seventy years of age were to be completely exempt from all debt laws.[37] This act was a watered-down version of a proposal that would have freed all those debtors too poor to provide for themselves while in jail who had been incarcerated for very small debts.[38] Its rather bland provisions accounted for the lack of disagreement occasioned by its passage. Only eight of thirty-six assemblymen and three of fourteen councillors who cast ballots voted in the negative.[39]

In spite of the passage of more progressive legislation in other states (New York, for example, had abolished the debtor's prison by 1831), New Jersey continued along with its policy of nonaction.[40] The Prison Discipline Society of Boston in 1830 noted that New Jersey was the most neglectful state in attempting to either improve the conditions that debtors were forced to live in or to abolish debtor laws altogether. As late as 1834, nearly half of the prisoners in the state were debtors, yet there was no firm commitment to change the situation by either party or by any other identifiable group in the legislature.[41]

Although legislation entitling a debtor's family to keep certain necessary items from the creditor's grasp received approval, little beyond the small concessions of the 1830 act was obtained before 1842.[42] The only general abolition law proposed was quickly muffled. During the 1835 session a bill to abolish imprisonment for debt in certain cases and to punish fraudulent debtors was presented before the Assembly. The first section of this bill called for the end of imprisonment without any restrictions. The Assembly committee to which this bill had been referred reported back to the house and recommended that it not agree to this section. The members of the Assembly, by a vote of 24–21 acceded to this suggestion and so the bill was dismissed. The party index of likeness on this vote was 93.[43]

During the 1842 session, the legislature did enact a general abolition law.[44] The leader of the 1842 Assembly forces in favor of abolition was Doctor Stephen Congar, a Whig representative from Essex. As chairman of the select committee on this subject, Congar, along with three other members of his committee, issued a slashing attack on New Jersey's debt laws. After describing imprisonment for debt as "the barbarous relic of a barbarous age . . . at war with the true principles of human society," the report questioned why New Jersey, in contrast to "many of her sister states" that had done away with such laws, "should . . . lag behind the spirit of the age, and cling with unreasoning pertinacity, to the exploded notions of the past." This appeal on humanitarian grounds was supplemented by the more practical analysis that New Jersey's debt laws, were "injurious to the pecuniary interests of the citizens of our state." In the spirit of this report, the committee presented for consideration a bill that called for the abolition of imprisonment for debt in every circumstance. Creditors, however, were to be protected from those individuals who attempted to remove any of their property from the state or who concealed their holdings with the intent of preventing them from being used for the payment of their debts. Such fraudulent debtors were to be deemed guilty of a misdemeanor, and upon conviction could be fined or imprisoned at the discretion of the courts.[45]

The liberal provisions of this bill met opposition in the Assembly on two occasions. Voting in these instances failed to clarify strong party attitudes on this issue. The general abolition provision of the committee's bill was altered by the passage of an amendment limiting it to abolition on execution only rather than on any civil process. Although eighteen of the twenty-three negative votes were cast by Whigs, a total of ten Whigs and fourteen Democrats combined to secure its passage. An amendment to allow the arrest of a debtor who intended to flee from his creditors rather than only when the intent to defraud had been established was defeated by a 28–22 vote. Again, no clear party or sectional divisions marked this voting. An equal number of assemblymen from both parties combined to defeat this restricting proposal.[46]

The vote on the final passage of the bill demonstrates the limited partisan interest on the question of imprisonment for debt. Forty-one of the forty-nine assemblymen who voted on this roll call cast affirmative ballots. Although all eight negative votes were cast by Whigs, the party index of likeness on this roll call was 74. All of the eighteen Democrats who voted, along with twenty-three Whigs, decided in favor of the bill. Aside from Cape May whose single representative voted in the negative, only one county delegation (Burlington) cast more negative votes than positive votes (1–4). That seven of the eight negative votes were cast by delegates from western counties is the only obvious deviation from the picture of general agreement over the approval of the bill.[47]

Unfavorable reaction on the part of those who were opposed to a liberalized debt law was strong. The state legislative election campaigns in the fall of 1842 found some Democrats attempting to discredit their opponents by charging that if the Whigs obtained majorities in the legislature, they would reimpose imprisonment for debt.[48] Indeed, three of the Whig candidates for the Assembly in Essex went on record in favor of such action.[49] The 1843 legislative session was to spend a good deal of its time in deciding upon the correctness of the work of their predecessors on this question.

Of the seventy-seven cleavage, Assembly roll calls voted upon in this session, twenty-two involved the passage of a new debt law. Presented by Henry W. Green, a Whig representative from Mercer county, this new bill went far toward repealing the rather liberal provisions of the 1842 measure. In particular, Green's version allowed the creditor to imprison the debtor. It also placed the responsibility for recovering the debtor's property on the debtor rather than on the creditor.[50] Led by Stephen Congar, a group of fifteen Democratic and five Whig assemblymen made a determined effort to defeat this bill. Congar introduced twelve amendments, each of which called for a revision of Green's bill to a more liberal position. Other amendments and procedural motions accounted for the remaining ten roll calls on this bill.[51] On all but two of twenty-two roll calls, this group of assemblymen occupied the minority position. Representing eleven counties, they provided an average of 81% of the minority votes cast on these roll calls. Their votes always defined a position that was opposed to the reimposition of restrictive debt laws. The core of this group was composed of Congar and six Democrats, two from Sussex, and one each from Middlesex, Hunterdon, Atlantic, and Cumberland. At least six of these seven men voted together on seventeen of the twenty roll calls in question. As a group they recorded over 50% of the total minority vote nine times and between 35% and 49% of it five times.

The seven county delegations that had none of their members in the minority group of twenty were all represented by Whigs in the Assembly. As it was in 1842, the strength of this proimprisonment group was found in west Jersey. Burlington, Gloucester, Salem, and Cape May consistently voted against all attempts to soften the tenor of Green's proposal. In the end, this version passed in the Assembly by a 34–20 margin.[52] The party index of likeness on the final roll call was 55. Indeed, on sixteen of the twenty-two roll calls, the party indices of likeness were ·lower than 66. Whig representatives were far more cohesive on these votes, recording an index of relative cohesion of 82 as compared to the Democrats' 66. As defined by their votes, at least in this particular session, the Democrats stood on the more liberal side of social reform, while the Whigs held to a more restrictive position.

This same pattern was evident in Council. On nine

Council roll calls taken on this bill, the Democratic minority of eight was quite cohesive in its opposition.[53] On seven occasions, including two passage roll calls, these individuals voted unanimously against the measure (roll calls 60, 75). Although the Whigs were only slightly less cohesive in favor of the bill, the alignment of the Whig representatives from Salem, Hudson, and Passaic along with the Democrats on these two votes was enough to defeat the bill, thus maintaining the more liberal legislation of 1842.

Although in this instance more Democratic legislators than Whig legislators voted to support reform legislation, the significance of the phenomenon can not be emphasized. The inconsistent voting behavior of both parties on debtor legislation prior to 1843 leads one to concur with the opinions of two of the leading Whig newspapers in the state that this matter "was not a party question."[54] Unanimous approval by the thirty Democratic and twenty-eight Whig delegates to the 1844 Constitutional Convention of a constitutional provision prohibiting imprisonment for debt in any action or in any judgment founded upon contract except in cases of fraud merely reinforces this conclusion.[55]

Legislative activity involving the state's judicial system reveals a similar lack of partisan concern and a reluctance to take positive action on the part of New Jersey's legislators. Although judicial reforms were proposed in the mid 1830s, it was not until the Constitutional Convention of 1844 that significant changes were made. At this time the office of the governor was separated from that of the chancellor. The Council was relieved of its responsibility of serving as the Court of Errors and Appeals, a practice that had its antecedents in colonial times. Most important, the local justices of the peace, formerly appointed by the Joint Meeting, were then limited in number according to the population of each township and elected by the popular vote of the eligible voters whom they would actually serve.[56]

Prior to these developments little of consequence occurred. Judicial legislation considered by the legislature often elicited the unanimous support of the state's lawmakers.[57] Hardly ever did the press refer to such matters in partisan fashion.[58] Although roll calls on judicial questions occasionally engendered moderate degrees of party voting, there is nothing to indicate that legislative parties consciously organized themselves around such matters.[59]

The judicial proposal that produced the highest level of party cohesion was less concerned with fine points of law than it was with practical partisan considerations. During the 1838 session, the legislature enacted a law to facilitate the administration of justice. In the Assembly the Whig majority voted 30–1 in favor of the bill, while the Democratic minority voted 3–13 against it. The party index of likeness of 22 recorded on the passage roll call was the lowest for the seventy-two Assembly, cleavage roll calls concerned with judicial matters voted on between 1829 and 1844. This bill increased the number of the state's supreme court justices elected in Joint Meeting to five and authorized them to preside over the circuit courts in each county.[60] In an instance where the Whig legislative majority would be able to fill these newly created posts with deserving partisans, Democratic opposition to this bill is not surprising.

Legislative response to social enactments fails to reveal any commitment by New Jersey's legislators, either as a united body or as representatives of political parties, to the multitude of reform movements that flourished in the Jacksonian period. In no way does legislative voting behavior suggest differing party attitudes toward the role of government in setting "the moral norms of society."[61] Roll-call analysis does show that certain parts of the state remained relatively consistent in their stance on certain questions. Counties in the western part of the state, for example, stood against a progressive common school law and the abolition of imprisonment for debt. It is quite apparent, however, that legislative parties were not a decisive force in the area of social legislation. Only rarely did they serve even the constituent function that at other times manifested itself.

Generally, social questions that elicited partisan voting behavior involved matters that directly affected the relative strength of the Democrats and their opposition in the state. Disagreement in these instances did not reflect differing party attitudes toward the need for social reform, but rather the desire of both sides to protect their organizations in order to compete effectively for political power. This same concern contributed in part to instances of party voting engendered by national fiscal resolutions, general banking and currency policy, the Joint Companies, and, after 1834, incorporation proposals for banks and manufacturing companies. In simple terms, where party as interest group was somehow affected by legislative decisions, then legislative parties consciously operated as meaningful determinants in the decision-making process.

Notes

1. Like most states, the abolitionist and the temperance movements took place outside of the formal political process. Legislation dealing with such matters as military reform, religious rights, and mechanics lien laws, although analyzed, are not presented in this chapter. Roll calls on these matters were few. The voting patterns that they produced do not contradict the patterns that are discussed in this chapter nor do they alter its conclusions. Tables in Appendix A summarize voting on these roll calls.

2. Nelson G. Burr, *Education in New Jersey, 1630–1871* (Princeton, New Jersey: 1942), pp. 250–69, indicates the nature of this support. Burr's account of the common-school movement in New Jersey was most helpful in providing necessary background on this subject. For further evidence of bipartisan support, *see Newark Daily Advertiser*, 17 January 1838; *J.N.J.L.C.*, 58th sess., 1st sitting, 1834, pp. 4–17; *J.N.J.L.C.*, 63d sess., 1st sitting, 1839, pp. 109–17; *P.N.J.G.A.*, 53d sess., 2d sitting, 1829, p. 95; *P.N.J.G.A.*, 54th sess., 1st sitting, 1830, p. 77; *P.N.J.G.A.*, 62d sess., 1st sitting, 1838, p. 19.

3. The legislation of 1816 authorized the state treasurer to invest $15,000 arising from the payment of the funded debt of the United States in various stocks and the legislature to appoint trustees composed of the governor, the speaker of the Assembly, the vice-president in Council, the attorney general, and the secretary of state to oversee the fund. In 1829 the legislature decided that $20,000 should be appropriated annually out of the income of the fund to support the schools of the state. This was increased to $30,000 in 1838. *P.N.J.G.A.,* 54th sess., 1st sitting, 1830, pp. 92–93; *N.J.L.,* 62d sess., 1838.

4. Burr, p. 252.

5. Ibid., pp. 250–51. The December 1828 and January 1829 issues of the *Trenton Emporium,* for example, contained copies of such appeals.

6. *P.N.J.G.A.,* 53d sess., 2d sitting, 1829, p. 95.

7. 1829 Council, U.R.C. 38, p. 98; 1829 Assembly, C.R.C. 42, p. 317.

8. *N.J.L.,* 53d sess., 1829, pp. 105–108. Each township was to elect trustees who were to choose school buildings and hire teachers. They were directed to report annually to the Trustees of the School Fund, who in turn, were to report annually to the legislature.

9. *P.N.J.G.A.,* 53d sess., 2d sitting, 1829, p. 98.

10. Levine, "Party-in-the Legislature," pp. 361–62, describes fully voting on township support.

11. 1830 Assembly, C.R.C. 97, p. 280; U.R.C. 38, p. 295: 1830 Council, U.R.C. 40, p. 107.

12. *N.J.L.,* 54th sess., 1830, pp. 118–21.

13. *N.J.L.,* 55th sess., 1831, pp. 145–47.

14. 1831 Council, U.R.C. 46, p. 116.

15. 1831 Assembly, C.R.C. 63, p. 229. Assembly cleavage roll call 62 was on a motion to give this bill a third reading. Voting on it revealed almost the identical pattern as on roll call 63 and so was not included in the discussion.

16. Party indices of likeness on roll calls 62 and 63 were 98 and 93, respectively.

17. *Newark Daily Advertiser,* 16–22 January 1838.

18. *N.J.L.,* 62d sess., 1838, pp. 246–51.

19. 1838 Assembly, U.R.C. 74, p. 637: 1838 Council, U.R.C. 89, p. 343.

20. 1838 Assembly, C.R.C. 69, p. 521; C.R.C. 71, p. 524. There were five other cleavage roll calls on this bill: C.R.C. 68, p. 520; C.R.C. 70, p. 523; C.R.C. 72, p. 525; C.R.C. 76, p. 529; C.R.C. 121, p. 635. Party indices of likeness on these roll calls were in the middle range, that is, 47, 25, 56, 77, and 60, respectively. The content of these roll calls was not made clear in the text. It thus became difficult to assess their significance.

21. This analysis has included voting behavior on the major legislation on education in the period as defined by Burr. Other legislation relating to education as well as voting on those measures discussed in this chapter are summarized in Appendix A.

22. Examples of the recommendations of governors are: *J.N.J.L.C.,* 55th sess.,

204   THE BEHAVIOR OF STATE LEGISLATIVE PARTIES

1st sitting, 1831, p. 12; *P.N.J.G.A.*, 61st sess., 1st sitting, 1837, pp. 121–29; and *J.N.J.L.C.*, 62d sess., 1st sitting, 1838, pp. 12–18.

23. *P.N.J.G.A.*, 64th sess., 2d sitting, 1840, p. 464.

24. *P.N.J.G.A.*, 66th sess., 2d sitting, 1842, pp. 594–95.

25. 1842 Assembly C.R.C. 22, p. 350; C.R.C. 23, p. 351; C.R.C. 96, p. 637. James Leiby, *Charity and Correction in New Jersey, A History of State Welfare Institutions* (New Brunswick, New Jersey: Rutgers University Press, 1967), p. 51. Leiby points to the influence of Dorothea Dix in persuading the legislators to pass the bill.

26. Ershkowitz, "New Jersey Politics," p. 256; *P.N.J.G.A.*, 55th sess., 1st sitting, 1831, pp. 12–21; *P.N.J.G.A.*, 56th sess., 1st sitting, 1832, pp. 12–21.

27. In 1830 the Assembly voted against postponing the prison bill (roll call 86, p. 261) and approved the engrossed version of the bill (roll call 95, p. 279). Party indices of likeness on these two roll calls were 98 and 80, respectively. Consideration of the bill was postponed in Council by a 9–4 margin, C.R.C. 42, p. 116. In 1831 the Assembly agreed to postpone consideration of the bill (roll call 57, p. 218). A party index of likeness of 89 was recorded on this roll call. During the 1832 Assembly, the motion to postpone the bill was narrowly defeated (roll call 58, p. 254). The motion to engross the bill was then defeated by a 19–26 margin (roll call 59, p. 255). Party indices of likeness on these roll calls were 93 and 98, respectively.

28. *Newark Daily Advertiser,* 24 January and 1 February 1833.

29. 1833 Assembly, C.R.C. 36, p. 353, and C.R.C. 17, p. 279, were on preliminary-passage votes with voting alignments similar to those on the final passage roll call.

30. *N.J.L.,* 57th sess., 1833, pp. 95–97.

31. 1833 Assembly, C.R.C. 49, p. 397.

32. *Washington Whig* (Bridgeton), 2 March 1833.

33. 1833 Assembly, C.R.C. 62, p. 431; C.R.C. 64, p. 444; C.R.C. 68, p. 451. *N.J.L.,* 57th sess., 1833, p. 151.

34. For example, *see Emporium and True American,* 17 August 1838. Between 1834 and 1839 ten separate appropriations, each approved by the unanimous votes of the state's legislators, were authorized. In this manner over $190,000 was allocated for prison construction. Only in 1841 did the prison again become a subject of partisan disagreement in the Assembly. At issue was the competence of the keeper of the prison and the question of whether to appoint a financial agent for the institution. The mean party index of likeness on the ten roll calls involving these matters was 22. Democrats were particularly cohesive, although in the minority. The roll calls reveal that the present keeper who was coming under attack was a Democratic appointee. This fact explains the partisan tinge given to these deliberations. The specific roll calls included 1841 Assembly, C.R.C. 3, p. 69; C.R.C. 6, p. 261; C.R.C. 7, p. 263; C.R.C. 11, p. 291; C.R.C. 13, p. 297; C.R.C. 14, p. 368; C.R.C. 15, p. 369; C.R.C. 16, p. 372; C.R.C. 17, p. 373; C.R.C. 49, p. 518. Leiby, pp. 39–43, points out that the prison was often a political issue after the 1850s.

35. Leiby, p. 36. The discrepancy between 150 cells and 300 cells is due to the difference between the actual terms of the prison bill and subsequent architect's plans.

36. Michael A. Lutzker, "Abolition of Imprisonment for Debt in New Jersey, *Proceedings of the New Jersey Historical Society* 84, no. 4 (January 1966): 1–29, is the chief source on this subject.

37. *N.J.L.,* 54th sess., 1830, pp. 114–16.

38. Lutzker, pp. 17–18.

39. 1830 Council, C.R.C. 21, p. 74; 1830 Assembly, C.R.C. 77, pp. 236.

40. David M. Schneider, *The History of Public Welfare in New York State, 1609–1866* (Chicago: University of Chicago Press, 1938), pp. 143–47. Lutzker also points to more progressive developments in other states.

41. Lutzker, pp. 16–20.

42. *N.J.L.,* 60th sess., 1836, p. 387.

43. 1835 Assembly, C.R.C. 57, p. 408.

44. Five Council roll calls dealt with this bill in the 1841 session; roll calls 26, 27, 28, 41, and 42, located on pp. 277, 277, 278, 300, and 301, respectively, of the journal for the 1841 Council. The bill was approved in Council but did not come up for vote in the Assembly.

45. *P.N.J.G.A.,* 66th sess., 2d sitting, 1842, p. 382–88.

46. 1842 Assembly, C.R.C. 47, p. 470; C.R.C. 77, p. 578. Party indices of likeness on these two roll calls indicate some measure of partisan division on whether to abolish imprisonment for debt. As defined by their votes on these roll calls, however, neither party consistently took a liberal stance. On roll call 47 the Democrats voted 14–5 for this more restrictive amendment, while the Whigs voted 10–18 against it. On roll call 77, defeated by a 22–28 margin, seventeen of the twenty-two votes in favor of the more restrictive position were cast by Whigs, with the negative votes evenly divided between the two parties.

47. 1842 Assembly, C.R.C. 79, p. 582.

48. Lutzker, p. 23; *Newark Daily Advertiser,* 6 October 1843.

49. *Newark Daily Advertiser,* 7 October 1843.

50. Lutzker, p. 24.

51. 1843 Assembly, C.R.C. 21, p. 360; C.R.C. 22, p. 361; C.R.C. 23, p 365; C.R.C. 24, p. 367; C.R.C. 25, p. 368; C.R.C. 26, p. 370; C.R.C. 27, p. 371; C.R.C. 28, p. 372; C.R.C. 29, p. 373; C.R.C. 30, p. 374; C.R.C. 32, p. 381; C.R.C. 33, p. 382; C.R.C. 34, p. 384; C.R.C. 35, p. 385; C.R.C. 36, p. 387; C.R.C. 38, p. 396; C.R.C. 40, p. 421; C.R.C. 41, p. 422; C.R.C. 42, p. 426; C.R.C. 43, p. 427; C.R.C. 44, p. 428; C.R.C. 45, p. 428.

52. 1842 Assembly, C.R.C. 45, p. 428.

53. 1843 Council C.R.C. 52, p. 253; C.R.C. 53, p. 254; C.R.C. 54, p. 255; C.R.C. 55, p. 255; C.R.C. 56, p. 255; C.R.C. 58, p. 258–59; C.R.C. 60, p. 263; C.R.C. 62, p. 264; C.R.C. 75, p. 278.

54. *New Jersey State Gazette,* 11 February 1843; *Newark Daily Advertiser,* 16 February 1843.

206 THE BEHAVIOR OF STATE LEGISLATIVE PARTIES

55. Bebout, Introduction, p. 75; *Proceedings 1844*, pp. 429, 615.

56. *Proceedings 1844*. Rosalind Branning, *Pennsylvania Constitutional Development* (Pittsburgh: University of Pittsburgh Press, 1960), also indicates that such reforms were common to this period.

57. In the Assembly, 74 of the 153 roll calls on judicial legislation were of the unanimous variety, while in the Council, 101 of 138 were.

58. An exception is *Newark Daily Advertiser*, 14 January 1833.

59. In 1836, for example, a motion to postpone consideration of Joseph Scott's revision of the Orphan's Court was approved by a 25–18 margin (Assembly cleavage roll call 82, p. 540), resulting in an index of party likeness of 45. In 1842 three bills involving judicial matters elicited moderate partisan responses. One bill concerned the selection of jurors, another the responsibilities of the sheriffs, and the third dealt with the jurisdiction of the court for small causes. Only two of the five roll calls concerning these measures dealt with attitudes about the judicial process (roll calls 40, 41, 42, 91, and 93). Assembly roll call 41, p. 451, was on a motion to amend the act relative to jurors so as to change the salary of people serving on grand juries from one dollar to one cent a day. This motion was defeated by a 21–25 margin, the Democrats voting 1–15 and the Whigs, 20–10. More interesting was the vote on Assembly roll call 93, p. 632, the passage of an act to regulate the collection of moneys. This measure provided that all litigation involving the claims of under $100 remain under the jurisdiction of the court of small causes. It also prohibited a plaintiff from moving his case to a higher court if the defendant had a number of cases pending where the total claims together exceeded the $100 limit. This bill was passed by a 36–12 vote, with the Democratic minority voting 20–0 in favor of it. Levine, "Party-in-the Legislature," pp. 385–386, provides other examples of partisan voting behavior.

60. *N.J.L.*, 58th sess., 1838, pp. 61–64: 1838 Assembly, C.R.C. 50, p. 461.

61. Ershkowitz and Shade, "Consensus or Conflict," p. 617; and Formisano, *The Birth of Mass Political Parties*, pp. 137–64, both argue that these attitudes existed. The New Jersey experience, however, offers no support for such arguments.

8
Legislative Voting Behavior: Party Legislation

Although over time legislative parties assumed a constituent role in the decision-making process, factors other than party also influenced legislative voting behavior. A particular range of questions concerned directly with the ability of parties to win elections and to enjoy the perquisites of power, however, consistently elicited conscious partisan responses from state legislators. Deliberations involving government printing contracts, elections, gerrymandering proposals, and resolutions on national issues involved state party organizations and party activists as definable interests. Like Joint Meeting appointments, cohesive party voting on these matters indicates the close ties between legislative

THE BEHAVIOR OF STATE LEGISLATIVE PARTIES

parties and state organizations when obvious partisan advantage was at stake.

I

The distribution of government printing contracts was an important source of patronage at the disposal of the legislature. Rather than relying on a state printing office, the Council and the Assembly, by joint resolution, awarded the printing of the laws, the legislative journals, bills and special messages, and even court proceedings to private printing firms.

Legislative voting behavior on resolutions concerned with the public printing as well as the political affiliations of those firms that received jobs indicates that the majority party in the legislature utilized printing contracts to reward publishers of newspapers that defended its actions and campaigned for its candidates. In five legislative sessions, the minority party offered little resistance to the choices made by the majority party. No doubt agreed upon in caucus, the selection of firms to handle the public printing received the unanimous approval of the legislature.[1] In those instances where divisive behavior was evident, the legislators' partisan identities clearly accounted for voting alignments. The mean party index of likeness on the thirty-five Assembly, cleavage roll calls recorded between 1829 and 1844 concerned with the distribution of printing contracts was 25. On both sides, partisan cohesion improved somewhat after 1833.[2] As one newspaper editor noted, "resolutions disposing of the public printing" were matters "upon which the strength of parties . . . [were] tested."[3]

Between 1829 and 1844, twenty-seven different firms obtained government printing contracts. All but two published newspapers, thirteen of which were affiliated with the National Republicans and then Whigs and twelve of which supported the Democrats. During the eight years of National Republican and Whig dominance, publishers of newspapers loyal to these parties received thirty-four of the thirty-seven printing contracts extended by the legislature. During the eight years of Democratic control, publishers of Democratic papers garnered twenty-six of the thirty-three contracts awarded.[4]

Certain publishers received preferential treatment. S. L. B. Baldwin, of the *Somerset Whig* (Somerville), for instance, was awarded contracts to print the proceedings of the Council for the 1838, 1839, and 1840 sessions and the state's laws for the 1842 session. Similarly Josiah Harrison, publisher and editor of the *Camden Republican,* and the publishers of the *New Jersey Journal* (Elizabeth), the *Newark Daily Advertiser,* and the *New Jersey State Gazette* (Trenton), all Whig newspapers, each received at least three contracts during the years of Whig control. For the Democrats, Joseph Justice, publisher and editor of the *Emporium and True American* (Trenton) was awarded the job of printing the Assembly records for the 1830 session and the state's laws for the 1830, 1831, 1832, 1834, and 1835 sessions. Bernard Connolly, of the *Monmouth Democrat* (Freehold), and James E. Gore, of the *Somerset Messenger* (Somerville), also were the recipients of at least three contracts.

II

Deliberations over the distribution of the public printing, like Joint Meeting appointments, clearly affected party activists in their efforts to wage successful election campaigns and to maintain efficient party organizations. These same concerns account for the interest of party legislators in the enactment of measures involving the creation of new townships and counties. When in the majority, both sides, in caucus, concocted elaborate gerrymandering schemes in order to reshape election districts so as to guarantee the preponderance of voters loyal to their cause in particular geographic areas. By establishing new townships where the electorate was known to be friendly, parties helped themselves by increasing their representation on the county board of freeholders and by filling local township offices with loyal partisans. Even more significant, by carving new counties out of existing ones, the major parties in New Jersey altered the balance of political strength in the legislature by insuring victory for their candidates in the elections needed to fill newly created Council and Assembly seats.

To be sure, not all proposals involving the creation of townships and counties or the redrawing of boundary lines elicited partisan responses.[5] Sectional loyalty and local self-interest were often key factors in deciding upon such legislation.[6] Prior to 1833, even in cases where party interests seemingly were involved, legislators occasionally found it difficult to respond as loyal partisans.[7] Moreover, in a large number of cases there was virtual unanimity in favor of proposed legislation (Table 25). Usually, however, where the potential political strength of the Democrats or their opposition was at stake, party representatives in the legislature, whether in the minority or the majority, voted to protect party interests.

Partisan efforts to reshape election districts and to create new counties were most intense in those sessions where legislative party majorities had been achieved after years of failure. During the 1838 and 1844 Assembly sessions, for example, more township and county bills were considered than in any other years between 1829 and 1844. The 1838 session marked the first time since 1833 that the Whigs achieved majorities in both houses of the legislature. Democratic majorities in 1844 were that party's first since 1837.

The address of the Democratic state convention of September 1838 reviled the Whig majority for creating the county of Mercer during the 1838 legislative session "at

TABLE 25

County and Township Roll Call Distribution, 1829-1844 Assemblies

Roll Call content	No. Unan. bills	No. Unan. R.C.s	No. Cleav. bills	No. Cleav. R.C.s	Mean Party Index of likeness on Cleav. R.C.s by category
New Townships*	13	14	17	60	15
New Counties*	--	--	10	33	26
New Cities*	5	6	--	--	--
Supplementary Townsp.**	11	11	6	6	51
Supplementary County**	9	11	6	8	37
Supplementary Cities**	11	14	6	8	40
General Matters***	--	--	4	7	30
TOTAL:	49	56	49	122	24

*Refer to bills that call for the formation of new townships, counties, and cities.

**Refer to supplementary bills to previous acts that dealt with the formation of cities, townships, and counties. These might involve the laying out of streets, changes in representation in the legislature, and the like.

***Refers to general legislation regarding the formation of townships, counties, and cities. Such matters will be discussed in the course of this chapter.

the dictation of a party caucus—by a party vote—purely for party purposes."[8] The return to power for the first time since 1833 not only explains the creation of Mercer, but also Whig attempts to create two new townships. Sixteen of the twenty-one cleavage roll calls relating to townships and counties decided upon in the Assembly involved the division of Harrington Township in Bergen County into two townships; the division of Galloway Township in Atlantic into two townships; and the creation of Mercer County from parts of Hunterdon, Burlington, Middlesex, and Somerset. The mean party index of likeness on the five roll calls resulting in the division of Harrington was 16. On the three roll calls involving the division of Galloway, it was 20, and on the eight roll calls dealing with Mercer it was 19.[9] Whether on passage votes, amendments concerning boundary lines, or motions to strike out whole sections of bills, the two parties always voted on the opposite sides of the questions. As might be expected, the Whig majority supported these gerrymandering proposals, while the Democratic minority stood opposed.

An identical situation occurred in Council. Except on a single roll call concerned with deciding upon a name for the new township to be created by the division of Galloway, the votes on these three bills found the Democrats and the Whigs in complete opposition to each other. On the six roll calls relating to these bills, party indices of likeness with one exception were 0. In that instance, the final passage of the Mercer County bill, it reached 10.[10]

The creation of Mercer by the Whigs proved to be an astute move, for that county returned only Whigs to the legislature for the next six years. Throughout the 1839–1843 legislative sessions, the Whigs, always in control, attempted similar gerrymandering schemes to strengthen their position on both the township and county levels. The creation of Hudson County and the division of Harrington Township in Bergen County, accomplished during the 1840 session, for instance, improved Whig prospects. The

Harrington bill, though voted upon and apparently approved by both houses during the 1839 session, did not become a law until 1840. Eighteen Assembly roll calls and five Council roll calls related to this bill were voted upon during the 1839 and 1840 sessions. In each instance Whig and Democratic legislators opposed each other. Always the Whig majority voted in favor of the bill; always the Democratic minority voted against it. The mean party index of likeness for the Council roll calls was 2 and for the Assembly roll calls it was 17. In both houses, the final passage votes on the bill produced mean party indices of likeness of 0.[11]

The frequency with which the Whigs attempted to improve their political position in the state through the enactment of township and county legislation fell off somewhat after 1840. Continued Whig success at the polls no doubt minimized the need to reshape township and county lines. The return to power of the Democrats in 1844, however, quickened the pace at which such legislation was introduced to a frenzy.

Democratic achievements in 1844 were truly impressive. Back in power for the first time since 1837, Democratic legislators created six new townships, redrew the boundary lines of several others, and carved Camden County out of part of Gloucester. Voting on these measures as well as on related legislation was along strict party lines.

Twenty-three Assembly, cleavage roll calls were taken on legislation involving the formation or the reshaping of eight townships. The mean party index of likeness on these roll calls was 9. On only one of these bills was the index on the final-passage roll call over 13.[12] A mean party index of likeness of 8 was recorded on four roll calls concerned with the creation of Camden County.[13]

Voting on a general measure designed to repeal an 1833 act supplement to an act relative to incorporations also reflects the same partisan interest in gerrymandering proposals. One preliminary passage vote, one amendment, and the final passage vote all registered party indices of likeness of 0. In each instance, the Whigs voted to prevent the enactment of this measure, while the Democrats voted to insure its passage.[14] The bill itself repealed an 1833 law that had required notice of applications to alter county or township lines to be advertised in the state's newspapers for six weeks prior to their presentation in the legislature.[15] Commenting on its passage, a writer for one Whig newspaper called its enactment

> an OUTRAGE. . . . [H]ow the majority [Democrats] can justify it, to their consciences and their constituents, is more than I can imagine. They knew six weeks ago, what county and township lines they wished and intended to alter, and the only possible reason for not advertising in time, must have been that they feared opposition which would have been incited by a knowledge of their intentions. . . . They feared the people—and therefore determined to wait until the close of the session, then *repeal the act* which requires notice to be given, and so introduce and pass their party projects with a haste which is in itself a proof of their unjust and outrageous character.[16]

As charged in these remarks and as demonstrated by their legislative performance during the 1844 session, Democrats took the initiative to strengthen their political position in the state. In pursuing such a program, however, they were no more at fault than their Whig predecessors. Quite simply, the enactment of legislation aimed at the redistribution of the state's electorate was part of the calculated efforts of both legislative parties, when in the majority, to guarantee the continued success of their state organizations at the polls.[17]

III

It is not surprising that party interest in winning elections also accounts for the close attention given by legislative parties to deliberations over election laws and disputed elections. Between 1829 and 1844 two major disputed elections were debated in the Council and the Assembly.[18] One involved the Congressional election of 1838, known in New Jersey history as the *Broad Seal War,* While the other concerned a state Assembly contest in Cumberland county. Legislative activity in both instances reveals the full and conscious influence of legislative parties on the decision-making process.

The 1838 Congressional election in New Jersey was a cause of great controversy in the state. Complete election returns indicated that five Democrats and one Whig had won seats in the U.S. House of Representatives, but William Pennington, the Whig governor responsible for validating the returns, exercised his prerogative before the votes from two Democratic townships had been reported. Pennington's action resulted in the election of six Whig Congressmen. The U.S. House of Representatives, containing a Democratic majority, refused to seat these individuals and recommended that the five Democrats and one Whig who had received the most votes be declared duly elected. Roll calls voted upon during the 1840 New Jersey legislative session concerning this dispute pertained to the decision of the House and to Pennington's role in the affair. With the reputation of their titular leader at stake and with the question of party control of the state's Congressional delegation still undecided, the Whigs, possessors of a three-seat advantage in the Council and a thirteen-seat margin in the Assembly, voted to protect their party's interests. At the same time, the Democratic minority, anxious to affirm the correctness of the Congressional decision to seat five of their candidates, opposed the passage of a series of resolutions that condemned the Congressional decision and that defended Pennington's action.

The various roll calls in both houses on these measures involved the presentation of documents relating to the case, decisions as to whether the lists of illegal voters should be printed, deliberations over Pennington's message that dealt with the affair, and the resolutions themselves. On twenty-three of the twenty-seven Council roll calls concerning these matters, party indices of likeness of 0 were recorded each time. The mean party index of likeness on all twenty-seven roll calls was 5. All but two of the twenty-two Assembly roll calls involving the election recorded party indices of likeness of 0. The indices recorded on the other two roll calls were 5 and 3, respectively.[19]

The disputed returns from one of the two townships, Millville in Cumberland County, also set off a fight over the seating of that county's Assembly delegation during the 1839 session. It, too, was decided along party lines. The Whig majority in the Assembly voted to seat a Whig candidate for a Cumberland Assembly seat even though irregularities in both the investigation of the election and in the counting of returns cast serious doubt over his claim to office. Each of the three Assembly roll calls on this matter recorded party indices of likeness of 0 as did three of the four Council roll calls on the same subject.[20]

The enactment of election laws, to the degree that they affected the political fortunes of the Whigs and Democrats, also evoked partisan disagreement. Forty-four Council roll calls pertaining to such legislation were voted upon between 1829 and 1844, mostly after 1838. Only five were decided by the unanimous votes of the members of that house. The mean party index of likeness on the remaining thirty-nine roll calls was 19. On twenty of these roll calls, an index of 0 was recorded each time. Forty-eight roll calls on election laws were also voted upon in the Assembly. Here six were the subject of unanimous votes, while forty-two occasioned noticeable disagreement. The mean party index of likeness on these forty-two roll calls was 27.[21]

The eleven unanimous votes recorded in the Council and the Assembly concerned the detailing of election dates, outlining procedures by which voters could exercise their franchise, and deciding upon the eligibility of voters.

Although such matters were an essential part of the electoral process the fact that decisions on these particular measures did not affect the two contesting parties in different ways explains the lack of division that they caused.[22] Those roll calls that elicited cleavage votes, however, directly involved alterations of the rules of the game or introduction of procedures that favored the party that happened to be in the majority in the legislature. Generally, the determination of these questions generated cohesive party responses on the part of New Jersey's lawmakers.

The activities of the 1843 and the 1844 legislative sessions provide the clearest examples of such partisan behavior. Until 1842 New Jersey was one of a small number of states that had continued to elect its Congressmen by the general-ticket method. A federal law of that year sought to abolish this procedure and ordered that all states adopt the single-member, district method for electing Congressmen. Each state was to be divided into specific Congressional districts, with one representative to be elected from each district.[23]

During the first sitting of the 1843 session, the Whigs, with a majority of two in the Council and eight in the Assembly, responded to the federal mandate by enacting a law prescribing the time and the manner of holding elections for the state's Congressmen. As arranged by the Whigs, the measure created five districts that apparently isolated the Democrats while guaranteeing the election of four Whig Congressmen.[24] The Democratic minority, quite aware of Whig intentions, made an unsuccessful attempt to alter the formation of these districts. Voting in the Council and the Assembly reflected the self-interest of both parties on this matter. Two roll calls were taken in the Assembly on the bill. The first was on a motion to postpone consideration of it to the next legislature; the second was on its passage. The motion for postponement was defeated by a 32–22 margin, while the bill was passed by the identical vote. Party indices of likeness on both bills were 3.

Eleven roll calls related to this bill were voted upon in the Council. Aside from the passage vote, these included motions for postponement, amendments to reshape the districts, as well as some procedural motions. In each instance, all of the Democrats opposed all of the Whigs that cast ballots.[25]

In 1844 the Democrats, with a six-seat advantage in the Council and a twelve-seat margin in the Assembly, redressed the injustice done their cause by the Whigs. In short, the Democrats rewrote the 1843 measure concerned with the establishment of Congressional election districts and fashioned a new bill that apparently favored their interests.[26] Two Council roll calls were taken on this bill. The first, an amendment to the bill's first section, resulted in a party index of likeness of 78; while the passage vote recorded an index of 0. Three roll calls were voted upon in the Assembly. Each of these votes resulted in a party index of likeness of 0.[27]

Sectional pressures occasionally took precedence over party demands in the determination of election laws. In particular, proposals that altered the representation of designated counties in the legislature were usually decided on sectional lines. During the 1830 Assembly session, for instance, four roll calls were taken on a bill concerning the representation of counties in the Assembly. This bill authorized the counties of Sussex, Warren, Essex, Hunterdon, Burlington, Gloucester, and Middlesex to increase the size of their Assembly delegations by one. It also provided that, following the next census, each county should send one assemblyman for each of its 6,000 inhabitants. No county, however, was to have its representation reduced, nor was any county to have more than five assemblymen, regardless of its population.[28]

With the exception of Bergen, whose delegates consistently voted in favor of the bill, the seven counties whose representation was to be increased supported this measure, while the remaining six counties voted against it.

Aside from the vote on a motion to strike out part of the bill's second section, which prohibited any county from having more than five representatives, the county configurations of those that stood to benefit from this bill against those counties that did not receive an increase in representation were far more significant than party. The mean index of likeness for these two county groups on these roll calls was 14. Party indices of likeness on these same roll calls never dropped below 80.[29]

The desire to increase the political power of one's own county or section in relation to other parts of the state also resulted in localized voting behavior on similar proposals during the 1837 and 1838 legislative sessions. That party interest, however, was usually the chief determinant in the passage of laws involving representation and the electoral process can not be denied.[30]

IV

Legislative parties were also extremely active with respect to the enactment of resolutions concerning national affairs. Between 1829 and 1844 the legislature took it upon itself to approve resolutions dealing not only with the fiscal policies of Andrew Jackson and Martin Van Buren, but also others concerning a wide variety of national issues. In 1830, for instance, resolutions were voted upon involving the right and the responsibility of the national government to enact protective tariffs and the right of an individual state to adopt and to act upon its own construction of the U.S. Constitution. One year later, a resolution was enacted that approved of the nomination of Andrew Jackson for the Presidency. During other years, resolutions on the government's public land policy, U.S. relations with France, the actions of South Carolina during the nullification controversy, federal tariff policy, and proposed revision of the U.S. Constitution were also considered. In 1844, even a resolution that demanded that the Congress refund to Andrew Jackson a $1,000 fine that he had paid in 1815 for placing New Orleans under martial law was proposed and enacted by the legislature.[31]

Resolutions on national affairs took one of two forms. Most stated only a preference for a particular policy or individual. On occasion, after stating such a position, the resolutions "requested" the state's representatives and senators to support the stand taken by the legislature, regardless of their own preferences. With very few exceptions, all national resolutions, no matter their form, were determined along party lines.

Legislative activity on resolutions invariably was initiated by the majority party in the legislature with the aim of putting New Jersey on record as opposed to or in favor of national administration policy. Given the state of national politics in the 1830s and 1840s, resolutions enacted in years when the Democrats controlled the statehouse looked with favor on administration policy, while those framed in years of Whig dominance were negative in tone. Legislative committees controlled by the majority party insured that these matters would be presented on the floor for consideration and the party caucus was employed to guarantee the proper phrasing of the documents as well as the party's full support.[32] Voting in both the Council and the Assembly testifies to the efficacy of party discipline in these affairs. Forty-five of the fifty-one Assembly roll calls concerned with national personalities and programs were decided by cleavage votes. Voted upon during eleven legislative sessions between 1830 and 1844, these roll calls recorded a mean party index of likeness of 6. The situation in Council was just as spectacular. Here, twenty-six of thirty roll calls, voted upon during nine sessions, were the subject of cleavage votes. The mean party index of likeness on these twenty-six roll calls was 3.[33]

Except for Joint Meeting appointments, no other category of proposals voted upon between 1829 and 1844 evoked such a high degree of partisan response from New Jersey's legislators as did these resolutions. Nor is this surprising. These expressions of party unity between the state organization and the national party leadership served two functions. On one level, the efforts of the state parties, when in power, to align their state officially with the policies of their national party leadership was one way in which they could acknowledge their debt for political services rendered to them by their national organizations.[34] More important, in a political age dominated by the contest for the Presidency, when even local and state election campaigns were conducted primarily on the basis of allegiance to national personalities and programs, the identification between the state-party organizations and their national leadership was an indispensable feature of politics. The passage of resolutions by the majority party simply contributed to this process of identification. As one Whig partisan put it, when describing the passage of an 1834 resolution that supported Jackson's Bank policies, "the all-convincing argument employed" to persuade Democratic legislators to support the resolution, was "that to sustain the party, the party must sustain the General."[35]

The ability of legislative parties to marshal their forces when deliberating over legislation that affected state-party organizations did not go unnoticed in New Jersey. During the 1840 Democratic state convention, for instance, the major speaker remarked on the record of Whig achievement during the 1838, 1839, and 1840 legislative sessions. With particular emphasis on the disputed Congressional elections of 1838, he noted that

> their [Whig] political acts . . . have been one continued series of oppression and tyranny. Scarcely an act of public utility can be pointed to. To secure and perpetuate the power of the minority [Whigs] has been their constant end and aim. . . . They have formed new counties for the avowed purpose of perpetuating their ill-gotten power.

They have increased taxation. And to cap the climax of their iniquity and outrage, they have denied the independent voters of New Jersey the right to choose their representatives.[36]

Such comments appeared with great regularity during election campaigns in New Jersey up through 1844. Although differences over fiscal policy, the Joint Companies, and the actions of national political figures served as important state-campaign issues, both parties, with equal vigor, castigated each other for the enactment of pernicious "political acts." Invariably leveled by the minority party in any given year, it was common to find accusations that the majority party enacted legislation to serve its own interests at the expense of the people's rights. The usual charges included the creation of new counties and townships and the enactment of election laws that gave advantages to the party in power, the appointment of unqualified individuals to unnecessary positions solely on the basis of their partisan identities, and the careless and extravagant stewardship of the state's finances.[37]

Legislative voting behavior on the public printing, elections, gerrymandering proposals, national resolutions, and Joint Meeting appointments substantiates the claims of partisans made in the heat of battle. Substantive legislation rarely produced absolute party unity in the legislature. As activists, however, party legislators could see the need for concerted action on matters clearly affecting electoral success and organizational stability. On questions that obviously affected party as a distinct institution with its own special needs, they responded as partisans, unaffected by various other interests that at times demanded their attention.

Notes

1. Unanimous approval was given in the following sessions: 1835 Assembly, U.R.C. 27, p. 384. 1836 Assembly, U.R.C. 9, p. 135. 1839 Assembly, U.R.C. 28,

p. 411. 1840 Assembly, U.R.C. 41, p. 474. 1841 Assembly, U.R.C. 44, p. 609. Although no direct reference concerning the use of the caucus to agree upon printing contracts in advance could be found, the distribution of appointments, invariably involving printers loyal to the majority party in the legislature, suggests that decisions were reached there.

2. 1829 Assembly, C.R.C. 20, p. 253; C.R.C. 22, p. 257. 1831 Assembly, C.R.C. 56, p. 216; C.R.C. 66, p. 231. 1832 Assembly, C.R.C. 72, p. 290. 1835 Assembly, C.R.C. 44, p. 364. 1836 Assembly, C.R.C. 125, p. 650. 1837 Assembly, C.R.C. 8, p. 45; C.R.C. 9, p. 47; C.R.C. 11, p. 51; C.R.C. 12, p. 51; C.R.C. 13, p. 104; C.R.C. 14, p. 105; C.R.C. 15, p. 109; C.R.C. 41, p. 280; C.R.C. 67, p. 368; C.R.C. 68, p. 369. 1838 Assembly, C.R.C. 113, p. 616. 1839 Assembly, C.R.C. 76, p. 588. 1840 Assembly, C.R.C. 43, p. 321; C.R.C. 69, p. 430; C.R.C. 70, p. 431; C.R.C. 71, p. 432. 1841 Assembly, C.R.C. 20, p. 386; C.R.C. 48, p. 517. 1842 Assembly, C.R.C. 9, p. 222; C.R.C. 27, p. 372; C.R.C. 48, p. 472; C.R.C. 49, p. 473; C.R.C. 52, p. 485; C.R.C. 84, p. 600; C.R.C. 85, p. 600; C.R.C. 100, p. 645; C.R.C. 101, p. 647. 1843 Assembly, C.R.C. 5, p. 184. Excluding the five roll calls voted upon in 1829, 1831, and 1832, the mean party index of likeness on the remaining thirty roll calls becomes 20. No record exists of any roll calls concerning printing, either unanimous or cleavage, for the 1830, 1833, 1834, and 1844 sessions.

3. *Emporium and True American* (Trenton), 12 November 1836.

4. The Elmer T. Hutchinson collection on New Jersey's publishers and printers before 1850, located in the Rutgers University Library, proved an invaluable source for discovering the political affiliations of New Jersey's publishers. Notable exceptions to the pattern of partisan appointments were George Sherman, copublisher of the *New Jersey State Gazette* (Trenton), who was awarded the contract for publishing the law reports by the Democrats in three sessions, and Edward Sanderson, Whig publisher of the *New Jersey Journal* (Elizabeth) and assemblyman from Essex during the 1839 and 1840 sessions, who was awarded the contract to publish the chancery reports by the Democrats in three sessions. Sanderson, in fact, was awarded this contract in every session between 1833 and 1843.

5. Citizens in various parts of the state for a variety of reasons petitioned the legislature to create new townships or to redraw boundary lines. For instance, see *New Jersey State Gazette,* 5 January 1833. In this instance it was argued that a new county was needed because it was inconvenient for many people to travel to the old county seat. For a discussion of county formation in New Jersey, see Harris I. Effross, "Origins of Post-Colonial Counties in New Jersey," *Proceedings of the New Jersey Historical Society* 81, no. 1 (January 1963): 103–122.

6. As noted in Table 25, party was the most important factor in the first two categories. The bulk of cleavage roll calls concerned the creation of new townships and counties. Similar distribution occurred in the Council.

7. Levine, "Party-in-the Legislature," pp. 412–15, discusses instances of such behavior.

8. *Emporium and True American,* 21 September 1838.

9. 1838 Assembly, C.R.C. 15, p. 318; C.R.C. 25, p. 387; C.R.C. 26, p. 388; C.R.C. 27, p. 389; C.R.C. 30, p. 396; C.R.C. 31, p. 413; C.R.C. 44, p. 431; C.R.C. 46, p. 434; C.R.C. 48, p. 449; C.R.C. 62, p. 500; C.R.C. 73, p. 527; C.R.C. 74, p. 528; C.R.C. 77, p. 532; C.R.C. 78, p. 533; C.R.C. 79, p. 534; C.R.C. 81, p. 538.

10. 1838 Council, C.R.C. 16, p. 201; C.R.C. 18, p. 208; C.R.C. 23, p. 223; C.R.C. 24, p. 228; C.R.C. 26, p. 247; C.R.C. 27, p. 248.

11. No explanation for the delay exists in the legislature's records. The final passage vote in the 1840 Council is C.R.C. 3, p. 37. Assembly roll calls on the Harrington bill are as follows: 1839 Assembly, C.R.C. 28, p. 419; C.R.C. 29, p. 420; C.R.C. 30, p. 421; C.R.C. 39, p. 468; C.R.C. 40, p. 469; C.R.C. 53, p. 523; C.R.C. 54, p. 524; C.R.C. 55, p. 524; C.R.C. 61, p. 546. 1840 Assembly, C.R.C. 23, p. 230; C.R.C. 24, p. 231; C.R.C. 25, p. 232; C.R.C. 26, p. 236; C.R.C. 27, p. 237; C.R.C. 28, p. 250; C.R.C. 29, p. 254; C.R.C. 30, p. 254; C.R.C. 31, p. 257.

12. 1844 Assembly C.R.C. 10, p. 294; C.R.C. 14, p. 337; C.R.C. 25, p. 532; C.R.C. 42, p. 505; C.R.C. 45, p. 517; C.R.C. 48, p. 525; C.R.C. 62, p. 575; C.R.C. 86, p. 618; C.R.C. 93, p. 629; C.R.C. 94, p. 630; C.R.C. 95, p. 630; C.R.C. 96, p. 632; C.R.C. 97, p. 632; C.R.C. 122, p. 694; C.R.C. 125, p. 671; C.R.C. 126, p. 672; C.R.C. 127, p. 672; C.R.C. 128, p. 673; C.R.C. 129, p. 674; C.R.C. 130, p. 675; C.R.C. 131, p. 676; C.R.C. 132, p. 676; C.R.C. 133, p. 677.

13. 1844 Assembly, C.R.C. 55, p. 552; C.R.C. 64, p. 578; C.R.C. 65, p. 579; C.R.C. 66, p. 580.

14. 1844 Assembly, C.R.C. 72, p. 587; C.R.C. 111, p. 659; C.R.C. 112, p. 660.

15. *Newark Daily Advertiser,* 23 February 1844.

16. Ibid. In contrast to party voting on this measure, the Assembly also approved another general measure in nonpartisan fashion. The bill concerned a supplement to an act approved in 1798 concerning the incorporation of the inhabitants of townships and the designation of their powers. 1844 Assembly, C.R.C. 113, p. 661. The vote was 32–9, registering a party index of likeness of 95.

17. Effross, p. 122, concludes that "the number of county incorporation bills that passed by bare majorities along partisan lines indicates that the welfare of the residents in the projected counties was, perhaps, not the paramount consideration in their establishment. . . . Even the cogency of economic arguments for creating new counties was subordinated to party efforts for political aggrandizement."

18. Apparently there was some dispute at the outset of the 1830 Assembly session concerning the seating of John Vail, an Essex Whig who served in that session. C.R.C. 2, p. 13, of the 1830 Assembly records concerned a motion to accept the report of the committee in relation to the memorial of Isaac Miller contesting the right of Vail to a seat in the Assembly. No evidence exists as to what the contents of the report were. Vail, however, did take his seat. The Democrats voted 6–24 against accepting the committee report, while the National Republicans voted 10–1 in favor of acceptance. A party index of likeness of 29 was recorded on this roll call.

19. 1840 Council, C.R.C. 7–C.R.C. 31, pp. 124–153; C.R.C. 33, p. 173; C.R.C.

36, p. 183. 1840 Assembly, C.R.C. 4–C.R.C. 22, pp. 196–229; C.R.C. 33, p. 275; C.R.C. 34, p. 276; C.R.C. 40, p. 286.

20. 1839 Assembly, C.R.C. 3, p. 8; C.R.C. 5, p. 290; C.R.C. 6, p. 290. 1839 Council, C.R.C. 3, p. 107; C.R.C. 4, p. 109; C.R.C. 5, p. 110; C.R.C. 6, p. 110. McCormick, *History of Voting in New Jersey,* pp. 116–119, describes this dispute. The remaining Council roll call recorded a party index of likeness of 10.

21. 1830 Council, C.R.C. 19, p. 68; C.R.C. 40, p. 115. 1833 Council, C.R.C. 20, p. 213. 1838 Assembly C.R.C. 22, p. 211; C.R.C. 26, p. 247; C.R.C. 27, p. 248; C.R.C. 31, p. 299. 1839 Council, C.R.C. 37, p. 342; C.R.C. 39, p. 348; C.R.C. 40, p. 353. 1840 Council, C.R.C. 34, p. 181; C.R.C. 35, p. 182; C.R.C. 38, p. 187; C.R.C. 39, p. 187; C.R.C. 44, p. 213. 1841 Council, C.R.C. 3, p. 31; C.R.C. 4, p. 33. 1842 Council, C.R.C. 70, p. 307. 1843 Council, C.R.C. 4–C.R.C. 12, pp. 116–21; C.R.C. 66, p. 266; C.R.C. 69–C.R.C. 74, pp. 273–76. 1844 Council, C.R.C. 44, p. 295; C.R.C. 49, p. 314; C.R.C. 50, p. 315; C.R.C. 58, p. 399; C.R.C. 72, p. 422; C.R.C. 74, p. 425; C.R.C. 102, p. 460. 1830 Assembly, C.R.C. 75, p. 234; C.R.C. 76, p. 235; C.R.C. 78, p. 238; C.R.C. 79, p. 240; C.R.C. 102, p. 288. 1833 Assembly, C.R.C. 26, p. 296; C.R.C. 72, p. 461; C.R.C. 73, p. 464. 1835 Assembly, C.R.C. 62, p. 427. 1837 Assembly, C.R.C. 54, p. 319; C.R.C. 60, p. 333; C.R.C. 61, p. 334; C.R.C. 114, p. 531; C.R.C. 115, p. 532. 1838 Assembly, C.R.C. 49, p. 460; C.R.C. 100, p. 585. 1839 Assembly, C.R.C. 65, p. 550; C.R.C. 88, p. 619; C.R.C. 93, p. 626. 1840 Assembly, C.R.C. 41, p. 295; C.R.C. 46, p. 329; C.R.C. 48–C.R.C. 54, pp. 331–43. 1841 Assembly, C.R.C. 66, p. 631. 1842 Assembly, C.R.C. 10, p. 227; C.R.C. 74, p. 571; C.R.C. 83, p. 597. 1843 Assembly, C.R.C. 3, p. 183; C.R.C. 4, p. 108; C.R.C. 52, p. 455; C.R.C. 74, p. 497. 1844 Assembly, C.R.C. 85, p. 615; C.R.C. 88, p. 622; C.R.C. 92, p. 629; C.R.C. 101, p. 643; C.R.C. 107, p. 655.

22. For example, an act passed in 1837 to provide for the election of a United States congressman to replace Philemon Dickerson was approved by the unanimous votes of the legislators; 1837 Assembly, U.R.C. 11, p 98.

23. McCormick, *History of Voting in New Jersey,* p. 129.

24. The first district included the counties of Cape May, Cumberland, Salem, Gloucester, and Atlantic. Although Atlantic had always been a Democratic stronghold and Cumberland had gone Democratic in 1843, this district was considered to be safely in the Whig column. The second district included Mercer, Burlington, and Monmouth. Since its formation in 1839, Mercer had always elected Whigs to the legislature. Burlington had done likewise since 1838. That Monmouth had consistently supported the Democratic cause did not change the fact that this district was also considered to be "safe" for the Whigs. Similar preponderance of Whig strength was apparent in the composition of the fourth and fifth districts. The former included Somerset, Middlesex, and Morris, all counties that had consistently returned Whigs to the legislature since 1838. The latter included the Whig strongholds of Essex, Hudson, and Passaic, as well as Bergen, a county that had consistently voted Democratic since 1833. Only the third district gave an ostensible advantage to the Democrats. Lumped

together in this district were Hunterdon, Warren, and Sussex counties that had been at the core of Democratic strength in New Jersey since the late 1820s.

25. *See* footnote 21 for information on roll calls.

26. McCormick, *History of Voting in New Jersey*, p. 129. It is interesting to note that for all of their hard work, neither the Whig plan of 1843 nor the Democratic plan of 1844 proved successful. *See* Levine, "Party-in-the Legislature," pp. 427–28, for further discussion of partisan voting behavior on election laws.

27. 1844 Council, C.R.C. 58, p. 399; C.R.C. 72, p. 422. 1844 Assembly, C.R.C. 92, p. 629; C.R.C. 101, p. 643; C.R.C. 107, p. 655.

28. *N.J.L.*, 54th sess., 1830.

29. 1830 Assembly, C.R.C. 75, p. 234; C.R.C. 76, p. 235; C.R.C. 78, p. 238; C.R.C. 79, p. 240.

30. If the party indices of likeness on the six roll calls voted upon during the 1830, 1837, and 1838 sessions concerning county representation in the Assembly were excluded, the mean party index of likeness for the remaining thirty-six cleavage roll calls relating to election laws would be 19.

31. Resolutions appear in the law books of the following sessions; *N.J.L.*, 57th sess., 1833, pp. 167, 168, 170; *N.J.L.*, 58th sess., 1834, p. 177; *N.J.L.*, 59th sess., 1835, p. 12; *N.J.L.*, 60th sess., 1836, p. 29; *N.J.L.*, 62d sess., 1838, pp. 25–28; *N.J.L.*, 63d sess., 1839, p. 239; *N.J.L.*, 64th sess., 1840, pp. 137, 140; *N.J.L.*, 65th sess., 1841, p. 140; *N.J.L.*, 68th sess., 1844.

32. *Washington Whig* (Bridgeton), 18 January 1834; *Newark Daily Advertiser*, 10 February 1834; Jeremiah Leaming to Samuel Southard, 11 January 1834, Southard Papers, P.U.L.

33. 1831 Council, C.R.C. 24, p. 122. 1833 Council, C.R.C. 2, p. 31. 1834 Council, C.R.C. 3, p. 43; C.R.C. 4, p. 45; C.R.C. 13; p. 148. 1835 Council, C.R.C. 2, p. 40. 1836 Council, C.R.C. 5, p. 40; C.R.C. 11, p. 142; C.R.C. 12, p. 143. 1841 Council, C.R.C. 32–C.R.C. 38, pp. 294–98; C.R.C. 45, p. 303; C.R.C. 46, p. 304; C.R.C. 51, p. 312. 1842 Council, C.R.C. 22, p. 201; C.R.C. 24, p. 206; C.R.C. 25, p. 207; C.R.C. 30, p. 211. 1843 Council, C.R.C. 27, p. 183; C.R.C. 43, p. 240. 1844 Council, C.R.C. 1, p. 143. 1830 Assembly, C.R.C. 6, p. 68; C.R.C. 87, p. 268; C.R.C. 102, p. 288; C.R.C. 103, p. 291; C.R.C. 104, p. 291; C.R.C. 108; p. 196; C.R.C. 110, p. 298. 1831 Assembly, C.R.C. 53, p. 212. 1833 Assembly C.R.C. 5, p. 89; C.R.C. 6, p. 90. 1834 Assembly, C.R.C. 4, p. 225; C.R.C. 44, p. 447. 1835 Assembly, C.R.C. 4, p. 114; C.R.C. 9, p. 121; C.R.C. 10, p. 123; C.R.C. 11, p. 124; C.R.C. 12, p. 126; C.R.C. 13, p. 128. 1836 Assembly, C.R.C. 3–C.R.C. 9, pp. 96–109; C.R.C. 22, p. 273; C.R.C. 23, p. 274; C.R.C. 41, p. 364; C.R.C. 110, p. 615. 1838 Assembly, C.R.C. 12, p. 181. 1839 Assembly, C.R.C. 8, p. 306; C.R.C. 23, p. 405. 1841 Assembly, C.R.C. 20, p. 386; C.R.C. 23, p. 419; C.R.C. 24–C.R.C. 30, pp. 419–33; C.R.C. 62, p. 622; C.R.C. 73, p. 651. 1842 Assembly, C.R.C. 13, p. 313; C.R.C. 14, p. 319; C.R.C. 15, p. 320. 1843 Assembly, C.R.C. 6, p. 242.

34. The appointment of Dickerson and Southard to cabinet posts and the work of the Democratic Congressional majority during the Broad Seal controversy would be examples of this relationship.

35. *Newark Daily Advertiser,* 10 February 1834.

36. *Address of the Democratic State Convention Which Assembled at Trenton on the 20th May, 1840, as Reported by Colonel James C. Zabriskie, Chairman of the Committee* (n.p., 1840), p. 7.

37. A reading of extant accounts of county and state party conventions confirms this point. The *Emporium and True American* provides accounts of Democratic state conventions, while the *Newark Daily Advertiser* provides similar information for National Republican and Whig meetings. For instance, *see Emporium and True American,* 21 September 1833, 7 August and 21 September 1838, 4 October 1839, 19 February 1841; *Newark Daily Advertiser,* 7 October 1833, 24 September 1834, 3 and 6 October 1838 and 14 March and 2 October 1839; *To the Electors of the County of Somerset, 25 September 1831, signed and printed by the Republican Convention held in Somerville on this date* (n.p., 1831); *Address of the Democratic State Convention Which Assembled at Trenton on the 20th May, 1840;* and *Address of the Hon. Hugh J. Garland Before the Democratic Mass Convention Held at New Brunswick, New Jersey, 8 October 1840* (New Brunswick, New Jersey: 1840), which provide evidence of these charges. Occasionally the state's governors made reference to similar activity, for instance, *J.N.J.L.C.,* 65th sess., 1st sitting, 1841, p. 13.

9
Conclusions

This study of legislative parties confirms the importance of party competition in shaping manifestations of party behavior in the New Jersey legislature. By examining the development of party activities in the legislature and the interaction of legislative parties with their state-party organizations, it suggests important insights into party role, party organization, and government operation in a single state during the period of development of the second American party system.

New Jersey's legislators were products of a highly competitive two-party system. Operating within an electoral environment that provided virtually universal, adult, white-male suffrage and frequent elections, the major parties maintained efficient organizations in order to elect their candidates to state legislative posts as well as to contest for Congressional and Presidential office. Democrats and their opposition enjoyed equal success in obtaining legislative majorities between 1829 and 1844. All legislators were elected to office as either National Republicans, Whigs, or Democrats. Their career patterns indicate that they were recognized party activists whose legislative tenure was regulated by the party organizations in which they played significant roles.

A constitutional framework that provided a limited role for the governor and that designated the bicameral legislature the most powerful branch of state government gave legislators responsibility for organizing the legislature, for appointing national, state, and county officials, and for enacting legislation. The ability of the legislature to exercise its power was facilitated by the presence of a well-developed internal structure of leaders, rules, and committees.

In these circumstances, legislators with the same political identities employed the instrumentality of the caucus to organize themselves. The caucus structure was mixed and accessible from without, allowing for the participation of party leaders who were not legislators. This arrangement enabled legislative parties to overcome obstacles to cohesive action created by the high rate of turnover among legislators. Party representatives in the legislature were thus in a position to correlate their behavior to the specific needs of the larger party organizations to which they belonged.

Throughout the period, legislative parties effectively sustained discipline with respect to control over the machinery of government and to the selection of the governor. The majority party in the legislature utilized the caucus to guarantee election of partisans to the offices of the Council and the Assembly and to secure dominance on legislative committees. The appointment of the governor in Joint Meeting was also managed in similar fashion.

Although a perfect situation for the operation of

genuine party government existed, the nature of party influence on legislative behavior was contingent upon the specific issue under review and on the moment in time when it was considered. Mobilization of legislative parties to furnish the patronage needs of competitive state-party organizations appeared as early as 1829. Between 1829 and 1844 the most effective operation of legislative parties was apparent on questions that reflected an understanding of party as a distinct institution with its own interests and needs. Roll calls on appointments, election laws, disputed elections, gerrymandering proposals, the public printing, and resolutions on national political issues invariably produced the highest indices of party voting in the legislature. Partisan direction of the enactment of legislation, as manifested by the few references to caucus activities, referred exclusively to deliberations on such matters.

In terms of controlling legislative machinery and of meeting the obvious requirements of party organizations, legislative parties were constantly operating and increasingly efficient forces between 1829 and 1844. Improved partisan cohesion over time on the entire range of issues subject to roll-call vote, however, suggests that the impact of party on legislative voting behavior developed dynamically in ways not solely related to predictable reactions to organizational needs.

Over time, legislative parties became convenient mechanisms for mediating the demands of individuals and groups seeking legislative favors. The emergence of this constituent role became noticeable after 1832 as party alignments in the state stabilized and as legislative procedures became regularized. Party influence on legislative voting behavior became especially intense between 1838 and 1844.

The mobilization of legislative parties and their control of legislative machinery in behalf of party needs contributed to this process by establishing conditions that allowed the effect of party to be felt, whether intended or not, on virtually all questions before the legislature. In the absence of other organized agencies capable of affecting voting alignments, legislators of the same political affiliation who met together in caucus and in committee and who consciously coalesced on matters of party concern voted together as a matter of convenience on issues totally unrelated to practical partisan considerations.[1]

The engagement of legislative parties in activities essential to the structure and operation of the state's government was not completely accidental. Conscious efforts of party legislators to shape the content of substantive questions that engendered partisan disagreement among national and state party leaders also contributed to party involvement in the decision-making process. Although rarely achieving the extremely high levels of party voting occasioned by "party" legislation, after 1832 deliberations involving banking and currency, the Joint Companies, and corporate privilege revealed clear partisan division among legislators. Following the Panic of 1837, legislative parties, in line with the pronouncements of state-party leaders, opposed each other even more strongly on these issues. Sectional and local pressures prevented absolute party unity on these questions, yet, consciously engineered party division in the legislature on them coincided with the appearance of party influence in general on the entire range of matters before the legislature.

The active efforts of legislative parties to direct voting on selected substantive issues in part depended upon the degree to which particular proposals affected competitive state politics. Andrew Jackson's attack on the Bank of the United States provided an issue around which state parties established their identities. The accommodation of New Jersey's parties to national party orientations on corporate and fiscal policy dominated the state's election campaigns between 1832 and 1844 and encompassed the efforts of party legislators to enact legislation in accordance with these positions. Only when such legislation involved special interests did erosion of party unity occur.

Differences of opinion among legislators on these issues

232   THE BEHAVIOR OF STATE LEGISLATIVE PARTIES

particularly after 1837 also encouraged party voting in the legislature on relevant proposals. Careful attention to partisan identification and allegiance on these sensitive questions, for whatever the reasons, increased the likelihood that the consideration of pork-barrel legislation and other nonpartisan matters would also feel the effect of party as a matter of course.[2]

Party influence on legislative voting behavior in New Jersey corroborates the substantive findings of a recent investigation of party voting based on a limited number of roll calls dealing with banking, corporation policy, and social reform in six state legislatures between 1833 and 1844. Although confined to these few issues and undertaken without consideration of the political and constitutional settings in which party legislators in different states operated, its results indicate that Democratic and Whig legislators opposed each other consistently on these questions.[3] Unlike the conclusions of this comparative study, however, the New Jersey experience does not confirm the thesis that partisan voting behavior on selected roll calls reflected the existence of "contrasting belief systems" between party legislators or between all individuals who identified themselves as either Democrats or Whigs. Nor does it assume a false dichotomy between the notion of parties as "electoral machines" and the notion of parties in the Burkean mold, suggesting that Jacksonian parties fit the latter category—organizations created and maintained solely to espouse and to implement public policy consistent with differing conceptions of how society should be governed.[4]

Lesislative parties in New Jersey were not parts of responsible parties committed to enacting comprehensive programs of public policy. Instead they were integral elements of state-party organizations whose major interests included self-preservation, winning elections, and enjoyment of the preferments of power. The accommodation of legislative parties to organizational needs contributed to rather than impeded the involvement of legislative parties as essential forces in the legislature's decision-making process. Conscious partisan attempts to shape legislation, however, remained confined primarily to questions that in some manner concerned competitive party organizations as interests. Despite increasing party influence in the legislature, it is clear that factors other than party also affected legislative voting behavior. The high percentage of legislation decided by unanimous consent as well as consideration of a disproportionate share of special bills further suggest the absence of both ideological conflict and of an agenda that required responsible party action.

The operation of legislative parties as agencies capable of satisfying partisan demands and of performing certain constituent functions did not preclude partisan disagreement on substantive issues. In fact, the existence of differing party positions in the legislature on corporate and fiscal policy contributed to the impact of party on legislative voting behavior. Division on these issues, however, was hardly the crucial factor in the development of New Jersey's legislative parties. Difference of opinion that did occur transpired within a limited framework of debate that did not reflect partisan conflict over the proper role of government or over the basic values of an evolving liberal-capitalist society.[5] The loyalty of party activists in the legislature to party organizations with their own vested interests and the development of legislative parties over time as convenient mechanisms for channeling demands confirms this point.

Notes

1. Although lobbyists operated in New Jersey, no large-scale interest associations capable of exerting pressure existed. The absence of organized pressure groups such as those that are present in modern industrial societies facilitated the process by which legislative parties took on constituent roles. For discussions of

the relationship between political modernization and pressure-group activity, *see* Douglas S. Gatlin, "Toward a Functionalist Theory of Political Parties: Inter-Party Competition in North Carolina," in *Approaches to the Study of Party Organization*, ed. William J. Crotty (Boston: Allyn and Bacon, 1968), pp. 217–246; Key, *Politics, Parties, and Pressure Groups*, p. 15–206; and Marshall, pp. 445–468.

2. The ability of party to perform constituent functions is underlined by the following date that gives the mean index of relative cohesion by party for each session between 1829 and 1844, as well as summaries of party cohesion for minority and majority positions.

Year	No. Assembly Cleav. Roll Calls	Democratic Mean I.R.C.	National-Republican/Whig Mean I.R.C.
1829	42	69.8	67.5
1830	110	64.6	71.3
1831	66	69.8	71.6
1832	89	71.9	69.2
1833	74	70.4	75.1
1834	74	66.1	78.6
1835	83	73.8	80.0
1836	131	71.9	85.4
1837	298	70.5	75.6
1838	122	84.3	83.9
1839	93	85.0	82.1
1840	81	87.3	87.7
1841	73	88.8	81.7
1842	101	79.8	78.9
1843	77	74.5	83.4
1844	134	80.0	81.9
Total:	1,648		
16-year mean:		75.5	78.4
Democratic Mean Index when Minority Party			80.0
Democratic Mean Index when Majority Party			71.1
N.R./Whig Mean Index when Minority Party			76.7
N.R./Whig Mean Index when Majority Party			80.0

Certain categories of legislation not discussed specifically in the preceding chapters further indicate the ability of legislative parties to perform constituent functions and to act in behalf of party interests. Over time, for instance, voting on roll calls concerning the formal operation of the Assembly felt the influence of party. The mean party indices of likeness for the 1829–32, 1833–37, and 1838–44 periods on these roll calls were respectively 75, 49, and 30. Increased party voting on legislation involving the granting of special privileges to communities reflect partisan desires to enhance in some fashion party strength. The deliberations over an 1838 bill to alter the charter of New Brunswick illustrates how such legislation involved party interests. The bill called for the mayor, alderman, and the recorder of New Brunswick to be chosen in local elections rather than by the legislators in Joint Meeting. The bill was supported by the Whigs and opposed by the Democrats in both the Council and the Assembly. In the Council, roll call 20, p. 210, recorded a party index of likeness of 0. In the Assembly, roll call 47, p. 435, a party index of likeness of 8 was recorded. Since New Brunswick was a powerful Whig stronghold, the bill guaranteed the selection of Whigs to fill offices regardless of which party had a majority in the Joint Meeting. Finally, voting on the calling of a constitutional convention engendered partisan cohesion, although once agreed upon, constitutional revision was undertaken in nonpartisan fashion. Bebout, "Introduction," pp. 66–69, suggests that "the question of the propriety of calling a convention furnished an issue out of which political capital might be made; but once it was decided, the safest course for both parties was to co-operate in making a good record, lest one be able to blame the other for the fiasco."

3. Ershkowitz and Shade, "Consensus or Conflict," pp. 593–613. These results are obtained despite some faulty methodological techniques that include preselection of roll calls with no stated premise for selection, use of percentage calculations with no indication of the actual numbers they represent, and poor definition of issue categories.

4. Ibid., pp. 591–92, 613–21.

5. This statement is based not only on the substantive findings of this investigation of New Jersey politics but also on several articles and books that together shaped my thinking on this rather large question. Louis Hartz, *The Liberal Tradition in America* (New York: Harcourt, Brace, and World, 1955); and C. B. MacPherson, *The Political Theory of Possessive Individualism: Hobbes to Locke* (New York: Oxford University Press, 1962), were particularly useful in suggesting the parameters of conflict in a liberal capitalist society. Converse, pp. 206–261; Edelman; McCloskey, Hoffman, and O'Hara, pp. 406–427; and Sorauf, *Political Parties in the American System*, pp. 30–31, 60, 131–32, all deal with this question in terms of the American political system.

Appendix A

Summarized in Appendix A are the 1,648 cleavage and 944 unanimous Assembly roll calls examined in this study. Roll calls were assigned to one of the thirty categories used in analysis. The mean party index of likeness for all roll calls in each category for a specified number of legislative sessions is also given. Summations for all sixteen sessions between 1829 and 1844 taken as a group as well as for the 1829–1832, 1833–1837, and 1838–1844 sessions are provided.

Although the definition of the majority of the categories employed in Appendix A should be evident from the analysis of legislative voting behavior presented in chapters 5, 6, 7, and 8, I have provided definitions for those categories whose contents may not be so clear.

Business-Government involvement refers to roll calls concerning direct government assistance in the completion of particular internal improvement projects, the regulation of particular aspects of the state's economy such as the regulation of fences, and the regulation of particular aspects of the state's economy in relation to the economies of other states.

Business-General regulatory refers to roll calls involving the regulation of particular business enterprises in New Jersey such as inns and taverns and horseracing. The bill authorizing limited partnerships, discussed in chapter 6, was also included in this category.

Enclosures refers to roll calls involving permission for individual citizens to improve their land either by enclosing it with fences, building dams, or draining their lands.

House operation refers to roll calls, procedural in nature, dealing with the operation of the Assembly. Roll calls on motions to adjourn or to postpone consideration of particular pieces of legislation are examples of the kinds of roll calls included in this category. High indices of party voting were recorded on these roll calls when they occurred at times when proposals affecting party as an interest were being discussed. For example, during the third sitting of the 1837 session, when the Democratic majority attempted to call a Joint Meeting, a series of procedural roll calls concerning adjournment and the activities of the Council occasioned highly partisan responses.

Miscellaneous refers to roll calls examined in each session that did not fit neatly into any other category and did not appear to warrant the formation of new categories. Many of the roll calls included here concerned the incorporation of benevolent societies and the incorporation of fire companies. Among the variety of roll calls categorized as miscellaneous were roll calls dealing with the sale of a government lot in Trenton, those concerning an act to prevent disturbances at singing schools, and those referring to a bill to prevent the exploding of firecrackers in the state.

Resolutions-Procedural refers to roll calls involving similar types of questions listed under house operation that were presented in the form of resolutions. For all intents and purposes, these roll calls could be included under the category of house operation.

Special privileges-Communities refers to roll calls involving the granting of special privileges to particular communities such as the right of citizens to vote by ballot at town meetings or the right of townships or counties to borrow money.

Transportation refers to roll calls involving the incorporation or the operation of companies engaged in the construction and management of transportation facilities. Excluded from this category are those roll calls specifically involving the Joint Companies.

TABLE A-1
Summation of Party Voting on Assembly Roll Calls, 1829-1844 Assemblies

Category	Number of Unanimous Roll Calls	Number of Cleavage Roll Calls	Mean Party Index of Likeness	Category	Number of Unanimous Roll Calls	Number of Cleavage Roll Calls	Mean Party Index of Likeness
Appointment of legislative officials	8	43	30	Military	10	28	77
Banking-special	22	128	66	Mining	15	9	74
Banking-general	3	55	48	Miscellaneous	60	97	63
Business-special	85	106	56	Natural Resources	10	11	78
Business-government involvement	15	48	72	Printing	11	34	27
Business-general regulatory	42	90	74	Religion	23	13	50
Constitutional reform	–	7	14	Resolutions-national	6	45	6
Counties and townships	64	124	25	Resolutions-procedural	11	16	43
Election	7	42	27	Social	57	101	72
Election disputes	6	26	2	Special privileges-communities	41	34	21
Enclosures	67	23	75	Specie	11	35	49
House Operation	87	150	55	State Prison	17	31	45
Insurance	39	15	70	Surplus revenus	–	27	86
Joint Companies	5	66	66	Taxation	13	39	63
Judicial	74	79	70	Transportation	125	126	71

Total number of cleavage roll calls: 1,648

Total number of unanimous roll calls: 944

TABLE A-2

Summation of Party Voting on Assembly Roll Calls, 1829-1832 Assemblies

Category	Number of Unanimous Roll Calls	Number of Cleavage Roll Calls	Mean Party Index of Likeness
Appointment of legislative officials	2	11	43
Banking-special	8	15	75
Banking-general	2	–	–
Business-special	13	8	88
Business-government involvement	4	14	72
Business-general regulatory	2	23	78
Constitutional reform	–	–	–
Counties and townships	16	5	70
Election	1	6	78
Election disputes	–	1	29
Enclosures	18	6	79
House operation	19	29	75
Insurance	4	2	86
Joint companies	1	44	78
Judicial	21	23	80
Military	3	12	74
Mining	3	2	85
Miscellaneous	5	18	76
Natural resources	4	–	–
Printing	–	5	68
Religion	4	1	83
Resolutions-national	–	7	15
Resolutions-procedural	–	–	–
Social	11	19	86
Special privileges-communities	5	–	–
Specie	–	3	95
State prison	1	6	86
Surplus revenue	–	–	–
Taxation	3	6	85
Transportation	22	43	77

Total number of cleavage roll calls: 309

Total number of unanimous roll calls: 172

TABLE A-3

Summation of Party Voting on Assembly Roll Calls, 1833-1837 Assemblies

Category	Number of Unanimous Roll Calls	Number of Cleavage Roll Calls	Mean Party Index of Likeness
Appointment of legislative officials	10	12	56
Banking-special	9	94	69
Banking-general	–	27	55
Business-special	58	43	70
Business-government involvement	5	27	70
Business-general regulatory	15	20	78
Constitutional reform	–	–	–
Counties and townships	24	24	40
Election	4	9	37
Election disputes	–	–	–
Enclosures	27	9	74
House operation	24	73	49
Insurance	14	6	83
Joint companies	4	20	45
Judicial	19	24	68
Military	5	15	79
Mining	7	5	84
Miscellaneous	21	51	64
Natural Resources	2	6	85
Printing	5	12	17
Religion	5	8	48
Resolutions-national	3	21	6
Resolutions-procedural	–	4	72
Social	20	16	65
Special privileges-communities	16	2	81
Specie	7	13	49
State Prison	10	8	49
Surplus revenue	–	27	86
Taxation	3	28	61
Transportation	65	53	75

Total number of cleavage roll calls: 657

Total number of unanimous roll calls: 382

TABLE A-4

Summation of Party Voting on Assembly Roll Calls, 1838-1844 Assemblies

Category	Number of Unanimous Roll Calls	Number of Cleavage Roll Calls	Mean Party Index of Likeness	Category	Number of Unanimous Roll Calls	Number of Cleavage Roll Calls	Mean Party Index of Likeness
Appointment of legislative officials	6	20	6	Military	2	1	77
Banking-special	5	19	40	Mining	5	2	36
Banking-general	1	28	41	Miscellaneous	34	28	56
Business-special	14	55	41	Natural resources	4	4	65
Business-government involvement	6	7	61	Printing	6	17	22
Business-general regulatory	25	47	70	Religion	14	4	44
Constitutional reform	–	7	14	Resolutions-national	3	17	7
Counties and townships	24	95	19	Resolutions-procedural	11	12	41
Election	2	27	21	Social	26	66	68
Election disputes	6	23	1	Special privileges-communities	20	32	17
Enclosures	22	8	72	Specie	4	19	32
House operation	44	48	30	State Prison	6	17	19
Insurance	21	7	54	Surplus revenue	–	–	–
Joint companies	–	2	36	Taxation	7	5	49
Judicial	34	32	65	Transportation	38	30	54

Total number of cleavage roll calls: 682

Total number of unanimous roll calls: 390

Appendix B

This appendix contains summaries of investigations of the significance of age, occupation, and length of legislative service on legislative voting behavior. Additional investigation of specific roll calls, as indicated in chapters 5 and 6, along with the material presented here, fail to reveal the quantitative significance of these factors on roll-call voting.

The tables present summaries of indices of likeness for paired groups of legislators designated by particular age, occupational, or legislative tenure characteristics. Indices were calculated for both the Council and the Assembly, although only Assembly data is presented here.

Three different combinations of age groups were tested for each of the sixteen legislative sessions between 1829 and 1844. Those individuals who were born before 1775 were compared to those who were born between 1775 and

1800; those born between 1775 and 1800 were compared to those born after 1800; and those born before 1775 were compared to those born after 1800. In each year, where reasonably large samples could be examined, the factor of age was of minimal quantitative significance.

Although differences in percentages do occur, only occasionally do they fall into the high ranges. Assuming that at least two-thirds of one group must oppose at least two-thirds of another group to indicate significant cohesion, one finds little cohesion when using age as a variable. Translating this assumption into numbers, a minimum index of likeness of 66 is needed to assert cohesiveness. Tables B-1, B-2, and B-3 show that this figure was only infrequently reached. A summation of the eleven-year sample in Table B-3 indicates that on only 91 of 1,267 roll calls, or less than 7.5% of the time, did indices of likeness drop below 66. Only six of the 1,267 roll calls recorded figures under 41. In 1835, no Assembly roll calls dropped below 65, while in 1840, 1841, and 1844 only two in each year were lower than this figure.

The results summarized in Tables B-1 and B-2, though less impressive, were based on comparisons of smaller groups of men. In Table B-2, for example, the number of assemblymen in the group containing legislators born before 1775 never exceeded five in any of the five years that were sampled. In spite of the possibility of distortion, 83% of all of the roll calls examined for those men born before 1775 and those born between 1775 and 1800 recorded indices of likeness over 66. Only 4% of the roll calls in this situation recorded indices of likeness under 41. Similar results occurred for the roll calls sampled in Table B-1.

The lack of significant results regarding the variable of service in the legislature are even more conclusive. Tables B-4, B-5, B-6, and B-7 summarize these findings. As illustrated in Table B-4 and in Table B-5, little difference existed in the voting patterns of men who served only one year in the legislature as compared to those who served two or more years. Whether service was in consecutive years or whether it occurred at intervals between 1829 and 1844, over 94% of all of the Assembly roll calls of the cleavage variety for these years revealed no statistical evidence in support of the importance of this variable. Comparisons between legislators who served at least two years in the Assembly, though not in consecutive years, with those who served two or more years in a row reveal similar results. As indicated in Table B-7, 80% of the roll calls in this sample recorded indices over 65, while 98% recorded differences over 40. Again, the small size of the groups being compared accounts for the lower percentage of roll calls falling into the 100–66 range than might have occurred with larger groups.

As with age and prior service, analysis of the effect of occupation was centered in the Assembly because of the small membership of the Council. Even in the Assembly, however, the problem of distortion inherent in the comparison of small groups could not be avoided.

Of the 340 assemblymen for whom information on occupation was obtained, 201 were farmers. The number of individuals in other occupational categories did not approach this total. The second largest group, businessmen, contained only 73 men. Moreover, in most years, the number of assemblymen of the same occupational group serving at the same time were few. Although various combinations of these groups were tested for all sixteen years, the small size of these groups makes the value of much of this analysis suspect. The following tables represent the results from those comparisons in which the largest number of men were involved.

For each of these six comparisons, over 92% of all of the roll calls in each sample produced indices of likeness over 40. Over 82% of all of the roll calls summarized in Tables B-8, B-9, B-11, and B-13 produced indices over 65. These statistics seem to indicate that occupation as an independent variable was not an important general influence on the legislative decision-making process.

In certain years and for certain combinations, however,

the statistical evidence concerning occupation does warrant further investigation. In the 1837 Assembly, for example, those legislators engaged in manufacturing, a trade, or in commerce voted in opposition to those engaged in the law quite consistently. Of the 298 roll calls that were examined, these groups produced indices of likeness under 61 a total of 123 times. The roll calls that resulted in these scores were categorized as follows: government operation and public printing—45; banks—19; surplus revenue—17; manufacturing—10; regulation of the economy—6; specie—6; transportation—5; judicial matters—5; creation of new counties—5; social legislation—2; special acts—1; insurance—1; and taxation—1. Most of the forty-five roll calls involving the operation of the government arose out of attempts to hold Joint Meetings during the second and the third sittings of the legislature. The content of many of these involved caustic remarks directed at the Whig members of the Council who refused to agree to resolutions calling for Joint Meetings. Party indices of likeness on these matters were high. Similarly, the roll calls involving specie, the creation of new counties, and banks recorded more than the normal amount of party voting. A closer look at the political affiliation of lawyers and businessmen serving in the Assembly indicates that the factor of party, more than the factor of occupation, directly influenced the decisions that were reached on a good many of these roll calls. In this particular session, contrary to the general findings relating to the occupational patterns of New Jersey's legislators, all six lawyers were Whigs and five of the seven assemblymen who were engaged in some form of business were Democrats. Given the nature of the roll calls involved, in this instance, party affiliation more than occupation, in quantitative terms, played a more significant role in determining voting behavior.

TABLE B-1

Indices of Likeness on Assembly Roll Calls for Assemblymen Born before 1775 and Assemblymen Born between 1775 and 1800

Year	No. Assemblm. born bf. 1775	No. Assemblm. born betw. 1775-1800	No. Roll calls	Number of roll calls with Index of Likeness between						
				100-91	90-81	80-71	70-66	65-61	60-41	40-0
1831	5	29	66	26	21	15	–	–	2	2
1832	6	27	89	34	32	15	33	2	3	–
1839	5	21	93	11	15	19	16	9	19	4

TABLE B-2

Indices of Likeness on Assembly Roll Calls for Assemblymen Born before 1775 and Assemblymen Born after 1800

Year	No. Assemblm. born bf. 1775	No. Assemblm. born after 1800	No. Roll calls	Number of roll calls with Index of Likeness between						
				100-91	90-81	80-71	70-66	65-61	60-41	40-0
1830	4	4	110	36	6	40	12	–	11	5
1833	4	4	74	27	4	24	2	–	14	3
1834	4	8	74	16	16	12	9	11	6	4
1839	5	13	93	31	34	14	4	2	7	1
1840	4	11	81	28	25	9	8	–	8	3

TABLE B-3

Indices of Likeness on Assembly Roll Calls for Assemblymen Born between 1775 and 1800 and Assemblymen Born after 1800

Year	No. Assemblm. born betw. 1775-1800	No. Assemblm. born after 1800	No. Roll calls	Number of roll calls with Index of Likeness between						
				100-91	90-81	80-71	70-66	65-61	60-41	40-0
1834	23	8	74	25	22	16	4	2	5	–
1835	30	9	83	35	33	11	4	–	–	–
1836	29	10	131	60	39	20	2	3	6	1
1837	25	11	298	98	100	50	18	8	23	1
1838	19	11	122	16	41	25	16	9	14	1
1839	21	13	93	21	23	33	5	4	5	2
1840	26	11	81	50	19	6	4	1	–	1
1841	36	18	73	27	30	11	3	1	1	–
1842	30	16	101	48	36	14	2	1	–	–
1843	26	19	77	27	34	10	3	2	1	–
1844	26	18	134	58	55	16	3	1	1	–

TABLE B-4

Indices of Likeness on Assembly Roll Calls for Assemblymen Who Served Only One Year in the Assembly and Assemblymen Who Served Two or More Years

Year	No. Assemblm. serv. only one year	No. Assemblm. serv. two or more yrs.	No. Roll Calls	Number of roll calls with Index of Likeness between						
				100-91	90-81	80-71	70-66	65-61	60-41	40-0
1829	21	22	42	15	16	10	1	–	–	–
1830	21	22	110	55	37	10	6	1	1	–
1831	29	21	66	26	22	16	2	–	–	–
1832	25	25	89	36	32	17	2	2	–	–
1833	29	21	74	35	24	10	3	2	2	–
1834	34	16	74	19	32	17	2	2	3	–
1835	21	29	83	24	28	12	7	9	–	–
1836	26	24	131	72	37	21	–	1	–	–
1837	23	27	298	116	117	44	12	5	4	–
1838	39	14	122	51	34	28	5	2	2	–
1839	30	23	93	42	35	14	2	–	–	–
1840	30	23	81	58	17	5	1	–	–	–
1841	27	26	73	11	13	33	10	3	3	–
1842	39	19	101	20	30	38	7	4	2	–
1843	32	26	77	35	31	10	1	–	–	–
1844	32	26	134	37	46	39	4	8	–	–

TABLE B-5

Indices of Likeness on Assembly Roll Calls for Assemblymen Who Served Only One Year in the Assembly and Assemblymen Who Served Two or More Years in Consecutive Order

Year	No. Assemblm. serv. only one year	No. Assemblm. serv. two or more yrs. cons.	No. Roll Calls	Number of roll calls with Index of Likeness between						
				100-91	90-81	80-71	70-66	65-61	60-41	40-0
1829	21	14	42	13	14	9	1	4	1	—
1830	21	17	110	45	37	20	5	1	2	—
1831	29	16	66	24	20	17	2	2	1	—
1832	25	23	89	32	29	23	2	2	1	—
1833	29	21	74	35	24	10	3	2	—	—
1834	34	10	74	16	25	19	5	4	4	1
1835	21	26	83	24	24	15	2	6	11	1
1836	26	19	131	65	41	19	3	1	2	—
1837	23	25	298	106	123	49	9	7	4	—
1838	39	10	122	38	29	37	11	3	3	1
1839	30	23	93	42	35	14	2	—	—	—
1840	30	21	81	43	28	9	1	—	—	—
1841	27	26	73	12	12	32	8	6	3	—
1842	39	18	101	25	27	37	8	3	1	—
1843	32	24	77	31	25	20	1	—	—	—
1844	32	25	134	32	40	46	8	4	4	—

TABLE B-6

Indices of Likeness on Assembly Roll Calls for Assemblymen Who Served Only One Year in the Assembly and Assemblymen Who Served Two or More Years, Not Consecutively

Year	No. Assemblm. serv. only one year	No. Assemblm. serv. two or more yrs. not cons.	No. Roll calls	Number of roll calls with Index of Likeness between						
				100-91	90-81	80-71	70-66	65-61	60-41	40-0
1829	21	8	42	17	9	11	1	1	2	1
1830	21	5	110	33	34	23	5	4	10	1
1831	29	5	66	18	18	18	5	2	5	–
1834	34	6	74	27	23	15	2	2	5	–
1836	26	5	131	42	35	29	9	7	8	1

TABLE B-7

Indices of Likeness on Assembly Roll Calls for Assemblymen Who Served Two or More Years in the Assembly Consecutively and Assemblymen Who Served Two or More Years, Not Consecutively

Year	No. Assemblm. serv. two or more yrs. cons.	No. Assemblm. serv. two yrs. not cons.	No. Roll calls	Number of roll calls with Index of Likeness between						
				100-91	90-81	80-71	70-66	65-61	60-41	40-0
1829	14	8	42	18	5	9	–	3	5	2
1830	17	5	110	37	26	22	6	5	13	1
1831	16	5	66	22	18	8	4	1	11	2
1834	10	6	74	18	24	8	6	3	15	–
1836	18	5	131	40	30	25	10	10	15	1
1838	10	4	122	18	30	27	18	8	18	3

TABLE B-8

Indices of Likeness on Assembly Roll Calls for Assemblymen Who Were Farmers and Assemblymen Who Were Lawyers

Year	No. Assemblm. farmers	No. Assemblm. lawyers	No. Roll calls	Number of roll calls with Index of Likeness between						
				100-91	90-81	80-71	70-66	65-61	60-41	40-0
1829	10	7	42	11	7	6	5	1	2	2
1830	10	7	110	22	25	24	11	9	8	2
1834	24	9	74	21	17	21	6	4	2	–
1835	29	7	83	39	26	9	3	1	1	–

TABLE B-9

Indices of Likeness on Assembly Roll Calls for Assemblymen Who Were Farmers and Assemblymen Who Were in Manufacturing, Trades, or Commerce

Year	No. Assemblm. farmers	No. Assemblm. mfg., tr., com.	No. Roll calls	Number of roll calls with Index of Likeness between						
				100-91	90-81	80-71	70-66	65-61	60-41	40-0
1830	10	8	110	37	36	14	9	6	7	1
1836	27	8	131	54	50	20	2	2	2	1
1839	28	9	93	28	25	23	5	5	6	1
1841	29	9	73	6	21	30	7	2	7	–
1842	34	10	101	24	25	28	9	4	10	1
1843	28	12	77	14	16	18	10	11	8	–
1844	22	16	134	23	19	28	16	18	30	–

TABLE B-10

Indices of Likeness on Assembly Roll Calls for Assemblymen Who Were Lawyers and Assemblymen Who Were in Manufacturing, Trades, or Commerce

Year	No. Assemblm. lawyers	No. Assemblm. mfg., tr., com.	No. Roll calls	Number of roll calls with Index of Likeness between						
				100-91	90-81	80-71	70-66	65-61	60-41	40-0
1829	7	6	42	14	14	1	4	2	6	1
1830	8	8	110	26	29	18	12	3	14	8
1835	7	7	83	26	11	16	6	5	17	2
1837	6	7	298	41	49	41	24	20	93	30

TABLE B-11

Indices of Likeness on Assembly Roll Calls for Assemblymen Who Were Farmers and Assemblymen Who Were in Manufacturing

Year	No. Assemblm. farmers	No. Assemblm. mfg.	No. Roll calls	Number of roll calls with Index of Likeness between						
				100-91	90-81	80-71	70-66	65-61	60-41	40-0
1831	25	6	66	18	19	14	5	2	7	1
1843	28	6	77	10	18	13	2	5	29	1
1844	22	9	134	15	28	18	8	15	50	–

TABLE B-12

Indices of Likeness on Assembly Roll Calls for Assemblymen Who
Were in Manufacturing and Assemblymen Who Were in Commerce

Year	No. Assemblm. mfg.	No. Assemblm. com.	No. Roll calls	Number of roll calls with Index of Likeness between						
				100-91	90-81	80-71	70-66	65-61	60-41	40-0
1830	4	4	110	23	7	27	5	--	36	12
1843	6	6	77	37	13	11	9	4	3	--
1844	9	7	134	58	53	17	2	1	3	--

TABLE B-13

Indices of Likeness on Assembly Roll Calls for Assemblymen Who Were Farmers and Assemblymen Who Were in Commerce

Year	No. Assemblm. farmers	No. Assemblm. com.	No. Roll calls	Number of roll calls with Index of Likeness between						
				100-91	90-81	80-71	70-66	65-61	60-41	40-0
1836	27	6	131	45	38	17	8	5	15	5
1837	22	5	298	75	88	69	32	10	22	2
1838	25	5	122	46	35	20	8	7	5	1
1839	28	7	93	41	27	20	8	2	2	--
1841	29	7	73	13	12	33	1	4	5	1
1842	34	8	101	46	30	15	5	3	6	--
1843	28	6	77	25	24	14	5	4	5	--
1844	22	7	134	19	30	29	16	13	27	--

Selected Bibliography

Manuscripts

Columbia University Library
    Peter D. Vroom Papers
Historical Society of Pennsylvania
    Roswell L. Colt Papers
New Jersey Historical Society
    Mahlon Dickerson Papers
    James Parker Papers
    William Pennington Papers
    Peter D. Vroom Papers
Princeton University Library
    Samuel L. Southard Papers
    Garret Wall Papers

Rutgers University Library
   Benjamin Cooper Papers
   Theodore Frelinghuysen Papers
   Elmer T. Hutchinson Collection
   New Jersey Letters Collection
   James Parker Papers
   Charles Philhower Collection
   Peter Voorhees Papers
   Peter D. Vroom Papers

Public Documents

Acts of the Fifty-Third General Assembly of the State of New Jersey. Trenton, New Jersey: A. W. Phillips, 1828.

Acts of the Fifty-Fourth General Assembly of the State of New Jersey. Trenton, New Jersey: Joseph Justice, 1829.

Acts of the Fifty-Fifth General Assembly of the State of New Jersey. Trenton, New Jersey: Joseph Justice, 1831.

Acts of the Fifty-Sixth General Assembly of the State of New Jersey. Trenton, New Jersey: Joseph Justice, 1832.

Acts of the Fifty-Seventh General Assembly of the State of New Jersey. Trenton, New Jersey: Printed at the office of the *National Union,* 1833.

Acts of the Fifty-Eighth General Assembly of the State of New Jersey. Trenton, New Jersey: Joseph Justice, 1834.

Acts of the Fifty-Ninth General Assembly of the State of New Jersey. Trenton, New Jersey: Joseph Justice, 1835.

Acts of the Sixtieth General Assembly of the State of New Jersey. Trenton, New Jersey: William Boswell, 1836.

Acts of the Sixty-First General Assembly of the State of New Jersey. Trenton, New Jersey: Printed for the State, 1837.

Acts of the Sixty-Second General Assembly of the State of New Jersey. Trenton, New Jersey: James Adams, 1838.

Acts of the Sixty-Third General Assembly of the State of New Jersey. Camden, New Jersey: P. J. Gray, 1839.

Acts of the Sixty-Fourth General Assembly of the State of New Jersey. Trenton, New Jersey: Sherman and Harron, 1840.

Acts of the Sixty-Fifth General Assembly of the State of New Jersey. Trenton, New Jersey: Phillips and Boswell, 1841.

Acts of the Sixty-Sixth General Assembly of the State of New Jersey. Somerville, New Jersey: S. L. B. Baldwin, 1842.

Acts of the Sixty-Seventh General Assembly of the State of New Jersey. New Brunswick, New Jersey: David F. Randolph, 1843.

Acts of the Sixty-Eighth General Assembly of the State of New Jersey. Freehold, New Jersey: Bernard Connolly, 1844.

Journal of the Proceedings of the Legislative Council of the State of New Jersey, Being the First Sitting of the Fifty-Third Session. Woodbury, New Jersey: P. J. Gray, 1829.

Journal of the Proceedings of the Legislative Council of the State of New Jersey, Being the First Sitting of the Fifty-Fourth Session. Bridgeton, New Jersey: Samuel B. Sibley, 1830.

Journal of the Proceedings of the Legislative Council of the State of New Jersey, Being the First Sitting of the Fifty-Fifth Session. Bridgeton, New Jersey: Samuel S. Sibley, 1831.

Journal of the Proceedings of the Legislative Council of the State of New Jersey, Being the First Sitting of the Fifty-Sixth Session. Woodbury, New Jersey: Joseph Sailer, 1832.

Journal of the Proceedings of the Legislative Council of the State of New Jersey, Being the First Sitting of the Fifty-Seventh Session. Camden, New Jersey: Josiah Harrison, 1833.

Journal of the Proceedings of the Legislative Council of the State of New Jersey, Being the First Sitting of the Fifty-Eighth Session. Somerville, New Jersey: Gore and Allison, 1834.

Journal of the Proceedings of the Legislative Council of the State of New Jersey, Being the First Sitting of the Fifty-Ninth Session. Somerville, New Jersey: Gore and Allison, 1835.

Journal of the Proceedings of the Legislative Council of the State of New Jersey, Being the First Sitting of the Sixtieth Session. Somerville, New Jersey: Gore and Allison, 1836.

Journal of the Proceedings of the Legislative Council of the State of New Jersey, Being the First Sitting of the Sixty-First Session. Woodbury, New Jersey: A. S. Barber, 1837.

Journal of the Proceedings of the Legislative Council of the State of New Jersey, Being the First Sitting of the Sixty-Second Session. Somerville, New Jersey: S. L. B. Baldwin, 1838.

Journal of the Proceedings of the Legislative Council of the State of New Jersey, Being the First Sitting of the Sixty-Third Session. Somerville, New Jersey: S. L. B. Baldwin, 1839.

Journal of the Proceedings of the Legislative Council of the State of New Jersey, Being the First Sitting of the Sixty-Fourth Session. Somerville, New Jersey: S. L. B. Baldwin, 1840.

Journal of the Proceedings of the Legislative Council of the State of New Jersey, Being the First Sitting of the Sixty-Fifth Session. Woodbury, New Jersey: A. S. Barber, 1841.

Journal of the Proceedings of the Legislative Council of the State of New Jersey, Being the First Sitting of the Sixty-Sixth Session. Belvidere, New Jersey: Daniel G. Fitch, 1842.

Journal of the Proceedings of the Legislative Council of the State of New Jersey, Being the First Sitting of the Sixty-Seventh Session. Morristown, New Jersey: S. P. Hull, 1843.

Journal of the Proceedings of the Legislative Council of the State of New Jersey, Being the First Sitting of the Sixty-Eighth Session. New Brunswick, New Jersey: L. R. Stelle, 1844.

New Jersey. *Manual of the Legislature of New Jersey.* 144th Session (1920).

Opinion of the Attorney General in Relation to Certain Bank Charters, read in Council, 8 February 1842. Trenton, New Jersey: Justice and Mills, 1842.

Report of the Committee of the Legislature Appointed to Examine into the Conditions, Affairs, Revenue, and Future Prospects of the New Jersey Railroad and Transportation Company. Trenton, New Jersey: Joseph Justice, 1837.

Report of the Select Committee on the Subject of Banks, read in Council, 28 January 1842. Trenton, New Jersey: Justice and Mills, 1842.

Report of the Treasurer of the State of New Jersey to the Legislature. Trenton, New Jersey: Franklin and Mills, 1843.

Rules and Orders to be Observed in the House of Assembly of the State of New Jersey, Adopted 26 October 1831. Trenton, New Jersey: Joseph Justice, 1831.

Rules for the Government of the General Assembly of the State of New Jersey, Adopted 24 October 1839. Trenton, New Jersey: Sherman and Harron, 1839.

264   THE BEHAVIOR OF STATE LEGISLATIVE PARTIES

Rules for the Government of the Legislative Council of the State of New Jersey as well as to Their Proceedings When Sitting as a Court of Appeals and a Court of Pardons. Trenton, New Jersey: Joseph Justice, 1829.

Rules for the Government of the Legislative Council of the State of New Jersey, Adopted 28 October 1835. Trenton, New Jersey: Joseph Justice, 1835.

Rules for the Government of the Legislative Council of the State of New Jersey, Adopted 25 October 1839. Trenton, New Jersey: Phillips and Boswell, 1839.

Rules for the Government of the Legislative Council of the State of New Jersey, Adopted 27 October 1842. Trenton, New Jersey: Sherman and Harron, 1842.

United States. *Census of the State of New Jersey, 1840, 1850.*

Votes and Proceedings of the Fifty-Third General Assembly of the State of New Jersey. Woodbury, New Jersey: P. J. Gray, 1829.

Votes and Proceedings of the Fifty-Fourth General Assembly of the State of New Jersey. Trenton, New Jersey: Joseph Justice, 1830.

Votes and Proceedings of the Fifty-Fifth General Assembly of the State of New Jersey. Newton, New Jersey: Grant Fitch, 1831.

Votes and Proceedings of the Fifty-Sixth General Assembly of the State of New Jersey. Newton, New Jersey: Grant Fitch, 1832.

Votes and Proceedings of the Fifty-Seventh General Assembly of the State of New Jersey. Woodbury, New Jersey: Joseph Sailer, 1833.

Votes and Proceedings of the Fifty-Eighth General Assembly of the State of New Jersey. New Brunswick, New Jersey: McCready and Stedle, 1834.

Votes and Proceedings of the Fifty-Ninth General Assembly of the State of New Jersey. Freehold, New Jersey: Bernard Connolly, 1835.

Votes and Proceedings of the Sixtieth General Assembly of the State of New Jersey. Freehold, New Jersey: Bernard Connolly, 1836.

Votes and Proceedings of the Sixty-First General Assembly of the State of New Jersey. Belvidere, New Jersey: George W. Clason, 1837.

Votes and Proceedings of the Sixty-Second General Assembly of the State of New Jersey. Newark, New Jersey: M. S. Harrison and Co., 1838.

Votes and Proceedings of the Sixty-Third General Assembly of the State of New Jersey. Newark, New Jersey: M. S. Harrison and Co., 1839.

Votes and Proceedings of the Sixty-Fourth General Assembly of the State of New Jersey. Belvidere, New Jersey: Wilson and Brittain, 1840.

Votes and Proceedings of the Sixty-Fifth General Assembly of the State of New Jersey. Freehold, New Jersey: Callender and Johnston, 1841.

Votes and Proceedings of the Sixty-Sixth General Assembly of the State of New Jersey. Trenton, New Jersey: Phillips and Boswell, 1842.

Votes and Proceedings of the Sixty-Seventh General Assembly of the State of New Jersey. Woodbury, New Jersey: A. S. Barber, 1843.

Votes and Proceedings of the Sixty-Eighth General Assembly of the State of New Jersey. Somerville, New Jersey: Thos. S. Allison, 1844.

Election Data

Historical Archive. Inter-University Consortium for Political Research. Ann Arbor, Michigan.

Newspapers (New Jersey)

Bridgeton Washington Whig. 1828–1832.

Emporium and True American (Trenton). 1829–1844.

Hunterdon Gazette (Flemington). 1830–1833.

Newark Daily Advertiser. 1829–1844.

New Jersey Journal (Elizabeth). 1843–1844.

New Jersey Mirror (Mt. Holly). 1838.

New Jersey State Gazette (Trenton). 1829–1844.

Palladium of Liberty (Morristown). 1827–1831.

Trenton Emporium. 1828–1829.

Printed Sources: Books and Pamphlets

Address of the Democratic State Convention Which Assembled at Trenton on 20 May 1840 as Reported by Colonel James C. Zabriskie, Chairman of the Committee. N.p., 1840.

Address of the Hon. Hugh J. Garland Before the Democratic Mass Convention Held at New Brunswick, New Jersey, 8 October 1840. New Brunswick, New Jersey: 1840.

Address to the Electors of Cumberland County. N.p., 1828.

Address to the People of New Jersey on the Present Crisis, Reported to the Democratic State Convention by the Central Committee, 11 September 1834. N.p., 1834.

An Appeal to the Legislative Council and the General Assembly of the State of New Jersey on Behalf of the Religious Society of Friends, Commonly Called Quakers. Philadelphia: Joseph Rakestraw, 1836.

Captain Stockton's Address to the People of New Jersey, on the Subject of the Delaware and Raritan Canal and Camden and Amboy Railroad. Camden, New Jersey: P. J. Gray, 1835.

Charters of Railroad and Other Companies Between Philadelphia and New York. Philadelphia: A. Waldie, 1833.

Colonel Scott's Letter to Judge Nevius, Mr. Lupp, and Mr. Wood of New Brunswick, on the Constitutional Organization of the Legislative Council of New Jersey, October 1841. Trenton, New Jersey: Justice and Mills, 1842.

Deeth, S. G. *A Christmas Present From an Independent Whig.* N.p., 1837.

Elmer, Lucius Q. C. *The Constitution and Government of the Province and State of New Jersey, with Biographical Sketches of the Governors From 1776 to 1845.* Newark, New Jersey: Martin R. Dennis, 1872.

Ewing. *An Appeal to the People of New Jersey.* Camden, New Jersey: Hineline and Curts, 1843.

First Joint Report of the Associated Delaware and Raritan Canal Company, Camden and Amboy Railroad and Transportation Company, to the Stockholders. Philadelphia: H. G. Leisanring, 1867.

Foot, Samuel. *Speech at the Mass Meeting at Millstone, New Jersey, 7 August 1844.* Somerville, New Jersey: S. L. Baldwin, 1844.

Free Railroads. A Review of the New Jersey Railroad Company's Pamphlets on a System of Free Railroads. Trenton, New Jersey: True American Office, 1861.

Gordon, Thomas F. *A Gazetteer of the State of New Jersey, Comprehending a General View of its Physical and Moral Condition.* Trenton, New Jersey: Daniel Fenton, 1834.

Halsted, Oliver S. *Address Delivered Before the Whigs of Newark, 4 July 1834.* Newark, New Jersey: J. B. Pinneo and Co., 1834.

New Jersey (Federal) Writers Project, comps., and eds. *Proceedings of the New Jersey Constitutional Convention of 1844.* With Introduction by John Bebout. N.p., 1942.

Plain Questions to the People of New Jersey in Relation to the Selection of a Governor by a Native New Jerseyean. N.p., 1844.

Potts, Joseph C. *The New Jersey Register for the Year 1837.* Trenton, New Jersey: William D'Hart, 1837.

Proceedings and Address of the New Jersey State Convention Assembled at Trenton, 8 January 1828, Which Nominated Andrew Jackson for President, John C. Calhoun for Vice-President of the United States. Trenton, New Jersey: Joseph Justice, 1828.

Proceedings of the Burlington County Jackson Republican Meeting. N.p., 1832.

The Proposition to Extinguish Exclusive Privileges in the State of New Jersey. Princeton, New Jersey: John Bogart, 1836.

Sitgreaves, Charles. *Manual of Legislative Practice and Order of Business in the Legislature of the State of New Jersey.* Trenton, New Jersey: B. Davenport, 1836.

The Slander Rebuked or the Private Character and Public Services of John Thompson. Camden, New Jersey: Henry Curts, 1844.

Speech by the Honorable Charles Sitgreaves of New Jersey in the House of Representatives, 9 February 1869. McGill and Witherow, n.d.

Speech of Captain R. F. Stockton, Delivered at the Great Democratic Meeting at New Brunswick, Wednesday, 24 September 1844. New York: Jared W. Bell, 1844.

Stockton, R. F. *Appeal to the People of New Jersey.* Princeton, New Jersey: John T. Robinson, 1849.

To the Electors of the County of Somerset, 25 September 1831, signed and printed by the Republican Convention held in Somerville on this date. N.p., 1831.

To the Independent Whig Electors of the Township of Woodbridge. N.p., 1832.

Secondary Sources

No attempt has been made to include in this bibliography all of the literature on the politics of the Jacksonian era. Although much of this literature has been examined, only those works which had a direct influence on this study have been included. The useful collection of genealogical compilations and histories of New Jersey's counties in the Rutgers University Library and in the State Library of New Jersey at Trenton, although important sources for biographical information on New Jersey's legislators, have also been omitted from this bibliography.

Alexander, Thomas B. *Sectional Stress and Party Strength: A Computer Analysis of Roll-Call Voting Patterns in the United States House of Representatives, 1836–1860.* Nashville, Tennessee: Vanderbilt University Press, 1967.

————; Elmore, Peggy D.; Lowrey, Frank M.; and Skinner, Mary J. P. "The Basis of Alabama's Ante-Bellum Two-Party System." *Alabama Review* 19 (October 1966): 243–76.

————; Carter, Kit C.; Lister, Jack R.; Oldshue, Jerry C.; and Sandlin, Winfred G. "Who Were the Alabama Whigs?" *Alabama Review* 16 (January 1963): 5–19.

Anderson, Lee F.; Watts, Meredith W., Jr.; and Wilcox, Allen R. *Legislative Roll-Call Analysis.* Evanston, Illinois: Northwestern University Press, 1966.

Barnes, Samuel H. *Party Democracy: Politics in an Italian Socialist Federation.* New Haven, Connecticut: Yale University Press, 1967.

Barton, Roger A. "The Camden and Amboy Railroad Monopoly." *Proceedings of the New Jersey Historical Society* 12 (October 1927): 405–18.

Belknap, George M. "A Method for Analyzing Legislative Behavior." *Midwest Journal of Political Science* 2 (1958): 377–402.

Bell, Rudolph M. "Politics and Factions, 1789–1801." Ph.D. dissertation, Department of History, City University of New York, 1969.

Benson, Lee. *The Concept of Jacksonian Democracy: New York as a Test Case.* Princeton, New Jersey: Princeton University Press, 1961.

Bogue, Alan. "Bloc and Party Voting in the United States Senate, 1861–1863." *Civil War History* 13 (September 1967):221–41.

Branning, Rosalind. *Pennsylvania Constitutional Development.* Pittsburgh: University of Pittsburgh Press, 1960.

Brimhall, Dean R., and Otis, Arthur S. "A Study of Consistency in Congressional Voting." *Journl of Applied Psychology* 32 (1948): 1–7.

Bruchey, Stuart. *The Roots of American Economic Growth, 1607–1861: An Essay in Social Causation.* New York: Harper and Row, 1965.

Burr, Nelson G. *Education in New Jersey, 1630–1871.* Princeton, New Jersey: Princeton University Press, 1942.

Cadman, John W., Jr. *The Corporation in New Jersey, Business and Politics, 1791–1875.* Cambridge, Massachusetts: Harvard University Press, 1949.

Carleton, William G. "Political Aspects of the Van Buren Era." *South Atlantic Quarterly* 50 (April 1951): 167–85.

Cave, Alfred A. *Jacksonian Democracy and the Historians.* Gainesville, Florida: University of Florida Press, 1964.

Chambers, William N. "Party Development and the American Mainstream." In *The American Party Systems: Stages of Political Development,* edited by William N. Chambers and Walter D. Burnham, pp. 3–32. New York: Oxford University Press, 1967.

Chambers, William N., and Burnham, Walter D., eds. *The American Party Systems: Stages of Political Development.* New York: Oxford University Press, 1967.

Chase, James S. "Jacksonian Democracy and the Rise of the Nominating Convention." *Mid-America* 45 (October 1963): 229–49.

Clubb, Jerome M., and Allen, Howard W. "Party Loyalty in the Progressive Years: The Senate, 1909–1915." In *Quantitative History: Selected Readings in the Quantitative Analysis of Historical Data,* edited by Don K. Rowney and James P. Graham, Jr., pp. 443–56. Homewood, Illinois: The Dorsey Press.

Converse, Philip E. "The Nature of Belief Systems in Mass Publics. In *Ideology and Discontent,* edited by David E. Apter, pp. 206–261. Glencoe, Illinois: Free Press, 1964.

Davis, Rodney O. "Illinois Legislators and Jacksonian Democracy, 1834–1841." Ph.D. dissertation, Department of History, University of Iowa, 1966.

Dawson, Richard E., and Robinson, James A. "Inter-Party Competition, Economic Variables, and Welfare Policies in the American States." *The Journal of Politics* 25 (May 1963): 265–89.

Derge, David. "Urban-Rural Conflict: The Case in Illinois." In *Legislative Behavior: A Reader in Theory and Research,* edited by Heinz Eulau and John Wahlke, pp. 218–27. Glencoe, Illinois: The Free Press, 1959.

Dunham, William J. "Mahlon Dickerson, A Great But Almost Forgotten New Jerseyman." Master's thesis, Department of History, New York University, 1951.

Duverger, Maurice. *Political Parties: Their Organization and Activity in the Modern State.* New York: John Wiley, 1954.

Dye, Thomas. "State Legislative Politics." In *Politics in the American States: A Comparative Analysis,* edited by Herbert Jacobs and Kenneth N. Vines, pp. 151–206. Boston: Little, Brown and Co., 1965.

Edelman, Murray. *The Symbolic Uses of Politics.* Urbana, Illinois: The University of Illinois Press, 1964.

Effross, Harris I., "Origins of Post-Colonial Counties in New Jersey." *Proceedings of the New Jersey Historical Society* 81 (January 1963): 103–122.

Erdman, Charles R., Jr. *The New Jersey Constitution of 1776.* Princeton, New Jersey: Princeton University Press, 1929.

Ershkowitz, Herbert, and Shade, William G. "Consensus or Conflict? Political Behavior in the State Legislatures During the Jacksonian Era." *The Journal of American History* 58 (December 1971): 591–621.

Ershkowitz, Herbert. "New Jersey Politics During the Era of Andrew Jackson, 1820–1837." Ph.D. dissertation, Department of History, New York University, 1965.

_____. "Samuel L. Southard: A Case Study of Whig Leadership in the Age of Jackson." *New Jersey History* 88 (Spring 1970): 5–24.

Eulau, Heinz. "Political Socialization of American State Legislators." *Midwest Journal of Political Science* 3 (1959): 188–206.

_____, and Wahlke, John C., eds. *Legislative Behavior: A Reader in Theory and Research.* Glencoe, Illinois: The Free Press, 1959.

Fallaw, Walter, Jr. "The Rise of the Whig Party in New Jersey." Ph.D. dissertation, Department of History, Princeton University, 1967.

Farris, Charles D. "A Method of Determining Ideological Groupings in the Congress." *The Journal of Politics* 20 (1958): 308–38.

Fee, Walter R. *The Transition from Aristocracy to Democracy in New Jersey, 1789–1829.* Somerville, New Jersey: Somerset Press, 1933.

Flinn, Thomas A. "Party Responsibility in the States: Some Causal Factors." *American Political Science Review* 58 (March 1964): 60–71.

Forbush, Bliss. *Elias Hicks, Quaker Liberal.* New York: Columbia University Press, 1956.

Formisano, Ronald P. "Political Character, Antipartyism, and the Second Party System." *American Quarterly* 21 (Winter 1969): 683–709.

_____. *The Birth of Mass Political Parties, Michigan 1827–1861.* Princeton, New Jersey: Princeton University Press, 1971.

Frankel, Emil. "Crime Treatment in New Jersey: 1668–1934." *Journal of Criminal Law and Criminology* 28 (May–June 1937).

French, Bruce. *Banking and Insurance in New Jersey.* Princeton, New Jersey: Van Nostrand Press, 1965.

Gatlin, Douglas S. "Towards a Functionalist Theory of Political Parties: Inter-Party Competition in North Carolina." In *Approaches to the Study of Party Organization*, edited by William J. Crotty, pp. 217–46. Boston: Allyn and Bacon, 1968.

Goldman, Perry M. "Political Virtue in the Age of Jackson." *Political Science Quarterly* 77 (March 1972): 46–62.

Goodrich, Carter. *Government Promotion of American Canals and Railroads, 1800–1890.* New York: Columbia University Press, 1960.

―――. "Local Government Planning of Internal Improvements." *Political Science Quarterly* 66 (September 1951): 411–45.

Guttman, Lewis, "The Basis for Scalogram Analysis." In *Measurement and Prediction,* edited by Samuel A. Stouffer. Princeton, New Jersey: Princeton University Press, 1950.

Haller, Mark H. "The Rise of the Jackson Party in Maryland, 1820–1829." *Journal of Southern History* 28 (August 1962): 307–326.

Handlin, Mary, and Handlin, Oscar. *Commonwealth: Massachusetts, 1774–1861.* New York: New York University Press, 1947.

Harlow, Ralph V. *The History of Legislative Methods in the Period Before 1825.* New Haven, Connecticut: Yale University Press, 1917.

Hartz, Louis. *Economic Policy and Democratic Thought: Pennsylvania, 1776–1860.* Cambridge, Massachusetts: Harvard University Press, 1948.

Hartz, Louis. *The Liberal Tradition in America.* New York: Harcourt, Brace, and World, 1955.

Heath, Milton S. *Constructive Liberalism: The Role of the State in Economic Development in Georgia to 1860.* Cambridge, Massachusetts: Harvard University Press, 1954.

Henry, Andrew F. "A Method of Classifying Non-Scale Response Patterns in a Guttman Scale." *Public Opinion Quarterly* 16 (Spring 1952): 94–106.

Hofstadter, Richard. *The Idea of a Party System: The Rise of Legitimate Oppositions in the United States, 1780–1840.* Berkeley, California: University of California Press, 1969.

Hyneman, Charles S. "Who Makes Our Laws?" *Political Science Quarterly* 55 (1940): 556–81.

Jacob, Herbert, and Vines, Kenneth N., eds. *Politics in the American States: A Comparative Analysis.* Boston: Little, Brown and Company, 1965.

Jewell, Malcolm E. "Party Voting in American State Legislatures." *American Political Science Review* 49 (September 1955): 773–91.

Keefe, William J. "Parties, Partisanship, and Public Policy in the Pennsylvania Legislature." *American Political Science Review* 48 (1954): 450–64.

Key, V. O., Jr. *American State Politics: An Introduction.* New York: Alfred A. Knopf, 1956.

———. *Politics, Parties, and Pressure Groups.* New York: Alfred A. Knopf, 1956.

Klein, Philip S. *Pennsylvania Politics: 1817–1832, A Game Without Rules.* Philadelphia: The Historical Society of Pennsylvania, 1940.

Lane, Wheaton J. *From Indian Trail to Iron Horse, Travel and Transportation in New Jersey, 1620–1860.* Princeton, New Jersey: Princeton University Press, 1939.

La Palombara, Joseph, and Weiner, Myron. "The Origin and Development of Political Parties." In *Political Parties and Political Development,* edited by Joseph La Palombara and Myron Weiner, pp. 3–42. Princeton, New Jersey: Princeton University Press, 1966.

Leiby, James. *Charity and Correction in New Jersey, A History of State Welfare Institutions.* New Brunswick, New Jersey: Rutgers University Press, 1967.

Levine, Peter D. "The New Jersey Federalist Party Convention of 1814." *The Journal of the Rutgers University Library* 33 (December 1969): pp. 1–8.

———. "Party-in-the Legislature: New Jersey, 1829–1844." Ph.D. dissertation, Department of History, Rutgers University, 1971.

Lockard, Duane. *New England State Politics.* Princeton, New Jersey: Princeton University Press, 1959.

———. *The New Jersey Governor: A Study in Political Power.* Princeton, New Jersey: Van Nostrand Press, 1964.

Lowi, Theodore J. "Party, Policy, and Constitution in America." In *The American Party Systems: Stages of Political Development,* edited by William N. Chambers and Walter D. Burnham, pp. 238–76. New York: Oxford University Press, 1967.

Lutzker, Michael A. "Abolition of Imprisonment for Debt in New Jersey." *Proceedings of the New Jersey Historical Society* 84, no. 4 (January 1966): 1–29.

McCloskey, Herbert; Hoffman, Paul; and O'Hara, Rosemary. "Issue Conflict and Consensus among Party Leaders and Followers." *American Political Science Review* 54 (June 1960): 406–427.

McCormick, Richard L. "Ethno-Cultural Interpretations of Nineteenth Century American Voting Behavior." *Political Science Quarterly* 89 (June 1974): 351–77.

McCormick, Richard P. *The History of Voting in New Jersey, A Study of the Development of Election Machinery, 1664–1911.* New Brunswick, New Jersey: Rutgers University Press, 1953.

_____. "Party Formation in New Jersey in the Jackson Era." *Proceedings of the New Jersey Historical Society* 83 (July 1965): 161–73.

_____. "Political Development and the Second Party System." In *The American Party Systems: Stages of Political Development,* edited by William N. Chambers and Walter D. Burnham, pp. 90–116. New York: Oxford University Press, 1967.

_____. *The Second American Party System: Party Formation in the Jacksonian Era.* Chapel Hill, North Carolina: University of North Carolina Press, 1966.

McFaul, John. "The Politics of Jacksonian Finance." Ph.D. dissertation, Department of History, University of California at Berkeley, 1963.

MacPherson, C. B. *The Political Theory of Possessive Individualism: Hobbes to Locke.* New York: Oxford University Press, 1962.

MacRae, Duncan, Jr. "The Relation Between Roll-Call Votes and Constituencies in the Massachusetts House of Representatives." *American Political Science Review* 46 (1952): 1,046–1,055.

McWhiney, Grady. "Were the Whigs a Class Party in Alabama?" *Journal of Southern History* 23 (November 1957): 510–22.

Marshall, Lynn L. "The Strange Stillbirth of the Whig Party." *American Historical Review* 72 (January 1967): 445–68.

Mathews, Donald. *United States Senators and Their World.* Chapel Hill, North Carolina: University of North Carolina Press, 1960.

Meller, N. "Legislative Behavior Research." *Western Political Quarterly* 13 (1960): 134–53.

Miller, Douglas T. *The Birth of Modern America, 1820–1850.* New York: Western Publishing Company, 1970.

Miller, Nathan. *The Enterprise of a Free People: Aspects of Economic Development in New York State during the Canal Period, 1792–1838.* Ithaca, New York: Cornell University Press, 1962.

Miller, Warren E., and Stokes, Donald C. "Constituency Influence in Congress." *American Political Science Review* 57 (March 1963): 45–56.

Mueller, Henry R. *The Whig Party in Pennsylvania.* New York: Columbia University Press, 1922.

Murray, Paul. *The Whig Party in Georgia, 1825–1853.* Chapel Hill, North Carolina: University of North Carolina Press, 1948.

Nadworny, Milton J. "New Jersey Workingmen and the Jacksonians." *Proceedings of the New Jersey Historical Society* 67 (1949): 185–98.

Patterson, Samuel B. "Dimensions of Voting Behavior in a One-Party State Legislature." *Public Opinion Quarterly* 26 (Summer 1962): 185–200.

Pessen, Edward. *Jacksonian America: Society, Personality, and Politics.* Homewood, Illinois: The Dorsey Press, 1969.

Pierce, Harry H. *Railroads of New York, A Study of Government Aid, 1826–1875.* Cambridge, Massachusetts: Harvard University Press, 1953.

Polsby, Nelson W. "The Institutionalization of the United States House of Representatives." *American Political Science Review* 62 (March 1968): 144–68.

Primm, James. *Economic Policy in the Development of a Western State: Missouri, 1820–1860.* Cambridge, Massachusetts: Harvard University Press, 1954.

276 THE BEHAVIOR OF STATE LEGISLATIVE PARTIES

Prince, Carl E. *New Jersey's Jeffersonian Republicans: The Genesis of an Early Party Machine, 1789–1817.* Chapel Hill, North Carolina: University of North Carolina Press, 1967.

Ranney, Austin. "Parties in State Politics." In *Politics in the American States: A Comparative Analysis,* edited by Herbert Jacob and Kenneth Vines, pp. 61–100. Boston: Little, Brown and Co., 1965.

Remini, Robert. *The Election of Andrew Jackson.* New York: J. B. Lippincott, 1963.

Rice, Stuart. "The Behavior of Legislative Groups." *Political Science Quarterly* 40 (March 1925): 60–72.

———. *Quantitative Methods in Politics.* New York: Alfred A. Knopf, 1928.

Robinson, W. S. "Ecological Correlations and the Behavior of Individuals." *American Sociological Review* 15 (June 1950): 35–57.

Schattschneider, E. E. *Party Government.* New York: Rinehart and Company, 1942.

Schneider, David M. *The History of Public Welfare in New York State, 1609–1866.* Chicago: University of Chicago Press, 1938.

Sellers, Charles G., Jr. "Andrew Jackson versus the Historians." *Mississippi Valley Historical Review* 44 (March 1958): 615–34.

Sharp, James R. *The Jacksonians Versus the Banks: Politics in the States After the Panic of 1837.* New York: Columbia University Press, 1970.

Silbey, Joel H. *The Shrine of Party: Congressional Voting Behavior, 1841–1852.* Pittsburgh: University of Pittsburgh Press, 1967.

Simms, Henry H. *The Rise of the Whigs in Virginia, 1824–1840.* Richmond, Virginia: William Byrd Press, 1929.

Snyder, Charles M. *The Jacksonian Heritage: Pennsylvania Politics, 1833–1848.* Harrisburg, Pennsylvania: The Pennsylvania Historical and Museum Commission, 1958.

Sorauf, Frank J. "Political Parties and Political Analysis." In *The American Party Systems: Stages of Political Development,* edited by William N. Chambers and Walter D. Burnham, pp. 33–55. New York: Oxford University Press, 1967.

———. *Political Parties in the American System.* Boston: Little, Brown and Company, 1964.

Stevens, Harry R. *The Early Jackson Party in Ohio.* Durham, North Carolina: Duke University Press, 1957.

Taylor, George Rogers. *The Transportation Revolution, 1815–1860.* New York: Holt, Rinehart, and Winston, 1951.

Temin, Peter. *The Jacksonian Economy.* New York: W. W. Norton and Company, 1969.

Thompson, Charles M. *The Illinois Whigs Before 1846.* University of Illinois Studies in the Social Sciences. Vol. 4. Urbana, Illinois: University of Illinois Press, 1915.

Thompson, Robert T. *Colonel James Neilson, A Business Man of the Early Machine Age in New Jersey, 1784–1862.* New Brunswick, New Jersey: Rutgers University Press, 1940.

———. "Transportation Combines and Pressure Politics in New Jersey: 1833–1836." *Proceedings of the New Jersey Historical Society* 57 (January 1939): 1–15, 71–86.

Truman, David B. "The State Delegations and the Structure of Party Voting in the United States House of Representatives." *American Political Science Review* 50 (1956): 1,023–1,045.

Turner, Julius. *Party and Constituency: Pressures on Congress.* Baltimore: Johns Hopkins Press, 1951.

Wallace, Michael. "Changing Concepts of Party in the United States: New York, 1815–1828." *American Historical Review* 74 (December 1968): 453–91.

Wallace, Paul A. *Pennsylvania: Seed of a Nation.* New York: Harper and Row, 1962.

Index

Adams, John Quincy, 28, 30
Adams Party, 29
age: influence on legislative voting, 113, 243–44, 247–49; of
legislators, 65
appointments, 37, 57, 102–3,
141–42, 192, 200, 220, 229–30;
in Joint Meeting, 45, 79–80; and
legislative parties, 93–99, 103–4.
See also Joint Meeting; party voting; roll-call analysis
assembly: data on, 31, 36, 51–52;
party voting in, 100–3; fifty-first
session, 154; fifty-third session,
98, 187–88; fifty-fourth session,
188–89, 196, 218; fifty-fifth session, 189–90; fifty-sixth session,

159–61; fifty-seventh session,
134, 193; fifty-eighth session,
96–98, 120–24, 134, 174; fifty-
ninth session, 131, 134, 162–64,
170, 196–97; sixtieth session,
98, 120–24, 131, 134, 141,
154–57, 165–66, 170–72; sixty-
first session, 52, 120–24, 141–
42, 154–57, 171–72, 219; sixty-
second session, 97, 127–31, 134,
154, 173, 190–91, 201, 210–212,
219; sixty-third session, 154,
173, 213; sixty-fourth session,
192, 213, 215–16; sixty-fifth session, 131–33, 154, 173; sixty-
sixth session, 133–34, 173–74,
192, 197–98; sixty-seventh ses-

278

282 THE BEHAVIOR OF STATE LEGISLATIVE PARTIES

legislative parties — *continued*
106–8, 125–26, 230–33; defined, 19, 21; and gerrymandering, 209–14; and legislation, 186, 191, 201–2; mobilization of, 103; and party competition, 15–16, 107, 228–33; and party organization, 103, 138–44, 207–14, 221–22
legislative party caucus, 28, 79, 106, 135, 141, 208–9, 229–30; and appointments, 93–94; and party organization, 20, 38, 46
legislative tenure: influence on legislative behavior, 113, 244–45, 250–53
legislators: data on, 64–87; age of, 65; and appointments, 79–81; economic interests of, 71–75; ethnicity of, 65; involvement in corporations of, 72–75, 125, 157, 171; occupational analysis of, 65–71; as party activists, 16, 80, 82–86; religion of, 65; tenure of, 76–79
legislature: elections to, 15; powers of, 37–38; rules governing, 51–52; work of sittings of, 44–45. *See also* assembly; council
Levine, Peter D., 145n
liability of stockholders, 123, 132, 173–74, 176
limited partnerships, 56, 167
lobby activities, 57–59
locofoco, 172
log-rolling, 123–25, 155
lottery, 194
Lowi, Theodore, 111n
Lutzker, Michael, 205n

McFaul, John, 144
Massachusetts, banks in, 125
mentally retarded, 185

Mercer County, 132, 210, 212
Middlesex County, 98, 212, 218; assembly delegation, vote of, 119–20, 123, 133, 155, 158–59, 163, 166, 189–90, 199
militia, 56
Molleson, George, 128
Monmouth County, assembly delegation, vote of, 133, 155, 158, 161, 188–89
monopoly, 158; as partisan issue, 169–70, 172, 174–78
Morris Canal, 159, 164, 167
Morris County, 170; assembly delegation, vote of, 120, 123–24, 133, 159, 163–64, 190

National Republicans, 34, 161, 193–95
Newark Daily Advertiser, 58, 84–85, 132, 142, 163, 193, 209
New Brunswick Bridge Company, 162
New Brunswick, N.J., 158, 162
New Jersey, 125, 127, 152; location between New York and Pennsylvania, 125, 195
New Jersey Railroad Company, 58, 162, 164, 175
New Orleans, 220
newspapers, partisan affiliation of, 209
New York City, 125, 127, 158, 162
New York State, 129, 137, 192, 195; political parties in, 105

occupation: influence on voting behavior, 245–46, 254–59; of legislators, 66–71
orphan's court, 55–56

Panic of 1837, 126, 137, 139–40, 231

Parker, James, 38
party activists, 16–17, 104
party cohesion: timing of in legislature, 100–103
party competition, 30–34; and appointments, 97; and issues, 138; and legislative parties, 15–16, 87, 107, 228–33
party conflict, limits of in New Jersey, 177
party: constituent role of, 230–33; definition of, 18, 232; formation in New Jersey, 28–30, 104; influence on legislative behavior, 135–37; as institution, 104, 222; as interest, 59, 106, 175–78, 202, 207–22; loyalty to, 105. *See also* legislative parties; party voting
party in office, 18, 107
party organization, 34–36, 38–39; and legislative parties, 138–44
party organization proper, 18, 20, 87
party voting: and appointments, 92–99, 192; and assembly roll calls, 99–103, 239–42; on bank bills, 117–125, 128–34, 157; and council roll calls, 99, 102; and county bills, 209–14; currency bills, 130–31; and corporation charter bills, 167–71, 173–75; and education bills, 188–91; and election bills, 216–19; and fiscal policy, 134–35; and imprisonment for debt bills, 196–200; and Joint Companies' bills, 158–66; and Joint Meeting appointments, 92–99; and judicial reform bills, 201; in the legislature, 16–17, 230–33; and limited partnership bill, 171–72; and prison bills, 193–94, 204n; and public printing bills, 208–9;

and regulatory bills, 178n; and resolutions on election disputes, 215–16; and resolutions on national issues, 219–20; and stockholder liability bills, 173–74; and taxation bills, 145n; and township bills, 209–14; and transportation bills, 152, 154–56
Passaic County, assembly delegation, vote of, 133, 200
Patronage. *See* appointments
Pennington, William, 140, 215
Pennsylvania, 137, 192, 195
Philadelphia, 125, 158, 162; banks in, 127, 129
Philadelphia and Trenton Railroad Company, 162, 164–65
physically handicapped, 185
Polsby, Nelson, 90n
Potts, Stacy, 157, 169
Prince, Carl, 39
prison, 55–56; construction of, 193–95. *See also* legislation
private legislation. *See* special legislation
progressive interpretation of Jacksonian era, 71
public legislation. *See* general legislation
public printing, as partisan concern, 208–9. *See also* legislation; party voting; roll-call analysis

Raritan River, 158
reapportionment, 271–19
relative index of cohesion, 109n
religion, 102
resolutions: in assembly on national fiscal policy, 134–35, 140, 176; in assembly on resumption of specie payments, 132; in council on railroads, 163; joint

resolutions — *continued*
resolutions, 45; party voting on national resolutions, 102–3, 219–20. *See also* roll-call analysis
resumption of specie payments, 143
roll-call analysis: age as variable, 243–44, 247–49; of appointments, 192, 94–99; of assembly bills, 99–103, 239–42; of banking bills, 116–37; of corporation charter bills, 167–71, 173–75; of council bills, 99, 102; of currency bills, 126–31, 135–37; of education bills, 186–91; of election bills, 216–19; of imprisonment for debt bills, 195–200; of Joint Companies' bills, 157–66; of judicial reform bills, 200–201; and legislative tenure as variable, 244–45, 250–53; of limited partnership bill, 171–72; methodological problems of, 16–17; and occupation as variable, 245–46, 254–59; of prison bills, 193–94, 204n; of public printing bills, 208–9; purpose of, 91; of regulatory bills, 178n; of resolutions on election disputes, 215–16; of resolutions on national issues, 134–35, 219–20; of stockholder liability bills, 173–74; of transportation bills, 152–57; of taxation bills, 145n
roll calls: classification of, 99; method of analysis of, 99–102
rules of legislature, 51–52
Ryall, Daniel, 171

Salem County, 132; assembly delegation, vote of, 120, 129, 133,

155, 158, 161, 163, 166, 193, 199, 200
school fund, 56, 186–90
second party system, 15, 54; formation in New Jersey, 28–30
sectional voting, 158–59, 198–99, 201–2, 210, 218–19
Seeley, Elias P., 55
seniority, 79. *See also* legislative tenure
Shade, William G., 235n
social reform, 185–86
Somerset County, 104, 212; assembly delegation, vote of, 133, 155, 159, 161–63, 166, 189–90
Somerville Somerset Messenger, 209
Somerville Somerset Whig, 209
Sorauf, Frank P., 41n
South Amboy, N.J., 159
Southard, Isaac, 142
Southard, Samuel, 56, 98, 104, 142, 161, 193
South Carolina, 219
speaker of assembly, 37, 46, 79
special legislation: defined, 44; disagreement on, 52–54
Specie Circular, 128
specie payments: suspension of, 126–27; voting on resumption of, 132–33
state's rights, 219
Stevens, Robert L., 162
Stewart, William D., 162–63
Stites, William, 47
Stockton, Robert F., 162, 164
suffrage requirements, 35
Sussex County, 170; assembly delegation, vote of, 119, 155, 158, 161, 189–90, 199, 218

Taney, Roger B., 134
tariffs, 219